Yvonne—

Hope you like the book !

Annie

Arnie Kuenn + Brad Kuenn

CONTENT MARKETING WORKS

8 Steps To Transform Your Business

Connect with the Authors

Arnie Kuenn
Twitter.com/ArnieK
LinkedIn.com/ArnieKuenn
Email: ArnieK@VerticalMeasures.com

Brad Kuenn
Twitter.com/BKuenn
LinkedIn.com/BradKuenn
Email: BKuenn22@gmail.com

Published by VM Press, Phoenix, Arizona.

PRAISE FOR CONTENT MARKETING WORKS

"The thing that Arnie & Brad truly get right in his extraordinary new book is that the strategy is not just about creating the content - it's actually using it with the intent to move the business."

- Robert Rose, Chief Strategy Officer, Content Marketing Institute

"The new question isn't should you do content marketing, it's precisely HOW do you do content marketing effectively. This is the actionable playbook for which you've been waiting. Recommended!"

- Jay Baer, New York Times bestselling author of Youtility

"This book can (and for many, should) serve as a first step to upgrading your content marketing practices. Arnie and Brad deeply understand the relationship between content, marketing strategy, traffic opportunities, and sales, and what's better, have made that information useful and accessible."

- Rand Fishkin, founder, Moz

"At the most recent Content Marketing World conference, I was asked for an agency recommendation. Without hesitation, Arnie Kuenn and Vertical Measures leapt to mind based on his years of demonstrated expertise. Get this book and experience that expertise for yourself."

- Brian Clark, Founder and CEO of Copyblogger Media

"Give people what they're looking for - it's a winning approach every time. And what they seek is content, answers to their questions! A focus on content is always a wise investment, so learn, invest and succeed!"

- Duane Forrester, Bing

"Content marketing works, but only if you follow the advice in this insightful book!"

- Andy Beal, author of Repped: 30 Days to a Better Online Reputation

"Many businesses and organizations big and small struggle to understand what the essence of content marketing truly is. But in this work, Arnie Kuenn, one of the true pioneers in this space, has explained how to attain content marketing success in a way that not only will everyone "get it," but they'll also be able to implement its principles and strategies immediately to get results. Well done Mr. Kuenn!"

- Marcus Sheridan, president, The Sales Lion

"For most marketers, content marketing is a giant failure-prone experiment. With Content Marketing Works, you'll realize that it's a practical, proven, and, most importantly, predictable process that you can replicate yourself."

- Pawan Deshpande, CEO, Curata

"One of the biggest proponents of transforming your business with inbound marketing is having a concrete content strategy. The Kuenns not only recognize how important is it for businesses today to embrace content in order to attract, engage, and delight customers, but they outline every step of the process from planning to sharing to analyzing your efforts. Whether you're just getting started with content or want to improve your existing strategy, read this guide. Your audience will thank you."

- Mike Volpe, CMO, HubSpot

"Content Marketing Works wisely emphasizes that content marketing is a process, not a project. Just as a magazine doesn't publish a single issue, nor should your content program. Arnie and Brad take a complicated and critical element of modern business and demystifies it with case studies, instruction, and an 8 Step guide. Nicely done."

- Larry Kim, founder and CTO, WordStream

"As someone who teaches Content Marketing, I can see this book being a valuable asset to my students as it takes them step by step through the entire process."

- Simon Heseltine - Adjunct Faculty, Georgetown University

"If you want to know how to do content marketing RIGHT from start to finish this is the book for you!"

- Melissa Fach - @SEOAware

"Arnie knows content marketing, he was preaching content marketing before it became all the "rage" in the Internet marketing world. Content marketing DOES work and no matter your skill level, you WILL learn from this book!"

- Matt Siltala, president, Avalaunch Media

"In succession to Accelerate, Arnie has managed to write another great book that addresses many aspects of content marketing that are missing from other books, but are still imperative to proper execution. He truly speaks with insight and experience, and gives actionable information that all levels of content marketers will find useful. A must-have for every content marketer's library."

- Rob Garner, Chief Strategy Officer, Advice Interactive; author of "Search and Social: The Definitive Guide to Real-time Content Marketing."

"From the why to the how, Arnie and Brad have laid it out with a practical approach that will save you months of costly mistakes."

- Andy Crestodina, Principal, Strategic Director, Orbit Media

"Successful content marketing isn't always about the big viral moment. Using a proven process that drives consistency is key. "Content Marketing Works" provides that proven process for success."

- Pamela Muldoon, Next Stage Media Group

"As somebody who is one of the most recognized experts in the world on content marketing strategies and whose company is responsible for training more students in hands-on content marketing workshops than anybody else, this book by Arnie Kuenn is a must-have for anyone serious about content marketing!"

- David Wallace, CEO, SearchRank

"To be successful at Content Marketing, you must go 'all-in.' In Content Marketing Works, Arnie Kuenn provides the guide for how to survive the immersion and come out smiling at your success."

- Ardath Albee, author, eMarketing Strategies for the Complex Sale and Digital Relevance

"With Content Marketing Works, Arnie and Brad Kuenn have delivered a well-researched and insightful exploration of today's content marketing landscape, including both basic and advanced techniques in a practical and enjoyable book that is a definite must-read for anyone serious about content marketing in our social media age."

- Brett Tabke, founder and CEO of Pubcon

"Content Marketing really does work! Know why? Because it's all about quality. Arnie and the team at Vertical Measures have always gotten this right! This book brings calm and focus to the overwhelmed and seasoned marketer, alike. And it even addresses how to overcome the doubting boss! A job well done."

- Stoney deGeyter, Author, The Best Damn Web Marketing Checklist, Period! and CEO of Pole Position Marketing

"Just when you think nothing more can be said about content marketing that hasn't been said before, Arnie Kuenn turns around and wows us (once again) with another incredibly valuable tome on how to convince the powers that be that content marketing works. And he does it very, very well, covering all types of specific, current examples and case studies, putting together a resource that will pay big dividends for any company trying to transition to a content culture. If you're having difficulty selling content marketing in to the c-suite, this is the only book you need. A phenomenal addition to the library of great content marketing books!"

- Jon Wuebben, Founder/CEO, Content Launch

"Since I first met Arnie on an SEO conference panel 4 years ago, both he and his company have grown to embody the true definitive of "content kings." In "Content Marketing Works", not only does he explain in simple, repeatable & logical steps how & why he deserves a crown himself, but also why this book should be on the desk of every business that desires to compete in a content-centric, content-hungry, online world."

- Grant Simmons, author, speaker, sailor - VP of Search Strategies, For Rent Media Solutions

"Arnie and Brad Kuenn nail it with this fantastic guide to content marketing."

- Eric Enge, CEO, Stone Temple Consulting

"Arnie delivers his best content marketing recipe. Bon Appétit."

- Thomas Ballantyne, DOM, Bulwark Exterminating

"Content Marketing Works" provides a step-by-step blueprint for solopreneurs, marketers and business executives. It outlines how to develop your business's content so that it drives measurable results."

- Heidi Cohen – Chief Content Officer – Actionable Marketing Guide

"Arnie delivers a powerful blueprint for success in today's world of organic search."

- Jim Bader – Sr. Manager SEO for a leading healthcare company

"A definitive how to guide for content marketing. Any businesses that have not embraced the reality that all brands are publishers needs to read and implement Content Marketing Works. Arnie shares the blueprint to getting the most from your online marketing efforts...just add a little creativity and the discipline to stay on track."

- Matthew O'Brien, CEO of MINT Social

"Content Marketing isn't a new concept - Arnie wrote that book years ago, and we've all bought off. From my experience however, successfully operationalizing content marketing programs remains an important topic. If you are one of the many looking for repeatable results through sustainable processes, and perhaps some internal program buy-off, Content Marketing Works is a must."

- Mike Corak, EVP of Strategy, Scottsdale Managing Director, ethology

TABLE OF CONTENTS

ACKNOWLEDGEMENTS

When I wrote my first book, Accelerate!, I understood why the acknowledgment section of a book is so important – and why it can get pretty long. As I said in that acknowledgement, an author's name goes on the cover, the author gets the credit for the book, and the author gets all the attention. But I now know for a fact that it takes a team to get a book published. In fact, I could never write it by myself. Without my son Brad, this book might never have happened.

People in our office and around the industry have been asking me to write "Accelerate 2.0" for a while. Anyone who has ever written a book knows how hard it is to write the first one, let alone the second one. So procrastinate I did. Until one day Brad says, "Come on pops, I'll help you!" - And help he did - Brad provided writing, deep research, expert knowledge, editing skills to help make this book happen. So, even though the book is written in first person, it was truly a team effort.

Once Brad and I decided to write this book we knew we had to assemble a team to get it done. That team consists of the following people (we sure hope we haven't forgotten anyone):

Quinn Whissen is pretty much the project manager making sure everyone set and hit their deadlines. Not only that, she wrote the bulk of Step 7 covering lead nurturing. She is our marketing manager, therefore will also be taking charge of promoting the book. This book literally could not have happened without her.

Ben Snedeker, an experienced author who helped me with Accelerate!, agreed to jump in again and served as our editor. His expertise was invaluable while working with us through the entire writing and editing process. If you are contemplating writing a book, you might want Ben on your team.

Ardala Evans was our proofreader. She is a long time, full time employee at Vertical Measures so she did much of this in her off hours. Her attention to detail coupled with her industry knowledge made for a very smooth proofing cycle.

The creative team for this project is made up of **Dan Dannenberg, Drew Eastmead, David Gould, and Erin Pritchard**. The cover and every graphic in this book was designed by this team. They dealt with our excitement, concerns, impatience, naivety and ever changing deadlines with patience and professionalism. When we had dumb ideas they told us, when we had too many ideas they tackled them, when they had great ideas they let us take all the credit (see first paragraph).

At Vertical Measures, it didn't stop there. **Kaila Strong**, our Senior Director of SEO Services, and **Zach Etten**, our Director of Digital Advertising, served as subject matter experts, making sure we were accurate when it came to the analytics and advertising topics. The entire VM team helped. They voted on cover designs and even naming the book. **Dave Murrow**, our Content Marketing Strategist, came up with the winning title of Content Marketing Works and **Chris Bird**, our President, came up with the winning subtitle, 8 Steps to Transform Your Business. So thank you to everyone at Vertical Measures.

We also want to thank **Joe Pulizzi** for taking the time to write the foreword. The timing could not have been worse as it was just weeks before his hugely successful conference – Content Marketing World, yet Joe found the time to help us out. Joe was the person who convinced us to change the direction of Vertical Measures in 2010 and go all-in with content marketing. What he has done for us, our business and this entire industry since we met has been amazing.

Most importantly, we would like to thank our families. The Kuenns are a loving and compassionate bunch. Together, we have achieved wonderful things and have so much to be proud of. Cherished are the family get-togethers, summer vacations and happy holiday memories; relished are the constant laughs with the Di Santo's and cheers for an Arizona Cardinal victory. We could not have done this without your constant love and support. To everyone - Thank you.

- Brad & Arnie

FOREWORD

After graduating from Bowling Green State University in 1995, I left for Penn State University to study (of all things) rhetoric, with a focus on persuasive writing and speaking. It was then that I first studied the works of Aristotle.

Aristotle, the Greek philosopher born in 384 BC, believed that our knowledge as humans is a result of how we perceive and interact with the world. In essence, the human brain is a tabula rasa, or "clean slate," capable of learning, changing and adapting, and not fated to any particular belief structure.

For you, this means your marketing can, and should be, a tabula rasa.

Let me explain.

Much of the way we behave as marketers is based on the past and the success of mass media. Glorious mass media helped us reach hoards of people with our messaging all at one time. We simply found out what channels our customers were hanging out in, and then bought space to promote our products and services in that channel (renting time). If we distracted enough of those people from the content they actually wanted, then the buy had a positive return.

If we woke up tomorrow and had a clean slate as marketers, would we really spend the majority of our marketing dollars on this type of approach?

Never in a million years.

We wouldn't go out searching for who is attracting our customers, and then rent time from those people. We would find a way to attract customers to us. We would create a beacon of light for our prospects and customers. We would help our customers live better lives and acquire better jobs, and because of this, they would ultimately reward us by buying our products or services.

If marketing was a clean slate, we would set up our marketing as publishing operations. We would own our marketing channels and tend to them consistently as critical assets to the business. And if we ever rented space, we would do it sparingly.

But we do. A lot. Because that's what we've always done. And the people in our marketing department have always done it that way too. We are marketing zombies, and we have no idea that there is a better way. Oh, we tinker with the idea, but we really don't take it seriously (do we?).

Content Marketing Works is your opportunity to clean slate your marketing. This book gives you permission to think and do differently from everyone else. This book is your ticket to becoming the leading informational resource for your particular niche. This book will not only change the way you market, but it will change the way you conduct business.

Before you dig in, do me a favor…put away your preconceived notions about marketing. Disregard what you've done in the past. The era of content marketing is before you. It takes patience and consistency, but it works. The promise is real.

Tabula rasa.

- Joe Pulizzi, Founder, Content Marketing Institute

INTRODUCTION

The "I" vs. "We"

As I mentioned in the acknowledgements (you read the acknowledgments right?), this book is a product of many people. I happen to be the lead author and the "face" of Vertical Measures, so I have most of the first person, real life experiences with our clients and at conferences. In light of that, we decided to write the book from a first person perspective even though Brad provided a lot of the research, his expert knowledge, writing and editing skills. This book would not have happened without him.

Let's Get Started

I think I know a little bit about you. You understand that the world of marketing has been radically changing in the last few years to a new kind of marketing. There's been a growing shift to something called content marketing. You want to engage this phenomenon and bring it to your company.

You're aware of the trend that today less money is being spent on traditional advertising — print, television, etc., because marketers are moving their money online. But when your executives hear that, they think it means "Advertise on Google!" Although that is certainly part of it, advertising online is just one aspect of **succeeding** online. The companies that are booming online right now are the ones creating *content* that engages their customers and brings in the business. Content marketing is still evolving. The truth is that, to some extent, everyone in this industry is trying to figure out the best approach, even the experts. This can make creating your own content marketing strategy a confusing endeavor. That's where this book comes in.

Many marketing books present themselves like the consultant who comes in and says, "Here's the strategy you need, but I don't actually implement. That's for you to figure out." But if you're going to be successful, you need to understand *how* to create and promote compelling content that brings in the customers — not just that you *need* to.

People like you spend thousands of dollars to hear people like me speak for 45 minutes at conferences about what it means to create that awesome content. We put up 20 or 30 slides and tell you what you should be doing and get you psyched about the possibilities. So, you walk away from the conference excited, ready to go. Then you get back to your office.

And then Reality Hits

Even if you are given the budget and approval to proceed (which makes you one of the lucky ones), you are now staring at your screen, saying to yourself, "Where do I start? I took notes. I have the slides, but how do I get going?"

Then you start thinking about how the speakers cited examples of Ford Motor Company doing this, or Coca Cola doing that, and now you start to tell yourself, "Sure, they have a million dollar budget, but I'm a three-person department with a $90,000 budget." So you struggle; thinking it just can't be done without a big budget and substantial resources. You just can't imagine how you're going to convince the boss let alone get all of this done, right?

You're exactly the one I had in mind when I wrote this book! I want to assure you that companies like yours, and mine, are creating effective and compelling content — and they're doing this successfully, without big budgets. Throughout this book I'll give you a few examples of small businesses that became big business through content marketing.

What will be different about this book?

Originally, I wrote *Accelerate!* to be the one you have on your desk that says *here's how you do it*. It was a hit! Over the last few years, I've been hearing that people want not only to know how to do this content marketing thing, but also how to get buy in from upper management. So I've added the tools to demonstrate a return on investment (ROI) to the powers that be. That way, once you know how to do it, you can convince your boss TO do it!

It's been three years since I wrote the original version of *Accelerate*. In Internet years that's a *very* long time. So much happens in the digital world; the only way to truly keep up is by reading, watching, and listening – every single day.

Over the last three years Google has made at least three major updates to their algorithm. First came Panda in early 2011. Panda's focus was the on-page elements of your website. It looked at issues like duplicate content, thin content and page load speeds. For Panda, if you had poor site structure and the Google bot thought you had multiple copies of the same content, it got interpreted as bad; so bad that you could incur a penalty.

On the other hand, if you took the lazy route and created very similar web pages over and over again, Panda was inclined to punish you too. For example, a realtor based in Phoenix, Arizona wants to be found for keywords representing the surrounding region. So, she creates pages like "Phoenix area realtor," "Tempe area realtor," "Mesa area realtor," and so on. But rather than put original content on each page, she copies 95% of the same content onto each page. Panda frowns upon that. Most likely Google would have penalized those pages (if not her whole site, depending on how much this pattern occurs on her pages).

Later in 2011, Google rolled out Penguin. This update primarily looked at off-page issues with the biggest emphasis on links pointing to your web pages. During much of the last decade, many SEOs spent a significant chunk of their effort obtaining links to their web pages. After all, they had been rewarded with higher search engine rankings for many years based on the number and quality of links pointing to their web pages.

But like almost everything in life, once people see the benefits in something, they'll try to exploit the situation; thus, the serious rise in spammy, scalable link building. People began doing whatever they could to get links to their web pages using keyword rich anchor text (example: *Phoenix area realtor*). After all, more is better, right? Well, it got out of hand, and Google levied the hammer with the Penguin update, and tens of thousands of sites (if not hundreds of thousands) were penalized (and continue to be penalized) for their backlink sins. In fact by 2013, Penguin created a new business for many agencies like ours diagnosing and removing these bad links.

To celebrate their 15th birthday, on September 27, 2013, Google launched a new algorithm called Hummingbird. This was not really an algorithm update, but actually a whole new algorithm. It is focused on "conversational search" since so many of us are using our mobile devices to search, and when using them we ask by speaking instead of typing full questions. Google claimed that search can be a more personalized way to interact with users and provide a more direct answer.

"What's the closest place to buy a Vitamix blender?" A traditional search engine might focus on finding matches for words, such as finding a page that says "Vitamix" and "blender" for example.

Hummingbird is designed to better focus on the meaning behind the query. It may better understand your actual location, if you've shared that with Google. It might understand that "place" means you want a physical store. It might get that "Vitamix" is a particular type of blender carried by certain stores. Knowing all these meanings may help Google go beyond just finding pages with matching words.

Google claims that Hummingbird is paying more attention to each word in a query, ensuring that the whole query — the whole sentence, or conversation, or meaning — is taken into account, rather than specific words. The goal is that pages matching the meaning of the query do better, rather than pages matching just a few words.

So over the course of three years, and as many new versions of their algorithm, Google made a strong statement about the type of content it was going to provide in its search results. Suddenly, **Content is King – again**.

Figure 1: Google Glass

The last three years were not exclusively centered on Google algorithm updates. Google also released a product called Glass. Essentially, Google Glasses look like a pair of eyeglasses, but are actually a wearable computer where the lens of the glasses are an interactive, smartphone-like display, with natural language voice command support as well as Bluetooth and Wi-Fi connectivity. Maybe you've seen someone wearing them? This little tidbit of wearable technology is changing the way we interact with the internet, and I assure you, marketers will need to keep up.

Beyond wearable technology, there has been an astronomical growth in mobile technology, in general. Yep, I used the word "astronomical" on purpose and I don't think it's an exaggeration. About four out of every five people in the world now have a mobile phone. Think about it, that includes the poorest people on earth, and the vast majority can't go a single day without their phone. A little less than half of Americans say they can't even go a few *hours* without checking their mobile phones. One in four people check their phone every 30 minutes, which is a lot of checking when you consider how many mobile phones are in the world. It is projected that the number of active cell phones will reach 7.3 billion by 2015, which is actually more phones than there are people on the planet.

Mobile technology has created some giants who have developed apps that click with mobile users. Facebook is one of those giants, who in 2014 will reach more than three quarters of the smartphone market, and it accounts for more than 20% of total time spent using apps each month. Since I wrote *Accelerate!*, Facebook has exploded in growth. It's now a public company and as of this writing claims to have 1.31 billion users, which is a 22% growth from 2013.

Continuing with the massive changes over the last three years; a few sites that barely existed then, claim gigantic user numbers today. For example Twitter claims more than 560 million users, Google Plus says it has 400 million users, Instagram boasts better than 150 million and Pinterest has over 70 million users.

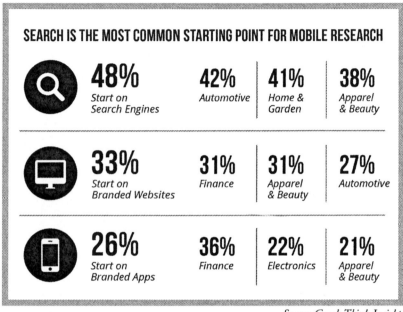

Source: *Google Think Insights*

Figure 2: Search metrics

What Have the Last Three Years Taught the Content Marking Industry?

Joe Pulizzi, founder of the Content Marketing Institute (he wrote the foreword), is leading the pack in answering this question. I first met Joe a few years ago when he was evangelizing content marketing to anyone who would listen. He wrote constantly and spoke at almost any event that would have him.

Joe made me *see the light*, and for that I am eternally grateful. We practice what we preach at Vertical Measures and consistently create quality content. Today we create 12-15 new pieces of content every month. Our business has more than tripled in the last three years – all based on the leads flowing to us from our content marketing efforts. We have worked with dozens of clients to help them implement their own content marketing. Everything from writing blog posts for them, to creating in-depth search, social, and content marketing strategies. Suffice it to say, we have learned a lot of lessons along the way too. All of which I plan to share with you in this book.

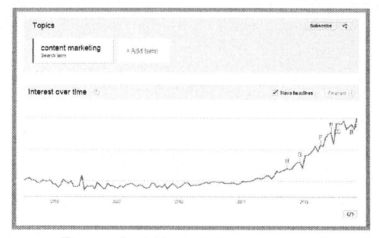

Figure 3: Google Trends for "content marketing"

30- Day Trials Never Work

You will go deep into the lessons I've learned as you read through each step covered in this book. But I'll mention here the biggest lesson that the last three years has taught us in this industry: Dipping your toes in the water never works. You've got to dive in headlong. Thirty day trials always fail. You need top-level buy in for a period of at least six months. Anything less is a recipe for disaster.

Now that companies have a few years under their belts of measuring what works and what doesn't, one thing has become clear: content marketing takes a real commitment of resources *and time* in order to pay off. There are plenty of case studies from the likes of Hubspot, Marcus Sheridan (another good friend and true inspiration), and even an MBA program by Bill Belew at ITU[1] demonstrating the level of consistent effort and the time

---

1   http://itu.edu/

line needed for content marketing to take hold.

Sure, there are always exceptions to the rules, but the best evidence suggests that content marketing must be sustained for at least 4-7 months before the return on investment (ROI) begins to take shape. This is truly one of those snowball-type efforts. If you stick with it, you'll begin to see the content you produced months ago pays off over and over again, generating new business for your organization. Both our clients, and our agency, now have content out there that was produced years ago, and yet it still generates leads for them (and us). **No other marketing platform in the world works this way** – and with this book, I'm going to give you the tools to understand this platform and get the ball rolling at your business.

Wouldn't It Be Nice To Have a Playbook For This Game?

To get your content marketing campaign off the ground, it would be pretty sweet to get a straightforward look at how the whole game works. In *Accelerate!* we introduced our original 8 Step Process (see Figure 4 on page xxviii); however, after a few years of living and breathing content marketing, our firm has made some adjustments based on the lessons we've learned and the changing industry. We've refined our 8 Step methodology, which I will cover in detail in the following chapters. In fact, instead of calling them *chapters*, I'm calling them *steps* to make it easier to follow and to reference later. The eight steps are:

1. **Strategy Development**
2. **Ideation**
3. **Content Creation**
4. **Optimization**
5. **Content Promotion**
6. **Distribution**
7. **Lead Nurture**
8. **Measurement**

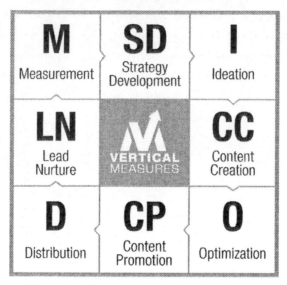

Figure 4: Vertical Measures' 8 Step Process

Each step is important but can only work when your strategy nurtures all of them. Think of a bicycle chain: When the chain is working your effort translates to acceleration! Break the chain and you're going nowhere—your content marketing strategy falls apart.

Look, if you own a website, you're a publisher. Period. And we all know what happens when a publisher stops publishing. As they have been saying forever in publishing, *Content is King.* A strong content strategy requires that you know how to develop, optimize, and promote your material. You need to find ways to get great content happening — and keep it happening, over and over again. Then you need to measure to determine what is working and what is not.

This book aims to give you a comprehensive understanding of what it takes to execute a successful content marketing strategy — no matter how big or small your organization might be. It is the classic "how-to" book following a step-by-step approach. We want to give you a portable field guide for your marketing team.

Our goal is to provide a book that can be there for you when you're brainstorming for your next piece of content, when you are getting ready to upload that content, and when you are ready to promote it. We want to keep you excited. We want to help keep the ideas coming. In our company, Vertical Measures, we do this for a living. And since you're now a publisher in the new world of marketing, you need to do this for a living, too.

Understanding the Shift to Content Marketing – the Basics

Before we dive into the eight steps, we need to get everyone on the same page. What exactly is content marketing? How important is search these days? How about social media? And what in the world do I do about mobile? It's critical that you understand these basics before you dive into the steps that follow.

There are nearly 3 billion people worldwide that are online.[2] When they want a product or service, they don't wait for an ad to appear on television, scour magazine ads or heaven forbid pick up a phone book. They go to the Internet and search via search engines or social sites because these methods promise fast results and relevant content — and generally deliver on that promise.

With the customer's attention shifting online, so has the focus of marketers, and it has required new marketing strategies as we begin to understand how users interact with the Internet and how the Internet works for users. Simply put, web users are consumers of content. Therefore, you need to deliver useful content that will engage your customers and keep them coming back for more. Most significantly, web users are *searching* for content to consume. This is key for any business's relevance and branding.

In fact, Vanessa Fox in her book *Marketing in the Age of Google* emphasizes, "Those businesses that don't realize that we've experienced a shift in consumer behavior and that customers and customer data are now centered on search will lose market share to those that do."[3] Fortunately, it isn't too

---

2   http://en.wikipedia.org/wiki/Global_Internet_usage
3   Vanessa Fox, Marketing in the Age of Google

late to get on board. You haven't missed the boat, but you don't have the luxury of *waiting* to build a content marketing strategy, either.

Content Marketing: A Definition

Over the last three years, we were frequently asked what exactly is "Content Marketing?" So we created our own definition.

- **Content marketing is the art of providing relevant, valuable content to your customers without selling or interrupting them.**

- **Instead of pitching your products or services, you deliver information that makes your prospects more informed before they buy.**

- **If you deliver consistent, ongoing, valuable information to your prospects, they ultimately reward you with their business and loyalty.**

Your Customers Are Online – Right Now

People spend an enormous amount of their time online, and that's where your marketing strategy needs to go. Your potential customers are online for a variety of reasons. The public relations firm Ruder Finn conducted a survey asking — why, exactly, do people go online? They categorized their results into the following seven reasons people use the Internet. Here's that list in descending order from most common reason to least common:

- To Learn (self-education, for research, to keep informed)
- To Have Fun (to pass time, to be entertained, to escape)
- To Socialize (to connect, to share, to discuss, to be part of a community)
- To Express Yourself (to opine, to entertain others, to emote, to be creative)

- To Advocate (to influence others, to activate support, to join a cause)
- To Do Business (to work, to manage finances, to sell)
- To Shop (to purchase, to compare)

The survey found a key demographic: "More than twice as many people go online to socialize (82%) than to do business (39%) or to shop (31%)."[4] Surprised? Here's the thing: The shift to reaching out to customers while they're using the Internet means that you have to engage them in what *they're doing* online. From the list above, it's evident that the critical mass for your content strategy will center on the top three reasons people are online: to learn, to have fun, and to socialize.

You may want them to shop on your site, for example, but you connect with them by providing some form of useful content that leads them to your site. Users *want* to engage with the content they find; that is, they *want* to stay on the page and interact with it or learn from it. If the content doesn't engage them, they move on (or bounce) and continue searching.

The Search Engines Have a Goal

The mission of any search engine — particularly Google, the giant in this arena — is to find the best and most relevant content for a person's search term. Here is Google's stated philosophy: "The perfect search engine would understand exactly what you mean and give you back exactly what you want." This is a pretty high bar, but it's what every search engine tries to do because that's what users demand. The competition among search engines is driven by the results they can bring back.

In order to provide search results, search engines need to know *first* what content is available on the Internet. So, programs (called web bots, web crawlers, or spiders) were developed to trawl the entire web with the goal of reading and analyzing every page that's out there and storing them for retrieval based on queries.

---

4   http://www.intentindex.com

As part of their cataloguing, bots measure the updating activity that occurs on a site, which affects the frequency at which it will return to read each site to look for new content. For example, bots check CNN.com almost continuously because the content is *always* updating, and generally users want the latest headlines and breaking news. On the other hand, the bot might read the website for, say, Todd's Garage and see that nothing has changed, so it will check back a week later and see that still nothing has changed, and again check back a month after that. The frequency of attention from the bots is reduced as the website remains stagnant. To a search engine, this can be a signal that the pages are old and dated. Thus, search engines reward sites that keep their content fresh and updated.

When bots read a page, they look for certain information on the page in order to understand it. In a way, bots read the text content on the page just as a human would. This is where your useful, written content comes into play.

Since the bot and algorithm are a computer program, and not a human, it also looks at the page in a different way than humans, too. Algorithms pay attention to on-page elements called title tags, H1s and Meta descriptions. They even look at the URL page name, which human users care little or nothing about. To the algorithm, however, this information defines the page from an organizational standpoint and can indicate how the webmaster views the page's meaning. Unlike humans, bots can't *see* images, so the title and the metadata that describe images are critical to a bot "knowing" that the image has keyword relevance (though in the near future users will probably be able to search by image, rather than by image metadata). This is true for video as well.

Relevance and Ranking in the Search Results

Using all of these clues, bots gather a huge amount of information about a page of content and determine its relevance to search. Therefore, this is the playing field when you develop your own content. As we get into Search Engine Optimization (SEO) later in the book, we'll consider different methods to optimize the ways that bots look at your web pages and help them understand how you *want* to be relevant.

From a search query, a search engine's job is to determine the person's intent. What kind of result does the searcher want to get back? The search engine must compare all the available content on the Internet to the query and produce a set of results that are relevant to the query, ranked in descending order of relevance. All this gets accomplished within a fraction of a second — something that continues to amaze me. Obviously, the Google algorithm (as with any other search engine algorithm like Bing's or Baidu's) is proprietary, so we can't know *exactly* how it works, but we can see it in operation and make some very good assumptions about what it does. Because a search phrase is not a standalone indication of specific meaning, search engines need to use other means for making a determination of meaning so that they can determine relevance. Effectively, the philosophy for determining relevance within a query is based on these premises:

- People will stay and engage a webpage, or they will bounce. They won't spend time with irrelevant content.
- People tend to search for the same kinds of things, but people are individuals, too.
- People will share relevant content with one another by linking their content to other relevant content.

In order for the algorithm to understand relevance in these terms, Google records each search session as part of its algorithm (yet another moment at which I'm astonished by Google). This has become increasingly important, as implied by all of the Google updates discussed in the beginning of this introduction. By recording sessions and analyzing the rate of bounce or engagement by page, Google can derive the relevance of that page for the average searcher relative to that particular keyword query. Sites that have high rates of bounce might be ranked lower in the result set. Conversely, sites that have high rates of engagement will be ranked higher in the result set.

Early on, Google concluded that linking from one web page to another is a particularly good way to determine relevance because content that is getting links pointing to it has been evaluated by a human and determined to be of value. Thus, links to content should represent relevance and act as a sort of voting mechanism. In fact, Google has become the dominant search engine because its engineers figured out this liking scheme before anybody else.

The downside to linking is that marketers quickly figured out this scheme and began to exploit it by developing link farms and other tactics, where links could be acquired wholesale in an effort to increase a site's rankings. So, Google constantly adapts its algorithm to penalize link farms and other paid-link approaches. The algorithm attempts to identify the *quality* of links as it indexes pages. Links to a page and search activity help comprise a page's value when determining relevance, counting as "votes" for the page. The more votes for a page, the higher it will rank against competing pages. One of the goals for your content strategy is to increase the number and quality of votes for your pages so that they will be the most relevant and engaging content for your target search terms. When you create your content, you might ask yourself, "Would someone find this useful enough to link to it?"

Understanding the Search Engine Results Page

Let's take a look at the Google Search Engine Results Page (SERP) from the searcher's perspective. We'll focus on Google, since it gets 70% to 80% of search traffic, but Bing has a very similar search results page. When a query is entered, less than a second later, pages of results appear, and the ball is now in the searcher's court to identify what results are relevant to her particular needs. Search engines are continually reorganizing their results page layouts in an effort to offer searchers an experience that leads them to their desired content faster. Despite these adaptations, the overall layout of the SERP has remained relatively constant.

Search results can be broken down into two large categories: Paid results and Organic results. Paid results — or *Sponsored Links*, as Google labels them — are segregated at the top of the page and to the right of the page. These results get a premium, front and center location in the results page, but they are limited to three or four results per query on the top line. More paid results appear in a narrower column on the right. While sponsors pay to have their pages listed in this category, these results still undergo a similar kind of analysis that organic results undergo so that they remain relevant to the search term.

THE BEST PLACE TO HIDE A DEAD BODY IS PAGE 2 OF THE GOOGLE SEARCH RESULTS

Organic results, on the other hand, represent the complete set of results possible for the keyword search. Organic results for some queries can amount to *hundreds* of pages of results. Nonetheless, the vast majority of searchers never leave the first page and practically never see page two.

Depending on what you search, the search engine might display: videos, a set of images, news items, or local search results. And in many instances, all of those types of media might appear in the results. Take, for example, a search of the term "Tom Hanks." Based on the algorithm's assessment of the available content and the relevance to the search term, people tend to want images of the movie star as well as information about him. The result set automatically includes images in addition to the text links, even though the searcher did not specify that images were sought. The amazing fact about this kind of relationship between search engine and user is that the searcher wants the best results but may not be able to articulate what the best results might be in terms of the simple query. Searchers rely on the search engine to do that for them.

This means that by diversifying the content you produce — for local search, images, video, etc., — you will create many more ways of being found online. In an offline context, this would be like placing ads on TV, radio, billboards, and in magazines. It's the same for the Internet; you create more opportunities for people to see your brand and engage with your products and services.

Everyone is Social and They're Talking Online

Since we're talking about what's happening online, we can't ignore social media. What began with computer-geek chat rooms has evolved into a worldwide cultural phenomenon. The Internet has become, not surprisingly, a zone of social interaction. People go to the Internet specifically *to socialize* by sharing information or media, participating in discussions, and being part of a community.

We can expand this social phenomenon to a certain extent to the category of *self-expression;* that is, opinions are given to be heard, as with sharing emotions and creativity, and often the one who engages in self-expression does so on a social media platform, such as Twitter or Facebook. The advocacy category is a very social one, too. The advocate influences others and works with groups for a cause — the advocate is not typically a lone crusader, but rather a member of a movement. Often times movements call for support, which take the form of grassroots, social campaigning. The members of the movement tend to have forums for discussion or blogs to keep each other updated on the current events connected to their cause.

You might ask, "So how does social media matter to my business?" Well, here's the skinny: It's pervasive, so chances are your customers are already engaged with social media. The number of people using social media has grown rapidly in the last few years and doesn't show signs of slowing down. Think of social media as a form of word-of-mouth advertising — which is the best kind of advertising — but it's a new word of mouth, where word travels much, much faster.

Perhaps the most incredible result of social media is that it's becoming a place for search. Searching Facebook, for example, is like picking the brains of millions of people at once. When people are talking about *your* product or service, and they search the social media where the conversation is happening, it becomes another place for them to find *your* brand. In fact, if I was to make a prediction about the future of search, I'd say it's here, on social media sites. So, just as you need SEO for search engines like Google and Bing, you also need to keep SMO, or Social Media Optimization, as a part of your strategy. You need to have a social media presence, and all your content on social media (yes, your profile counts as content) needs to be optimized.

In light of SEO and SMO, your content marketing strategy will be barbell-shaped, in a sense. You need to network via social media in order to develop your online presence as much as you need to pay attention to search — if you're planning on succeeding. It's through social media that your content will circulate most rapidly and you will get some of the best links pointing to your pages. A successful social media campaign will increase your search presence, while at the same time bring traffic to your site. In addition to content development for search engines, this book will look closely at how your content and social media presence will interact and how you can optimize both.

Going Forward: Searchers Are Telling You How to Market to Them!

Between Google and Bing, we have the big two search engines determining search relevance by a very similar set of criteria. This is fortunate for us online marketers because we can, to a large extent, standardize our marketing strategies for the web and not have to spend an enormous amount of energy managing multiple approaches for different search engines…at least for now. The key to ranking in search, as well as to creating a buzz in social media, is good, solid content. Period. So, as a producer of content, you are now a publisher. You need to see yourself that way.

Publishers need to make engaging, useful content happen. If they don't

— if *you* don't — you won't succeed. As they say, publish or perish. This means you need to create engagement. You need to create relevance. In a sense, you need to learn to read the minds of the searchers in your market. The good news — the *really* good news — is that the web gives you free marketing data that will guide you toward creating relevant subject matter. It's like a sneak peek into the minds of your customers!

In some ways, your customers are doing your work for you. *Sweet!*

Developing a Content Marketing Mindset

As I've been saying, if you have a website, you're a publisher, and you have to think like one. This means producing fresh content on a regular basis. Print publishers create content to survive, because that's their business. On the Internet, it's the same for you. You need to keep thinking about content ideas all the time. You should encourage your entire staff to do the same.

A content marketing mindset means always being on the lookout for new content possibilities. Keep a little notebook on hand, or use your phone's voice recorder, so that when you get a great idea for a top-10 list, you can record the idea. When you attend an event, bring your camera (most likely your phone) so you that can post images of the event on your blog or social channels.

You can't create something cool once and let it sit idly online, expecting it to be cutting edge or consistently relevant to users. Instead, your job is to keep producing fresh material, even repurposing your best content, so that it reappears in a fresh form and gives you as many different opportunities to be found online as possible.

The bottom line is that achieving the goals in a content marketing strategy takes some serious effort. For any marketing person, to add *publisher* to the number of hats they already have to wear requires a major commitment of time and energy. I've found that many businesses don't have the budget to add more bodies to their staff in order to tackle the objectives in a content marketing program, so they have to juggle existing resources. How can businesses make it work?

Top down buy-in is critical, especially for small businesses. Key executives need to recognize that a content marketing strategy is crucial to their success on the Internet, and they need to understand that they, too, will have to participate. Once the top has bought in, you can get the rest of the staff involved. There is a place for everyone to help create content.

Above all, top-down buy-in means that you can look to anyone and everyone to provide inspiration and new ideas for content. Foster a fun environment where creative expression is valued. The more you encourage creativity, the more you can gain from your content marketing strategy. **And always remember, just because you wrote it, took a picture of it or shot a video, it doesn't mean you have to publish it.** But you have to start creating content with the *intent* of using it.

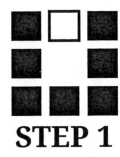

STEP 1

STRATEGY DEVELOPMENT
The Only Way to Succeed

With massive search engine updates and changing trends in technology and gadgetry, the landscape of content marketing is changing dramatically. Not only are content marketers required to create relevant, quality content, they need to create something that drives engagement and information for users across various platforms including wearable technology and mobile websites. When *Accelerate!* was published a few years ago, I would speak at conferences or workshops and ask the audience if they had ever heard of the term, "content marketing." By a show of hands, only small percentage had actually heard of it, let alone implemented it into their business plan.

Today, many businesses are employing entire content teams to manage and create content for their website. **This is for good reason: content marketing works!** These strategies have proven to be effective in gaining more traffic, more leads, and ultimately more business. While many companies understand the importance of content marketing, have researched the benefits, and are willing to make the initial investment in content marketing. – they are, unfortunately, stuck and have no idea where to start.

A solid content marketing strategy should act as a blueprint that will guide your efforts. It should be flexible so that ultimately it can be improved based on the identified successes and failures of your content. These strategies should help plan the following:

- Target audience
- Who will be producing the content
- What content will be produced
- Where the content will be published
- Promotional and social engagement
- Lead generation and nurturing
- Sales and revenue increases
- Measured results

Your strategy should not only focus on creating relative content, but also promoting, sharing, and engaging with the audience after it's published. Some would have you believe "if you build it they will come." It's just not true. It's more important than ever to use various social channels to generate user engagement and *promote* your content. Social media is very much a part of this strategy, and you will find success if you align your efforts between search and social for a holistic content strategy. The key is to create content that is easily sharable, compatible with mobile devices, and gets engagement from social channels like:

Source: http://www.ebizmba.com/articles/social-networking-websites

Figure 5: Social metrics comparison by platform

Business Success through a Solid Content Marketing Strategy

You won't find success without a well-planned and properly executed content strategy. Let's take Mint.com for example: Mint.com had 100,000 accounts in 2007, they were hitting a dead end in generating new leads and were looking for new ways not only to boost revenue for the company, but also to develop something that would provide value for their customers. Aaron Patzer, who launched the company in 2006, began doing some research on content marketing. He determined that it had the potential to be the answer for more leads (and more business), while delivering useful, helpful, information to an untapped market online. He was competing against banks that had massive budgets for advertising and marketing campaigns, so he developed a strategy that focused on quality blog posts, slideshows, videos and infographics to boost his brand awareness. He offered something his competitors weren't offering: engagement and approachability.

Mint.com built a unique personal finance blog; rich in informative content and topics that spoke to a young professional crowd. They chose this untapped target audience because they felt it had been neglected in their niche industry – and they were right! The company went from 100,000 accounts in 2007 to an amazing 600,000 in 2008. Eventually their blog, continuously updated with useful content that addressed common issues, would become #1 in personal finance. Their brilliant infographics and engaging articles became regular viral hits on Digg and Reddit. By 2009, the company grew to 2 million accounts, becoming the largest company in the personal finance market. Patzer would later sell the company to Intuit for $170 million. Today they have over 10 million customers, track more than $80 billion in credit and debit transactions, and hold nearly $1 trillion in loans and assets. A big part of that success came thanks to a solid content marketing strategy.

The company continued to fine-tune their content marketing strategy, and used the new found success to develop apps for the iPad, Tablet and Kindle. They realized that while you can find success online, people aren't just sitting at a desk, surfing the web. Much of that traffic comes from mobile devices. By creating content that is mobile friendly, they can tap into that younger audience from anywhere around the world. Of their 10 million users, more than 50% were coming to Mint straight from their smartphones.[5] Mint.com uses a content marketing strategy that *any company* can incorporate on a limited budget. They created robust content on different landing pages; for every popular finance query on Google, they targeted a page and content to it. They leveraged various social networks to create a conversation and engage with their audience. They got creative with their Facebook fan page and included Mint haiku contests, quick customer tips, and promotions for referencing the brand to a friend. Even if people considered personal finance boring, Mint was able to create topics that spoke to a younger audience and piqued their interest. One of my favorites was a series titled, "Train Wreck Tuesday" which featured sometimes humorous disasters in personal finance. Readers could even submit their own train wreck stories.

They had a "What's in your Wallet" feature where various people from all industries were asked finance questions like, "What type of credit card do you use?" and "What brokerage accounts do you have?" Mint streamlined their services to take only 10 minutes to set up and five minutes to automate payments for customers. Once people found Mint's content, they were quickly convinced that this was a leader in the industry, and built trust with the brand. This shows the true power of content marketing and the massive success that can be found by following through with a strategy.

Content Marketing Should be a Continuous Practice

If anything could impress on you only one thing from Mint.com's success, it would be that persistence pays off. A solid content marketing plan can take 4–7 months before noticing a return on investment. This is not a marketing campaign with a finish line. Your content marketing strategy should be treated as a philosophy and a continued practice that is combined with

---

5   http://vator.tv/news/2012-08-29-mintcom-tops-10m-users-5x-growth-in-3-years

all marketing efforts. Follow through with each of the steps and evaluate your successes and failures so that you can constantly improve and develop the strategy. You need to distribute your content efficiently to your customers and potential customers. When they look for answers online, you want them to find *your* content, *your* brand. To make that happen, you have to research, create, promote, distribute, and optimize all the content that you produce and then measure its performance. And you have to keep on doing it. All the time.

Be the Expert

Content marketing allows you to establish your brand as the expert in the industry, build trust with an audience, and turn that trust into business. Consider Valeria's point of view. She works a full-time job at a local hospital as a Registered Nurse. She loves taking care of her patients, but she wants to move up in her career and have a bigger impact in the field of healthcare. Valeria is a mother of two and has a lot of responsibilities at home, so she wonders if she even has the time to go back to school and earn an advanced degree to become a Nurse Practitioner.

One day she went online to find information to help her make a decision, and started with a question that is directly related to her needs, "How to become a Nurse Practitioner?" She clicked on a related article from the University of Tucson that offers a BSN-MSN bridge program online. Instead of the article advertising the program, it discussed the skills required to be a nurse practitioner and what it takes to be successful in the field. The article gave solutions to common challenges they face, including balancing work/home life. The article linked to a video with a title that caught Valeria's attention, "Top 5 Biggest Pet Peeves for Nurses" – the video shows funny reenactments of hospital employee interactions such as an empty coffee maker, overly suave doctors, and patients who have all the answers.

Even if Valeria is not ready to commit to the online degree program, she found the article useful and informative, and the video entertaining enough to share with friends in the healthcare industry. Valeria is able to trust the university because they demonstrated competence through their content without overselling their degree program. The

University of Tucson showed that they are not only experts in the health-care field, but caught Valeria's attention with their video title. On top of that, she is reading and watching all of this on *their* website where they have a good chance of capturing the lead! This is the direction your content strategy needs to go. In your industry, *you are the expert*; therefore, you can be the trusted solution and offer something the audience wants.

Like the fictitious University of Tucson, many organizations are just now starting to understand that, along with their "traditional" products and services, one of their new products has to be *information*. They specifically targeted someone like Valeria, a working adult with preexisting knowledge in the healthcare field. Their content offered information she could use in the real world, which built her trust in the brand. The trend is no longer about interruption-driven marketing techniques like television, radio or even newspaper ads. Businesses are now focusing on producing information – in the form of useful online content.

And just in the case of Valeria, people are willing to gather information and news from non-traditional sources. Most print news outlets have seen their readership shrink and migrate toward online content. In some cases they have made a complete shift to online content, shutting down their print operations altogether. Television and radio have made a similar shift to online content. You will often see them plugging their Twitter #hashtags, mobile apps, or online site during their broadcasts. The result, on the Internet, has been to blur the line between what was traditionally three different media forms (print, radio and television) into one: online information with mixed content forms, including text, images, audio, video and more. The bottom line: online content consumers will decide whether or not to accept the information based on the content's *quality and usefulness*.

This means that if your business publishes engaging content in a variety of forms, your customers will see your brand as a reliable source of information about your market. If your content is *high quality and useful*, it will position you as the trusted solution for your customers. The goal, then, for your content strategy is simple:

- **Provide quality content that solves the toughest problems your market faces.**

- **Position yourself as the trusted solutions provider for your industry and spread the word about it.**

- **Have people rely on you for your expertise as they become your customers.**

An engaging content marketing strategy enables you to be seen as a *source of information* for your customers and continue on as their *source for products or services*. Since Internet users have undergone a shift in what they accept as authoritative, you need to make the same adjustment. Demonstrating expertise in your field means showing the world what you do and how you do it.

With University of Tucson, their robust content demonstrated their knowledge in the healthcare industry and established themselves as an authoritative resource. Although the video took a humorous approach, it still gave viewers an insight on the real life idiosyncrasies that take place every day in the hospital, appealing to people interested in that field. The University of Tucson accomplished three very big things for their business and content marketing strategy: they generated a lead, got Valeria to share their content that could bring in more leads, and demonstrated their expertise in the field. Valeria now trusts them enough to revisit the site for more information and resources. When she's ready to take the next step in her career and go back to school, there will be only one place for her to choose. This is the kind of success that comes from a solid content marketing strategy, and it works in any market, whether it be an online university or small hobby shop. The key for any content marketing strategy is to develop engaging information – whether it's humorous, informational, or both – and to put it into action.

Create Personas around Your Target Audience

Your content marketing strategy must establish a target audience. Some marketers use the term "finding their personas" to describe the process of understanding their audience; others call it "target demographics." You can think of a *persona* as a marketing concept with a human face, human personality, and human needs and wants. Just as Mint.com targeted young professional adults and University of Tucson targeted working nurses, your niche audiences should be considered with every piece of content you create. We'll go deeper into this process in the next step, but take time to understand your audience's needs. You'll start by taking a look at how certain demographics are interacting with content in your niche. You can identify this market by:

- Researching various blogs in your industry.
- Observing who engages with the content.
- Studying how the audience is finding your existing content or the content of your competitors.
- Auditing your current website or blog to see which topics or content drew the most engagement and feedback.
- Monitoring your web analytics to view useful data about your potential target audience.

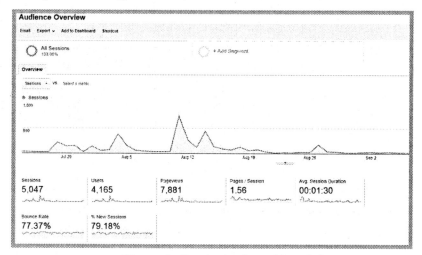

Figure 6: Google Analytics Visit Behavior

These patterns should tell you a lot about where your customers are coming from, where they are in their buying process, or what content they search for. Check out your current social interactions. If you do not have much engagement on your social channels, take a close look at how the audience communicates with your competitors' social channels? You should be able to get a clearer view on what type of content your audience likes to comment on and share, and this will be valuable information to have when researching or creating new content topics later in the strategy.

> **"Social media is the greatest free-market research environment ever because people out there are acting on their own and being more honest than they'll be in a focus group. You can survey people, but if you ask the wrong questions in the wrong way, they'll tell you what you want to hear. You want to hear the truth because you don't want to make an expensive mistake developing the wrong thing."**
>
> **–Brian Clark (@BrianClark)**

Who will Create your Content?

At the front end of this strategy, you can gain a lot of momentum researching your audience and developing ideas for content. The last thing you need is to hit a speed bump. And yet, now is just about the time that most companies run into one of the biggest speed bumps in this process: finding the resources to *develop* and *manage* a content marketing strategy. Conceptualizing, writing, and publishing quality content is a collaborative effort. You've got to foster a teamwork culture for content strategy across the company, from your sales department to designers and copywriters. Like many of us, you may not have the luxury of hiring a complete staff devoted to content marketing, and sometimes you need someone to wear many hats if it's not feasible to build a content creation team.

Responsibilities of a complete content marketing strategy include (but not limited to):

- Content/editorial management
- Content production
- Project budgeting, integration with other efforts
- Optimization
- Promotion/Distribution
- Audience development
- Research and measurement

Indeed, there are a number of hats you need to wear. In my opinion, one of the most critical hats is the director or manager. This role requires a blend of all responsibilities to oversee not only the content creation, but the promotion, distribution, and measurement of the content marketing strategy's success as well. Pay close attention to your content creators and producers, whether they write copy, design, or edit video, they have a huge impact on your content marketing strategy. Keep in mind, you may have a content producing goldmine in your company's existing staff, and you could mine them for content or resources. Remember – your main goal is to generate conversation with your content. The newly enlisted content team should listen to the target audience and begin creating content around their needs and questions.

> **"Communication and storytelling skills are critical these days. I would much rather have a group of amazing communicators, who can understand the business, wrap compelling and engaging stories around that business and communicate them brilliantly, than someone who can help me grind out an extra percentage point on my calls to action. It's not that those tasks aren't important – but they can't help me differentiate my brand. Great communicators will help me to be different."**
>
> **–Robert Rose (@Robert_Rose)**

Where will the Content be Published?

A big part of this strategy is planning exactly where this content will be going so that it reaches the right people. Just as a publisher would, you should establish a strategy that addresses each channel – including blogs, social media, websites, and email newsletters – that way you can take advantage of the strengths that each channel offers in engaging customers. Where will it be published across the web? What social channels will you use to promote it? A complete content marketing strategy makes efficient use of all targeted channels.

If you don't have a blog on your website yet, you're starting out behind the eight ball. By continuously posting quality content on your blog, you will benefit your rankings in Google and establish your brand as an authoritative resource in your niche industry. I generally recommend posting on your blog 3–5 times every week. Promote these posts on social media to reach a broad audience and generate the maximum amount of engagement.

Popular distribution channels allow you to post your original content and speak to an even broader audience. Networks like YouTube, Pinterest and Slideshare allow you to set up an optimized profile, which can direct people to your website or lead capture form. You don't want to miss out on this kind of low hanging fruit!

YouTube has established itself as a massive influencer in content marketing. By creating original video content, such as a how-to, expert interview, or even quick product review, you can support your thought leadership and build trust with a large audience.

If you regularly speak or create webinars, Slideshare offers an excellent opportunity to redistribute existing content. It can be used to distribute slides from a presentation, pages from a free guide, or even HD video from a relevant webinar series. When people search for common questions related to your slideshow, Google will list your slides on Slideshare as a trusted resource for information.

Pinterest has continued to gain more and more followers over the years. It's been able to take a snapshot of current trends and interests from people all over the world. Not only can Pinterest be crucial when establishing a target audience's needs, it can also be a way to show off your products, infographics, and other content by pinning it to optimized boards. This way your content can get prominent placement for your followers to engage, share, and re-pin, over a huge network.

It's imperative that we take mobile into consideration as we talk about publication and distribution. Content gets shared on mobile devices today more than ever before, and the trend shows no signs of slowing down. Be sure to create content that is not only going to generate traffic to your pages, but is also readable on mobile devises and easily shared from mobile platforms. Imagine someone shares an article on Facebook. You check Facebook's mobile app on your smartphone while you're on the subway, and you see the share. When you open the article to read it, it turns out that the website is not compatible and the article is nearly impossible to read. The obvious solution is to optimize your content to be fit for tablet and smartphone reading. When a user with a smartphone comes to your site, the objects on the screen will automatically adjust to fit the screen; you build once, and it fits nicely on all devices, from PCs to tablets and smartphones.

In fact, social media is an extremely useful way to promote and generate traffic to your content. After an article, video, or infographic is published, be sure to share it across various social channels to build a buzz around the piece. Your content marketing strategy should include scheduled posts on these channels, and real-time responses on comments or other user engagement. This type of attention shows the audience that you are an active member in the industry, and they will return to you for business or follow your brand for more information later. If you plan to post content on any social channels, be sure your company profiles are set up ahead of time and ready to receive content.

Establish Your Strategic Goals

In order to track content success, and guide your campaign, you need a strategy with specific objectives. By implementing these goals, you'll be able to discover what's working and then make changes along the way to hone in on an effective formula. Below are some of the goals you may want to consider for your organization.

Promote Thought Leadership

How do you want your customers – and the world, for that matter – to perceive you? Your brand lives in the content. To get your content marketing strategy rolling, you need to get people talking, mentioning, referencing, linking to, and especially, sharing your content. As your brand consistently provides valuable information to your customers and potential customers, so will the perception that you are a leader in the industry.

This begins with an online search for your brand and its executives, then tracking how many times you see them appear, as compared to similar searches for your competition. Are you generating enough thought leadership with your content? This kind of assessment needs to be done with some degree of regularity to keep track of how your brand, your key staff, and your product fit in with your community. Increasing your thought leadership, and influencing the audience's perception of your organization, comes down to distribution and promotion of your content. Your brand will start building an authoritative voice and authority in the industry as you are consistently generating shareable content, distributing it through multiple channels and promote it throughout your network. The more you promote and distribute new, useful content, the more you will boost your thought leadership within the industry.

Still to this day, I hear professionals say that their success within the industry speaks for itself, and there is no need to reinstate it to followers. I tell them that confidence is great, and their track record may be great too, but if they want to remain the expert in their industry they need to become a source of information for their customers. The reality is that each organization is competing with all kinds of content that attempts to engage its potential customers. If an organization's content isn't where their potential customers are looking, they will go somewhere else for expertise. So by promoting their expertise or content, businesses can remain a trusted solution in their industry.

People look online not only for products and services but to stay current in their field, keeping on top of what's hot right now, sharing tips on how problems are solved, and what tools work best. In other words, they aren't shopping: they're socializing and learning. If an organization wants to build on their thought leadership, they must be a source of information online and join the conversations that are happening in the industry. The best way to emphasize an organization's expertise is to produce and distribute content that demonstrates an inside knowledge of the keys to success within the industry and that offers real solutions to the problems customers in that industry face.

Reputation Management

Keep in mind that reputation management is a major production in its own right, and there are entire strategies to clear up a smeared reputation. This book does not aim to give a crash course in reputation management, nor are we giving you a comprehensive strategy for it (for that you might check out Andy Beal's book *Repped*). A reputation that has been marred often requires a major effort to clean up, months of work and, unfortunately, a considerable financial investment. For the scope of this book, I want to concentrate on how your content strategy can fit into your reputation management plan to *prevent* such problems.

Online reputation management is all about your presence online. As you craft your strategy (and eventually the content), you need to develop it around the goal of maintaining a high-quality reputation, ensuring that your customers and potential customers will find good mentions, excellent content, and exceptional reviews.

If there's one thing that can be said about the boom of social media, it's that conversations are everywhere on the Internet. These conversations can take the form of comments on blog posts, forums for customer rants, or user reviews, for example. You don't have ultimate control over these conversations, but you do have the opportunity to *participate* in these conversations.

The Internet is full of venues for consumers to vent their frustrations with products or services they've received. There are forums devoted to customer complaints and this can be found by potential clients or leads if good content doesn't outweigh it. Customers take the time to comment on a product they've received, sometimes even updating the original content with user-generated content (UGC). While this is great for consumer awareness, it can be challenging to present a balanced view of your product if there is vocalized negative press out there, especially when it seems to overshadow the good press.

Believe it or not, the solution to this problem is pretty simple: don't wait for a problem to develop. Proactive reputation management ensures that the organization's own content fills the search engine results page when searching for related questions, services or products. By ensuring that the organization's quality content is visible, it becomes much harder for negative content to rise up to page one on the search engine results page (SERP). Just like you, most searchers generally don't go past page one of the SERP. Organizations (even individuals) that want to manage their reputation with a content marketing strategy should focus on keeping page one filled with quality content that reinforces a positive brand image. When customers search for your brand, they should find nothing but positive information about your firm. A smart content strategy ensures that they'll find exactly that.

Take Vertical Measures, for example. A search for our company name returns with a variety of content – most of which we created internally, using staff as contributors. A Google search for "Vertical Measures" shows our brand image, top articles, and related content from distribution sites filling the results page (see Figure 7 on the following page). The No. 1 result is our domain, optimized to show 6 subpages on our website including our contact page. It's followed by our social channels and positive reviews on Yelp and other review sites. Nearly all the content on this page is content that we have developed and promoted, which is exactly how it should be.

Figure 7: Vertical Measures in the SERPs

Lower Customer Service Cost

Great content should solve the audience's problems. This has a hidden benefit that often gets overlooked. For customer service based industries, a lot of money is spent addressing customer complaints or employing staff to handle phone calls to answer questions. If you produce content that answers these concerns, customers will not only have a stronger relationship with your brand once they see you offering help, but they will also be able to solve the problem on their own without requiring the time and effort of a live representative. Content such as white papers, manuals, user guides, or simple FAQs on your website can help educate and empower your customers, resulting in fewer complaints and service calls.

This is extremely helpful for companies that send employees to homes or businesses on calls. Informative, quality content educates your customers on products or services, but also helps them understand your industry better. Educated customers are much more likely to share their knowledge with other customers or people asking questions in forums. Educated, empowered customers call your contact center less. In fact, they can even do some of that work in social media on your behalf – free of charge!

Customer Retention

Another common strategy uses your content to improve customer retention. This essentially means producing articles, videos, or other content that keeps people engaged and actively listening to your brand. You should keep your audience informed on new products, services, promotional giveaways, or updated information that they find useful. Social media is an awesome way to leverage your content so that customers keep coming back for more. It's a great way to keep followers up to date on industry news and service information that matters to them. While it's true that social media has changed the way customer outreach works, it isn't the only way. Email newsletters are still a great way to boost customer retention efforts. You can include email content in your strategy that delivers news and announcements, links to related articles from other industry leaders, or lure leads in with an attractive discount on a product or service.

Content that addresses customer support is a valuable way to build retention. Free guides, videos, FAQs and tutorials are huge when helping customers make better use of a product or service. This can also be done in the form of webinars, which can also be used for lead generation and retention. As a retention piece, they help customers understand how to use the product, while at the same time enables them to ask questions of product specialists.

Case studies have hidden benefits, too, and shouldn't be overlooked. They aren't just about proving the value of your product to prospective buyers. They show your clients how others are using your product, which provides them with new ideas for their own application. Hearing success stories from other companies in similar industries can be very inspiring – perhaps all the inspiration they need to sign a renewal contract, even if they have yet to see these results for themselves.

Lead Generation

If your company provides a service and doesn't necessarily sell products on your site, lead generation is especially important. So important, in fact, that lead generation, or Lead Gen, becomes the biggest goal for your company's content marketing strategy. Of B2B marketers polled, 78% stated that generating leads is the top challenge they face today. Content marketing is not only an effective way to generate quality leads, but it can also be more cost effective than other marketing alternatives.

One of my favorite types of content are free guides, whitepapers or case studies. These documents often contain interesting graphics and offer a robust amount of information. They can be written for niche audiences to help lead them towards making a buying decision. When executed well, a free guide can generate a large number of leads by simply placing content behind a lead capture form and requiring users to give some information before gaining access. Your content marketing strategy should include gated content that tracks leads and follows up with an informative newsletter, or other information source, that relates to their specific needs.

On the flip side, by researching your competitor's free guides, you can find some inspiration on what customers are asking about and looking for. This knowledge will come in handy when brainstorming and conducting competitive audits in the next step.

Increase Revenue

Bottom line: content isn't just there to increase traffic and get Facebook "Likes." Every part of this step requires that you have a clear understanding of your business goals and your target audience in order to achieve your one master goal: increased revenue. You can do this by developing a strategy that addresses the needs of your audience through the content you create. Your content must have a specific use for the customer. It should be geared toward an action, leading them down the sales funnel. Remember Valeria's interaction with the University of Tucson's content? Tucson built a trusting relationship with Valeria, which ultimately lead her to enroll at UT in their nurse practitioner program.

If you have created a piece of content that interested or engaged your target audience, they will be more willing to take an action and learn more. You've got to ensure that it helps users make a decision on what to buy or promotes an *action*. Action is good! Even if the action is only to share the article or a response in the comments; you have lift off. This is where the quality really matters – treat your content as a way to showcase your knowledge and leadership within the community. Your business and reputation does not speak for itself, so you must be the leading voice and your content will drive the charge. This approach gives credibility to your brand, ultimately leading to more revenue.

Search and Content Optimization

Any set of objectives for a content strategy would be incomplete if it ignored search engine optimization (SEO). Without considering SEO at the development stage, your content suffers major limitations before you even create it. Extending our bicycle metaphor from earlier, search and social optimization are like the tires of your bicycle. You can have a really hot bike – carbon frame, alloy parts, low spoke count wheels, aero rims– the works – but if your tires are low on air, you're going nowhere fast. By ensuring that each piece of content is optimized for search and has links to it, you give that content the best chance to be found in natural search.

Content development and search engine optimization go hand in hand. On-page SEO is about assuring that each content page has the nuts and bolts in place so that the page content will have the best chance for ranking highly in search. This means that your content needs to get plenty of links, both internal (your pages linking to other pages on your site) and external (other websites linking to your pages). Onsite SEO factors need your attention, factors like: title tags, optimized metadata, and assurance that the pages don't have excessive load time. As you develop content, keeping these SEO factors in mind ensures that content goes live in tip-top condition, improving your search engine rankings.

Every time a search engine bot crawls a site and finds fresh content, that site will be considered more authoritative, which increases its chances for higher rankings. Bots have a phenomenal amount of data to troll, so in an effort to conserve energy, they revisit a site more frequently only if that site has been providing new content to index. If the bot doesn't find fresh content on a site, it will lengthen the cycle that it returns to index again. If it finds fresh content, it increases the frequency it returns, even to the point that it may, hypothetically, never leave. Just by frequently producing new content, you give your whole site a boost in the search rankings.

On top of fresh content, Google and other search engines pay close attention to links in order to understand the importance of any page on the web. Every link is a vote for that page, so it's worthwhile to make an effort to attract links to your pages. Link attraction is about focusing on developing content that users want to share, which encourages natural linking. We will cover link attraction in detail in Step 4. For now, keep in mind that when someone consciously links to a piece of content, it's the strongest way to show that a piece of content has real value.

Measuring Successes and Failures

Many times, businesses assume that website traffic is the only thing they need to track for their strategy. After all, isn't the fundamental goal of content marketing to get people to our website? They want their content to be present in the search results, and they limit their objectives for their content right there. "We have to have a site, right? We let people know what we do and how to find us, right?" Well, sure, you want users to visit your site, but there is much more to be measured that will improve your content marketing strategy.

Certainly, increasing traffic to your site is important; however, unless you have advertisements on your site, and you're getting paid for page views, there isn't much to be gained from increased traffic, apart from reinforcing brand recognition. The ultimate goal for your strategy is to increase your conversion rates and generate sales for your business. Think about it: you may have an active Twitter following that gets a lot of engagement, or a Facebook page that gets a ton of likes, but the bottom line is that those channels alone do not convert followers into customers! The content that you promote on social media, then, needs to invite conversion from your pages. Your content should always work to funnel the traffic that you're getting to your conversion pages.

Your content will only add value to your business when it's relevant, engaging, and *useful*. Content that fails in this regard won't have a chance at going viral in social media channels, and rather than gaining valuable traffic, it will instead lead to high bounce rates. On the other hand, when you generate engaging content, you'll find that bounce rates drop and conversion rates go up. That's when you'll see your content take off in social media, too. It's a win-win!

The beauty is that you can objectively measure traffic increases and conversion rates, which means that you can have solid metrics for your social media campaign. For example, if you see increased traffic to your site and an increased rate of conversion when that traffic lands there, then your brand is strengthened, your mindshare has increased.

The ultimate goal of any content marketing strategy is to generate more traffic, more leads, more business. In the final step of this book, I'll help you use all these tools to measure the successes and failures of your content marketing strategy and provide tips on how to tweak your approach so that you can attain these very reachable goals.

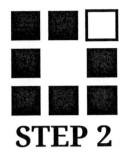

STEP 2

IDEATION

How Any Business Can Generate Hundreds of Useful Content Ideas

Now that you have a strategy — or maybe a better word is "blueprint" — in place, it's time to dive in and generate some great content topics. What makes a content topic great? That's for your audience to decide. Understanding what people are searching for will help generate brilliant ideas and useful content while improving your content marketing strategy. By doing some in-depth analysis, you can discover how people see products and services in your niche market.

You can discover *how people search* for the products and services you offer by analyzing long-tail keywords and spotting trending topics on related sites on which they spend their time. First, you need to understand the trends and how keyword phrases are used. Then you can develop your content to address your audience's needs and provide useful information that brings them to your brand. Going a step further, you can research what works for your competitors' content and enhance *your own* strategy based on the successes you find. By tailoring your content to answer your audience's specific questions or search queries, you'll be able to guide them to your products or services.

Keyword search analytics reveal how people search for content related to your industry. In combination with trending information, keyword research from Google Analytics and other resources can give you major insights into how your content can be found. Trending topics offer important insight into your customer's interests and needs, giving you more critical data. Trending data can come from multiple sources: social media, news, answer sites, and Google itself – places where conversations and content demonstrate your potential customers' interest. It's as if you have a window into the real issues your audience faces, giving you a chance to address those issues head on.

When you do research, you're investigating how searchers perceive products like yours and how they look for your services. With the information derived from this research, you can then develop your content and efficiently promote it where it's being discussed. The success of your entire content marketing strategy relies on research. If you drop the ball in the research department, your strategy doesn't stand a chance. Research is fundamental to subsequent steps in this plan, influencing every aspect of your strategy.

Find Information about Your Audience's Needs

The web is full of tools that determine what people are talking about, what they're searching for, what their community does or does not tolerate, and how your content could fit into the mix. Ignoring or rejecting the critical process of market research leads to misguided decision-making and lost opportunities.

> **In content marketing, don't just rely on your gut;**
> *go where the data leads you.*

In order to establish your target audience, you must identify their interests, their desires, and especially what they buy to fulfill those needs and interests. Before the explosion of the Internet, you had to survey consumers or create focus groups in order to conduct this kind of research. Not long ago, it would have been impossible to ask every person if they were interested in a particular kind of product. Information was gathered through demographic research and samples within demographics, but the Internet has changed the game. You now have endless information about your customers at your fingertips.

Chances are, the demographic you want to target interacts with the Internet in ways that will enable you to understand how they behave in your market. This information is valuable to all kinds of businesses, whether they are completely online or have a brick-and-mortar storefront. As you conduct research on your online audience, you'll be able to spot trends on local, national, and even global levels. Throughout this step, these are the resources you should use to research your market and find inspiration for great content:

- Google Analytics and Adwords Keyword Planner
- Content Inventory
- Social Media
- Competitor Analysis
- Ask your Staff and Customers
- Google and Bing Suggest
- Question and Answer Sites
- Curation websites
- Editorial Calendar

Keyword Research Using Google

Before you head down the ideation and research path, it's important to understand the keywords that are important to your business. Keep in mind that this is not the same type of keyword research you might conduct for an advertising campaign. This research is for content ideation. Generally the goal of keyword research for advertising is to find as many keyword combinations as possible to load into your ad campaign. With ideation, we focus on the longer phrases that people are searching for to build content around. There are many keyword research tools on the market, but for the purpose of this book, we'll take a look at Google Adwords Keyword Planner.

This tool allows you to enter multiple keywords to discover related keyword phrases and to compare search volume data. The results show all of the synonyms and related keywords for the terms you enter. Google refers to these results as "ideas" and for good reason: the huge amount of information that comes back can offer tons of ideas for content that incorporates these keyword combinations. For example, a search for "Grand Canyon" brings up all search terms that include the words "Grand" and "Canyon." You can get hundreds of results for a single term. You can also enter multiple terms to get variations on a number of ideas. By adding on the term "travel to," the results now include related terms to both entries as well as combinations of both, such as "Travel to Grand Canyon from Las Vegas," "Travel to Grand Canyon," etc.

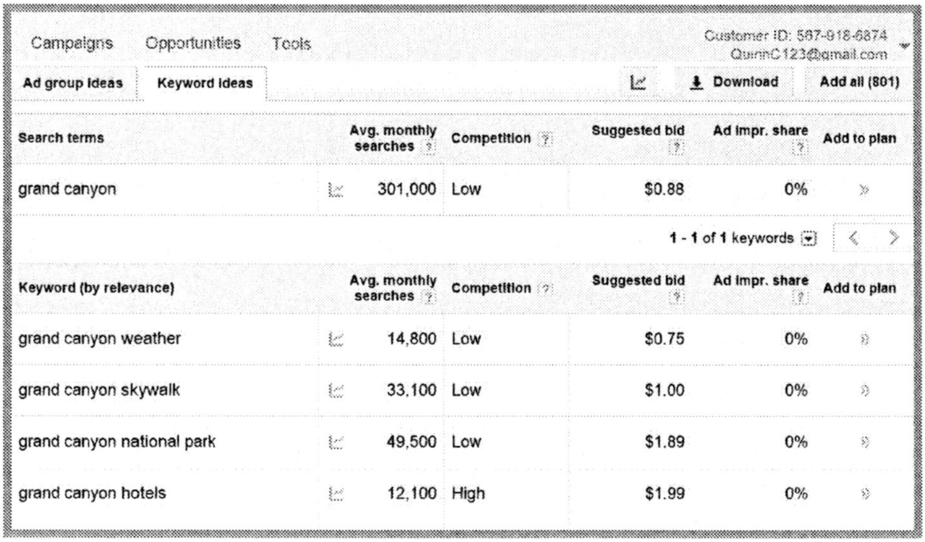

Search terms	Avg. monthly searches	Competition	Suggested bid	Ad impr. share	Add to plan
grand canyon	301,000	Low	$0.88	0%	

Keyword (by relevance)	Avg. monthly searches	Competition	Suggested bid	Ad impr. share	Add to plan
grand canyon weather	14,800	Low	$0.75	0%	
grand canyon skywalk	33,100	Low	$1.00	0%	
grand canyon national park	49,500	Low	$1.89	0%	
grand canyon hotels	12,100	High	$1.99	0%	

Figure 8: Google Adwords Keyword Tool for "grand canyon"

The analytic data that this tool offers includes:

- The competition for each term
- Number of global monthly searches
- Number of local monthly searches
- A bar graph depicting search volume by month
- Estimated average cost per click (for paid search)

The result set of "ideas" is an excellent way to identify new keyword combinations. By entering a single term, you get hundreds of possible variations with useful data on each term listed for easy comparison.

Monthly search volume is the first metric you should examine. In these columns you'll see the 12-month average number of user searches for the keyword. The monthly search volume is given in two columns, and it's important to know what they mean:

- "Global" monthly searches refers to searches for that term by searchers located anywhere in the world

- "Local" results refers to search activity of searchers located in the nation that you've selected (defaulting to the country you're in).

The Local Search Trends column displays, at a glance, the fluctuation of keyword traffic over the past year. Each bar on the graph represents one month of the calendar. This allows you to compare, conveniently on a single page, trend information between keywords. The competition for each term is also represented by a shaded bar graph. Here, the darker the bar, the more advertisers are bidding on the keyword. Bear in mind, for this graph, that competitiveness is relative to all keywords across Google, rather than the set of results you are working with. This standardizes the meaning of the competitiveness factor because it doesn't change with the result set. This will be useful when you prioritize the content topics later.

While the competition indicator is derived from paid search data, you can apply the data to organic search, as well. Businesses that want to rank in paid search will often optimize for the same terms in organic search so that their results appear in the Search Engine Results Page (SERP) multiple times. This means that the competition data for paid search will apply just as well to organic search. The average cost per click provides another indication of the value of each term in paid search. The price for a keyword goes up as websites bid for it. So, higher-dollar keywords are also going to be more competitive.

The biggest advantage to using Adwords is that it allows you to compare with relative ease multiple data points for a large number of keyword variations. You can use this tool to narrow in on a handful of terms that have good volume and competition and which are trending in a way that fits in with your strategy. Google AdWords works especially well as a first round keyword tool, helping you discover a variety of keywords to hone in on that will inspire your content creation efforts.

While Adwords allows you to discover how your audience searches the Internet, Google Analytics can provide a lot of information about the inbound searches that have landed searchers on *your domain*. It's a great tool for checking up on your keyword optimization efforts. This set of analytics reveals many of the keyword searches that landed searchers on your site and whether or not they converted while there. You'll see listed the specific phrases that bring traffic to your site. The search terms in this list can help you to anticipate variations on those terms. On top of this, you can find other opportunities for expanding the long-tail phrases within your content.

If your site has a search box, you can view the data for it in Google Analytics under Site Search. This will reveal what terms visitors are entering into the search box. In other words, you see exactly what they are searching for on your site. The data can reveal if your content is hard to find or that maybe it doesn't exist on your site. There you go – your visitors have just told you what content your site should have!

Inventory of Your Current Content Portfolio

It's critical that you take inventory of the current content housed on your site and your social channels. It can be a daunting task for larger sites, but it's important to know your starting point. Besides, when conducting inventories of your content, you are bound to find many pages that have old, inaccurate information on them. Some pages might need to be deleted all together.

Your existing content can provide a lot of information about how you can improve, what type of content you should create, and how to optimize your posts to be found easily in search or to be shared. Here are some things to look for:

- Where is your content being published on your site?
- How is your content currently organized on your site?
- Are you generating engagement with your content?
- Do you have a FAQ page that offers quick answers for visitors?

If your content is organized by category, are their some categories that are leaner on content than others? If you spot areas on your website that are in need of more information or updating – use this as an opportunity to create some great content for your audience. Are you publishing content on hard to find pages or an offsite blog? You want to ensure that regularly published content is easy to find to generate the most traffic and engagement with each piece. Sometimes great content ideas don't get the traction they deserve because they are not optimized when published.

For even more ideas, see how we recommend analyzing your competitors' content below. You can do the same exercise for your own content, thereby generating ideas for new content and steering your effort in the direction that has given you the most success. When you inventory your content, especially with a SWOT chart (below), you can identify your good ideas and give them a second chance at success.

Social Media

Social media channels have the power to reveal in real time your potential customers' interests. This can be enormously valuable to your business. Research through social media is an effective way to better understand how your potential customers think. In addition to understanding what they're talking about, you'll also see *how* they say it, giving you a great sense of the language they use to describe your products and how they perceive your market.

By paying attention to the conversations around the topics and concepts relating to your business, you'll spot trends in what people are saying, you'll become aware of the subtleties in the ways your customers phrase search requests, what content they respond to, and what invites user engagement. When you get to know the dynamics in your potential customers' conversations, you can develop rich answers to their most pressing questions, delivering those answers in terms that make sense to them.

Every social media site has its own community culture and etiquette. Each site brings a different kind of demographic data. Even if the same person is active on multiple social media sites, they behave differently on each site. Therefore, it's valuable for your business to approach social media in a similar way. The top three social sites can help you answer these questions:

Twitter: What #hashtags or trending topics are booming in your industry? What are people talking about and asking for?

Facebook: What type of content gets the most Shares and Likes in your industry? Are you posting as much content on Facebook as your competitors?

LinkedIn: How is your company viewed compared to your peers? Do you contribute or publish content that establishes your brand as a thought-leader in the industry?

To remain competitive you must keep abreast of social trends. This requires that you keep close watch on your competitors' social profiles to see how they engage their users, and you need to check back often. As you create content, continue to engage with social networks to keep current with the changing social trends. That way, you can engage your potential customers' right where they are, acting as a resource for their needs.

What are Your Competitors Doing?

Some of the very best content ideas come by keeping an eye on what your competitors are doing. It's likely that your competitors are already online, engaging with their customers and generating content that promotes their products and services. Create a list of your top several competitors and search for each brand on Google, Bing and in social media. By looking at what your competitors are up to, you'll gain an understanding of where your content can fit into the conversation.

One great way to measure the success of your competitors' content is to see who links to their pages. As we've described, one key way that Google and Bing measure content relevance is by links to pages. It follows that if your competitors are getting links to their content, then it must be working. Moz has a free tool that can quickly answer the question "how many links is a page getting?" Check out www.opensiteexplorer.org. Using this tool, and by specifically sorting by strongest pages, you can see the links pointing to any particular page (as long as it's in the Moz database). There you can analyze exactly the types of content that get the most links on your competitors' websites. Links imply that this content is being shared the most online, and you can use that data to develop your own shareable content.

As you investigate the pages your competitors produce, ask yourself:

- What kind of content seems to be attracting the most links on their site?

- How are they engaging their visitors?

- Is their content getting ranked up in news sites?

- Are their blogs popular on bookmarking sites?

- How are they using social media?

You can even go a step further and complete a SWOT content analysis for each of your selected competitors (see tables on the following page).

STRENGTHS	WEAKNESSES
Content that is likely to produce the greatest ROI (Return On Investment). What type of content are they creating really well? Are they engaging with the audience on social media? Are they promoting each piece of content?	Where are your competitors failing with their content? Is their content optimized around long-tail keywords and published correctly on their site? What areas or customer needs are they ignoring?

OPPORTUNITIES	THREATS
How would you build on their content to make it better? What long-tail keywords are they not utilizing that you can begin to target? What value can you provide to the audience that sets your content apart?	What obstacles might you face to improve the content created by your competitors? Does the competitor have more available resources, such as budget or staff? Do they create content that you cannot create such as infographics, mobile applications, etc?

By analyzing how your competition engages with their audiences, think about ways that you can replicate their success and improve the content that you deliver to your audience. During the SWOT analysis, you will find places where your competitors are missing big opportunities, giving you an advantage as you fill those gaps.

Directly Ask Your Staff and Customers

It turns out that one of the easiest ways to generate great content ideas happens to be right under your nose. Who better to ask than your staff and customers, themselves? I strongly recommend you identify all the people on your staff that connect with prospects or customers, and poll them. Look at anyone and everyone on your staff: it could be the delivery people, folks in accounting, front desk staff and especially your salespeople. Whether you go in person or use email or a survey product, all you need to do is ask them one question:

"What do they get asked all the time?"

Regardless of which department they work in, their answers will help generate ideas on what type of content your audience is looking for and would find useful. The questions your employees are asked will be the same ones those potential clients are searching for online. They are exactly the questions you should be answering with your content.

Figure 9: Team ideation meeting

Of course, it's always good to survey your existing customers, too. Use email or phone to ask them honest questions that will help you build trust and address their needs:

- What made you trust us?
- What information do you wish we had provided upon first contact?

- What information do you wish we had explained upon completion of services?
- What information were you looking to find when you began searching for a company like ours?
- What do you wish we would do better?
- Did you read online reviews about us?

You can get a huge amount of information from employees and existing customers, alone! Use these resources to get a jump start on content brainstorming. The information you discover can generate enough topics to fill weeks or months of content in your editorial calendar. (We will cover editorial calendars later in this step).

Using Google and Bing Suggest

Google and Bing both use a keyword suggestion feature to help searchers find what they are looking for more efficiently. Keyword suggestion instantly offers the top related keyword phrases as the searcher types the keyword phrase into the search box. The suggestions can change drastically as the searcher types each letter in the search box.

When the phrase appears that most closely conveys the idea that the searcher wants to express in the search, the searcher can select it from the list and go right to those results.

For example, say a family is looking to take a vacation to the Grand Canyon. The parents use online search to find information on nearby hotels and attractions to plan and book their trip. They might start their search by typing in: "visit the Grand Canyon." With every letter they type, the search suggestions become more and more specific. The parents' opening search is actively refined to help discover the best possible result for them.

Google

visit the grand 🎤

visit the grand **canyon**
visit the grand **canyon in march**
visit the grand **canyon from las vegas**
visit the grand **canyon in february**
visit the grand **canyon in may**
visit the grand **ole opry**
visit the grand **canyon in april**
visit the grand **canyon from phoenix**

Figure 10: Google Suggest

Searches related to visit the grand canyon

best time to visit the grand canyon   **fly to** visit the grand canyon

visit the grand canyon **from las vegas**   **map of arizona**

best way to visit the grand canyon   visit the grand canyon **skywalk**

visit the grand canyon **from phoenix**   **best place** visit the grand canyon

Figure 11: Google Related

From a research point of view, this information is a mini gold mine. By looking at Google suggest you can learn that people are frequently searching for visiting the Grand Canyon during specific months of the year because the search refines to show months. You can see that they want to know how to get to the Grand Canyon from Phoenix and Las Vegas. If I had a business that benefited at all from people visiting the Grand Canyon – like a hotel, helicopter service, rafting company, restaurants, chamber of commerce, visitors bureau, conventions, bus service, and so on – I would write 12 blog posts describing what it's like to visit the Grand Canyon during each month of the year. I would include things like weather, number of visitors, sunrise and sunset time, and more. And then I would create some content telling them how to get to the Grand Canyon both from Phoenix and Las Vegas. So in just a couple minutes of research, Google Suggest gave me 14 great content ideas!

This is a good place to remind you what content marketing is all about. When someone searches for "visit the Grand Canyon in October" and because you have created a piece of content that expertly answers this question, they see you in the search results and click on your listing. Where does that take them? – To your website! They are now reading your content on your website. You just won by being helpful!

If you're in the hospitality business, or own a nearby hotel, you want them to see your web page. You want them to engage with your content. Chances are very good that if you don't pay attention to the way this family, and all the travelers like them, are searching and discussing vacations in your area, you won't be able to bring that traffic to your website.

Google's other search feature, Instant Search, revolutionized the idea of search suggestion. Instant Search goes one step beyond keyword suggestion by actually populating the entire search results for the closest related keyword match. Instant Search is so fast that the results will update instantly as the searcher types new letters into the search. While these search features weren't designed for keyword research, you can get a lot of useful information from looking at how Keyword Suggest and Instant Search work to drive traffic toward particular keyword phrases in the search session. The technology has now been adopted by other major search engines, such as YouTube (see Figure 12 on page 37).

Start by typing a keyword phrase you're researching into the search engine and take note of how the refined search starts listing possible content ideas that you can later create. Keyword suggestion is designed to help the searcher target the search to the results that match his or her intent.

To start leveraging these search terms, you have to be able to anticipate the complex variations in search that individuals will use. You can get clues to these varied searches through a number of ways. Market research is a great way to start. Look at the questions people are asking about your industry on answer sites. The phrases that people use to ask questions can be the same kinds of questions they enter directly into a search engine for answers. Believe it or not, many clues are also actually sent directly to your business. Look at your customer service emails and other correspondence from individuals seeking information directly from you; they may use phrases that could appear in search. The comments you get on your company's blog posts are fantastic clues into how people communicate about your product or industry, what they're interested in, and what specific terms they're using to express their interest.

Figure 12: Youtube Suggest

"Hummingbird signaled Google's strong intent to look at queries more flexibly and get away from treating any given search string as a rigid and literal entity with a fixed result. We have to expect searches to get interpreted more often and we need to get away from being fixated on specific strings and think more in terms of concepts."

- Dr. Pete Meyers (@dr_pete)

Yahoo! Answers

Yahoo! Answers is still one of the biggest answer sites today, receiving hundreds of millions of questions and answers. The site gets a huge variety of questions, ranging from dating to homework to home and garden.

The way Yahoo! Answers works is simple; participants will submit questions to be answered by the community. When asking a question, the participant categorizes it by topic, making it easier to search and easier to answer. As an incentive to ensure that answers are accurate and free of spam, Yahoo! developed a point system. Answers are ranked by other users, and the "best answers" are given the most points. Users that accumulate points have proven to be reputable and are granted certain privileges, such as the ability to ask, answer, vote, and rate more frequently. With Yahoo! Answers, you can browse by category and see what kinds of questions are most popular, newest, or have received the fastest answers. In a way similar to polling customers and staff, these questions and answers can help you better understand the audience's needs and generate endless content ideas. Because every user has to categorize a question by topic before submitting, it's easy to research questions that pertain to your market. You can use your keyword phrases to sift through and browse questions that are being asked, either within niche categories or as a broad search. For example, after searching for the keyword "visit the Grand Canyon" over 400 questions and answers came back. Here are the top three questions:

1. "Where to stay when visiting the Grand Canyon?"
2. "Is visiting the Grand Canyon really worth it?"
3. "When is the best time to visit the Grand Canyon?"

If I own a business near the Grand Canyon or in the travel industry, these questions (and the hundreds that follow) give me a few ideas about what specifically people are after. All three of these questions revolve around planning a trip. So, right away I can infer that to be successful in this market, I have to find ways to provide information or services that focus on Grand Canyon visitors. Many questions in this search reveal that people are looking for fun activities around the Grand Canyon, including restaurants, parks, hotels, etc. Notice an opportunity for some content that will offer solutions to this problem? How about a Top10 list of coolest places to see the sun set? Or a resource page that offers information about nearby hotels to stay at? Answer sites can be bountiful sources for content ideas.

Figure 13: Yahoo! Answers

LinkedIn and Quora: B2B Networks with Big Questions

By now, most business professionals have a LinkedIn profile. LinkedIn is primarily a social networking site where members post their resume to their profile and add friends and industry colleagues to their network. Members are encouraged to include, in their network, colleagues from past professional experiences as well as current assignments, and then to develop a network of colleagues by industry.

Although LinkedIn has primarily been a social networking site aimed at business professionals, with more than 120 million networked individuals, LinkedIn can be used as a market research tool. The site boasts the ability for linked professionals to collaborate on projects and expand their ability to communicate across their industry through LinkedIn Groups. This key communication tool brings networked individuals together through invitation to the group. The group feature connects the members on a discussion board, and updates members by email when new information is added to the board.

In order to use it for research, you should join as many industry related groups as possible. Then you can monitor what is happening in the discussions. Often you will see a lot of activity around specific questions members are asking. Jot these ideas down as questions and topics you might address on your blog or website.

> **"Get a sense of which types of content are most popular on LinkedIn in your industry with LinkedIn's Trending Content tool, unveiled in March 2014. The interactive tool highlights the most popular content being shared on LinkedIn for various audiences and topic segments. Monitor this to understand what content your company should be creating and sharing on LinkedIn to generate the most engagement."**
>
> **– Barry Feldman (@FeldmanCreative)**

Quora is another great place to go for B2B organizations. It functions much the way Yahoo Answers does, but is more oriented to business. Quora has become an important player in the Q&A space. Like the others, it's meant to be a useful knowledge-indexing tool, a database of information provided by users. However, Quora is a *continually improving* collection of questions and answers because users review, edit, flag as useful/not useful, and even organize the content. The creators' goal was to have each question page become the best possible resource for someone who wants to know about the question.

Much like LinkedIn, you can monitor what's happening in your specific field of interest. When you see a lot of activity around specific questions, take note of these ideas as future topics you might address on your website.

Curation Sites and other Resources

If you diligently follow the steps outlined in this chapter, I'm confident that you'll end up with a list of hundreds of content ideas for your organization. But if you still feel the need to explore and add to that list, you can check out curation sites such as Alltop, Buzzfeed or Reddit. Curation sites gather the top performing content, across the web, related to niche industries. These lists can give you a snapshot of trends and popular topics that are bringing engagement and discussion around the world.

Alltop.com is quickly becoming one of the most popular curation sites available today. Alltop.com allows users to search for curated lists from a broad range of industries. Each page lists the top performing content alphabetically from various distributors around the Internet.

Figure 14: Alltop.com curation site

As you sift through Alltop, look at the content titles and topics that catch your eye. Do you think that your niche audience would find this useful? Is this something that your clients are asking all the time? Record these topics and take specific notes on how you can improve that existing piece of content. This will help later on when creating new, updated content that will offer even more value to your audience. Tracking curated content that's being searched for, engaged with, and shared can help you generate myriad content ideas for your business.

Leveraging Long-Tail Keyword Search

"Long-tail" keywords are the set of keyword searches that can be described as "niche searches." By practical definition, a "short- tail" keyword includes three or fewer words in the term, for example: "Grand Canyon." A long- tail keyword includes four or more words, such as: "Visiting the Grand Canyon Skywalk." Longer and more specific keyword strings generally have much lower volume per term than short-tail searches. Long-tail searches happen all the time, but they are hard to track because they don't always get enough volume to register in the analytic data. However, the sum total volume of these small-volume searches within a market can actually rival, in many cases, the volume for a popular short-tail term. A website that can rank for a large percentage of long-tail searches can compete with the huge volume of popular short-tail terms.

Not only that, it appears that searchers prefer to click on long-tail searches. The table below actually shows much higher click through rates for 7, 8 and 9 word phrases (see Figure 15 on page 43).

Words:	Total(%)	Organic(%)	PPC(%)
Total	31.28%	30.82%	0.46%
1	16.94%	16.46%	0.48%
2	99.08%	98.63%	0.45%
3	89.03%	88.68%	0.35%
4	86.11%	85.73%	0.38%
5	79.94%	79.6%	0.34%
6	82.05%	81.68%	0.37%
7	128.29%	127.46%	0.83%
8	130.63%	130.04%	0.59%
9	117.37%	116.63%	0.74%
10+	17.41%	17.31%	0.10%

Figure 15: Long tail keyword statistics

Ultimately, the way to leverage what people are searching for is to have a lot of content pages. The way to make this happen is to focus on being the source of expert information in your industry. An expert consistently provides content that is informative, engaging, and timely. By targeting lots of your pages based on the long-tail terms you've discovered in your research, you'll be able to compete against short-tail terms for traffic. While it can be tough to find ways to generate a large amount of content pages, two page types are perfect for going after long-tail terms:

Blog Articles: Blog posts are a fantastic way to address the pressing issues your customers face. When you regularly update your blog, you expand the content on your domain and give yourself numerous opportunities to incorporate new long-tail terms into your content.

Product Pages: Product descriptions are another great way to target long-tail searches. Product descriptions that spell out the make, model, color, and other options give customers searching for specific product details the ability to find them. Product descriptions are a very practical way to optimize for long- tail, and optimization for long-tail searches tends to be very predictable.

By having a lot of useful content on your site that *anticipates* the searchers' needs, your content can be found when those terms do get searched. As you continuously add new content, you increase your chances of grabbing more and more targeted search traffic.

I tell 95% of the businesses we work with that the best way to generate content ideas, create the content, and boost traffic to your site – not to mention beat the competition – is to leverage long- tail keywords. After devoting a year of effort, I would much prefer to have one hundred or two hundred new pieces of content ranking highly in the search engines, consistently bringing in more traffic, leads and revenue, over hoping I can produce a few blockbuster pieces with high search volumes.

Content/Editorial Calendar

Editorial calendars have been used by publishers to manage their content and ensure timely publication to readers for many years. Now that you've generated a stack of ideas using the strategies covered in this step, it's time to organize and develop those topics by using an editorial calendar. This is a critical part of the content marketing strategy. You will greatly benefit your content marketing program if you use this tool, and you'll get a clear outlook on current projects and upcoming content. I'm often surprised to find that many online businesses fail to adopt this tool into their content marketing strategy.

Similar to an editor in the traditional publishing industry, businesses should employ or designate an existing team member as a content marketing strategist who will track and manage an editorial calendar. An editorial calendar is crucial because it helps the strategist manage the broad range of media, including written articles, videos, and engagement on various social media channels. There are many ways to format and lay out an editorial content calendar; however, every editorial calendar should include, at minimum, an annual look, and detailed content roll out plans by month, always staying 60 to 90 days ahead. Your content editorial calendar should be available for all team members to view, either in a shared document online or saved somewhere on your business' shared drive.

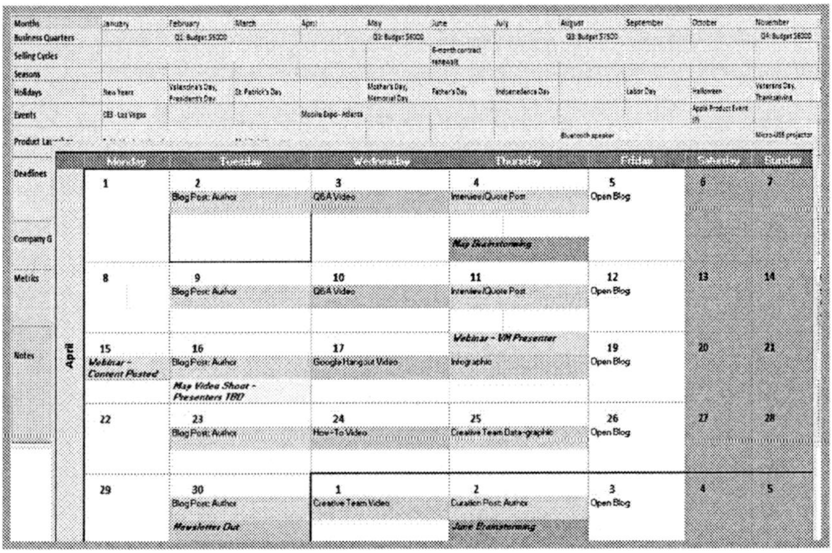

Figure 16: Content editorial calendar examples

The best editorial calendar plans a company's general content strategy a year in advance, with every piece of content that the organization intends to publish detailed two or three months ahead. It will include, not only the date of launch, but the steps included in meeting those goals, as well. The content strategist – or team – should frequently review the calendar to make improvements based on results and current trends, manage current projects, and brainstorm new ideas.

This calendar includes your content marketing plans for the year at a glance and offers a separate sheet to be used for each month, which includes a deeper look into each content project. A great way to collect ideas for the full year view of your editorial calendar is to gather team members to brainstorm for events coming up in the year ahead, like holidays, office openings or annual events. Here are some annual milestones you can consider when brainstorming for the coming year:

- **Business Quarters:** What are your quarterly goals? What resources do you/will you have each quarter? What is your quarterly content marketing budget? Having this information at hand can make it easier for the calendar manager to stay on track with goals, resources and budget.

- **Selling Cycles:** Does your business have specific cycles or trends throughout the year? Include any information regarding your selling cycles that can aid content producers and editors in their projects.

- **Seasons:** Does natural seasonality affect your business or does your industry have its own conceptual seasons? This data can be useful when brainstorming content ideas.

- **Holidays:** What major holidays or industry-specific holidays could you create content around? Additionally, the actual holiday dates are important for developing publishing schedules.

- **Events:** What industry events will you attend? What events will happen near you? This information is crucial to plan content projects ahead of time.

- **Product Launches:** What product launches should customers be aware of? Typically, some content will focus on specific product launches throughout the year.

- **Deadlines:** What are the current production deadlines for content that the team has set to meet? Deadlines that are already set in stone should be recorded so you can plan other content projects around them.

- **Company Goals:** What are your specific goals for the business? What do you hope to accomplish through these content projects?

- **Metrics:** What overall metrics will you track? Will you look at links, traffic and conversions? Outline goals upfront so content producers and editors can work to create content to effectively meet them.

An editorial calendar is more than just a spreadsheet filled with calendar dates, holidays and writer deadlines. A quality content calendar should be able to help your team track the creation and publication of each piece of content every month. The calendar should list specifics for the content, and include information such as:

- **Title/Description:** What is the title of the content piece? Describe the piece so others can identify the main theme and message.

- **Status:** What is the current status of this project? This column could be color-coded or labeled with different categories like "in progress," "on hold," or "with editor" so the standing of the content project is easily identifiable.

- **Type of Content:** This piece is what type of content? Types of content include blog posts, articles, videos, podcasts, slide shows, whitepapers, etc. This information is important for resource planning and identifying content trends and popularity.

- **Producer/Designer:** Who will be responsible for the creation of each piece? This person will be in charge of both completing the content piece and of managing the project throughout.

- **Editor:** Who is the editor for each content project? The editor is generally the last person who sees the content piece before it is distributed. This person is responsible for double-checking spelling and grammar while fact-checking content as well.

- **Target Audience:** Is this content piece intended for potential customers, current customers or another audience? What demographic are you targeting? It is important to identify this information before content distribution.

- **Distribution Channels:** Where will this content live? On what social networks will you share this content? Be sure the content distribution channels match where the target audience hangs out online for maximum content exposure. One the content is live, this is a good place to enter the URL.

- **Promotion:** What promotional efforts will take place to distribute this content piece? Will this content piece be leveraged by another digital marketing channel? Perhaps a content piece can be used in other online marketing efforts, giving your content a longer life cycle.

- **Meta Data Tags:** What tags or keywords are associated with this content piece? Be sure to check with the SEO team on the best tags and keywords to use with each content piece for maximum SEO potential. What good is your quality content if it can't be found? Ensure your content is optimized not just for your audience, but for search engines too.

- **Metrics:** Against what success metrics will you measure this content project? Are there baseline measurements? What are they? These metrics and baselines will depict whether or not a content project is successful.

- **Notes:** Are there any specific instructions or notes regarding this content piece? Are there updates to the project's status? Add anything extra worth noting in this column.

You should look into customizing your editorial content calendar to fit your organization's specific needs. Consider these additional columns:

- **Image Link:** If the content project is text based, having an Image Link column could help the person posting the content. The link could be to a website or to a folder or image on your shared drive.

- **Social Updates:** This could be the same as the Promotion column, but could also be an additional section. If you plan on sharing this content across social networks (which you should!), you may consider including Tweets, Facebook status updates and Google+ posts that can easily be copied by all that have access to the document.

Overall, there are many ways to adapt these editorial calendar suggestions to fit your own needs. The important part is getting your content projects organized in such a way that your team and project manager can easily digest them. Using an editorial calendar for content marketing projects is important in more ways than one. Not only will your content be organized in a way that makes sense – chronologically by month – you will have a record of all of your past content projects. This can be an essential tool when measuring your content marketing strategy's progress. Having a list of past content projects on hand allows for easier reporting and quick recognition of milestones and achievements.

If you use outside writers to create your articles or blog posts, editorial calendars can be used to efficiently track deadlines and payments. With months planned ahead, these calendars can make working with outsourced writing staff easier because you can assign projects well in advance and give your writers, or researchers, plenty of time to construct great content. Editorial calendars can also assist with managing multiple guest contributors by tracking specific dates and avoiding possible duplicate content.

Best of all, content marketing project organization can aid in brainstorming future projects and provide content repurposing and refreshing ideas. Essentially, being organized has a direct effect on your level of inspiration! As you determine what type of content is working within your field, an editorial calendar can also be a great way to generate new ideas and create different topics. Content strategists should review the calendar to spot topic areas that are lean in content, and deserve more focus. This can greatly help balance your content portfolio and ensure that you answer your readers' questions. Planning for future content topics can give your team plenty of time for research and production. Write down these new ideas and plan ahead for upcoming months. If your company's process involves various stakeholders, this can alleviate bottlenecks and stress during deadlines.

By using a calendar to manage the processes involved with producing your content, you can log where your content is published, and track the successes of each piece you create. While it's recommended that you plot a year out, that doesn't mean that you can't adapt your calendar to changing trends. The calendar is a guide to keep you on track with your content objectives, and it can be updated as necessary. It's very important that you consistently post content on your blog or website in order to gain followers and more traffic to your site. An editorial calendar allows you to plan when to post different topics related to your industry, publishing high priority topics first that will offer the most value to the reader. A properly scheduled calendar can also provide enough foresight for upcoming projects so that you can use it to promote product releases or company announcements. For example, if your company is holding a conference or attending a big trade show, you can publish scheduled content leading up to that event. You can plan for a running series of articles to help cover a large topic over a few posts, or schedule themes for your content based on the seasons, or holidays.

Editorial calendars not only ensure that the content will be delivered on time, but they also help manage where all the content is going; whether on your blog, YouTube channel, webpage, or other distribution sites. Once the post goes live, the content strategist can then track the metrics to evaluate successes and failures.

Every company that produces content needs an editorial calendar. It is an essential tool for tracking content projects, generating new ideas, and planning for the future. Once you've researched the necessary markets, ran a thorough inventory of your content, and examined your competitors' portfolio, then you can begin to organize these new found topic ideas within the content calendar.

To help get your content organized and improve your content marketing strategy, you can get a free download of a Content Editorial Calendar Template. You can find it here: VerticalMeasures.com/calendar.

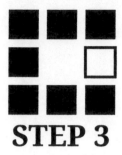

CONTENT CREATION
You Are Now A Publisher

Now that you have spent some time brainstorming and coming up with topics that can answer popular questions and provide value to your audience, it's time to take those topics and ideas and begin creating quality content.

Obviously, your content marketing strategy centers on consistently delivering useful content to your audience. The type of content that you produce will be catered to the demographic that you want to target, and you'll need to provide a variety of content across the whole spectrum that appeals to that demographic. To do that, you've got to free yourself up to experiment with forms of content that might seem edgy or outside the box.

Your website is not only a place to inform your customer base of your products and services, leading to a sale, it is also your *platform for publication*, and that's a beautiful thing. Publication on the web should not be a frightening endeavor. Instead, it should be, well, fun! Publishing isn't about inflating your site with useless fluff. Instead, you'll add interesting media that engages and educates your visitors, encouraging them to return.

Publishing is about consistency. Sporadic bursts of creative energy don't sustain a print publication, and it won't work well for your site, either. Model content production after the periodical industry and provide content on a regular schedule. The content can take many forms: lists, contests, images, video, infographics... you name it.

To Become the Trusted Solution, You Must be the Expert

Your goal as publisher is to generate engaging pages that position you as the expert in your industry. See, there's this one enduring problem that comes with an open and free Internet – anyone can put anything out there. While this is great for free speech, it has made web users a bit wary about the claims that are made online. Web users are famously cynical about advertising on the web. Ads that make claims of expertise fall short on the consumer. You can gain your customers' trust by actually *being the expert*, demonstrating in your media that you are the trusted adviser in your industry. In the world of publishing, there's an old saying, "Show, don't tell." This describes the posture your content needs to take. Don't just *tell* the consumer that you're the expert, expecting them to buy into it – everyone on the Internet makes the same claim, so what's the difference with you? You need to *show* that you *are* the expert; prove it up front with your informative, educational, and awesome content.

> **"You can't position yourself as an influencer — not in a way that has any staying power, anyway — any more than you can position yourself as being clever or attractive. That determination isn't yours to make. It's up to the "influenced" to decide if you are influential. I think that's one of the challenges marketers struggle to overcome. We focus on the symptom not the ill. To try to be seen as an influencer is likely to fail; but to create content that's inherently valuable, or surprisingly human, or unexpectedly useful, *that's* how, over time, you'll be seen as an influencer. Chasing the term itself will, ironically, pretty much guarantee that you'll never achieve it."**
>
> **– Joe Chernov (@jchernov)**

Content that *tells* the audience that it's coming from an expert feels hollow to them. That's called advertising, and the web is full of it. Anyone can say that they're the expert. How do you know it to be true? Experts prove it naturally by showing you. When your pages reflect an understanding of the real needs of your potential customers, and responds with solutions to their needs, then you've demonstrated you know your stuff, and your knowledge can be trusted.

Expert content takes a variety of forms. For example, it can be your blog talking about the current atmosphere in your industry and how it could affect your customers. It can be an article that solves a common problem that your customers experience. It can be the slideshow you presented at your last conference. This kind of content exudes confidence in your ability to solve your customers' problems. It even goes one step further – it demonstrates that you are the leading solutions provider in your industry, and that other solutions providers actually turn to *your* company for expertise.

Get Going With Content

Engaging content is genuine and believable. It appeals to our human sense of curiosity and can even inspire awe in us. The very best content has an un-self-conscious immediacy that makes it accessible to the audience it engages. Content that excels in this way has a tendency to get noticed, passed around, and, sure enough, attract links too.

The content development process centers on an ability to keep inspired. It's about seeing opportunities to nab raw materials and turn them into marketable content. It means being prepared, like bringing a digital camera to a conference or keeping a small video camera in a desk at the office. All it takes is a proactive mentality and a little creativity.

Let's be honest, content is the fun part of this business! It's where you get to showcase your knowledge and creativity. This is your big opportunity to invite the world to get to know your company, to exhibit how your team tackles the toughest problems in your industry, and to provide the solutions people actually need.

A big part of any content marketing strategy is trying out new ideas. It's not about trial and *error*; it's about trial and *testing*. When you try a new idea, measure its success. As I'll detail in Step Eight, I recommend that every time you create content, you follow up with measurement. That way, you'll discover what works for your target audience, and you can continue to produce the content that works. The results will reduce the risk of wasted efforts in the future and will guide you into your next endeavor. If you don't measure, then you'll end up throwing your ideas against the wall to see what sticks. Who has time to waste like that? You can't be afraid to try new things in a content marketing strategy. Heck, that's true for any marketing strategy. When you step out and take a risk with a new content idea, you've got to track its success; otherwise, you won't know if your risks are paying off.

After following the ideation process laid out in Step Two, you should have a plethora of content ideas that you want to be seen by as many people as possible, right? Most importantly, you want your content to reach not only a lot of people, but the *right* people. Success is not measured only by the number of hits a page gets. Ultimately, if your page gets a thousand views, but only 10 people commit to buying your product, then those 10 people were the most important visitors. It may sound like I'm reducing this to quality over quantity. I'm not. I don't think you have to pick quality or quantity. In my opinion that's a false dichotomy. I'm of the opinion that in this business it's about both quantity *and* quality. You don't need to worry about having one big, fat, fantastic idea that gets a million hits on day one.

To go with a baseball analogy, all you've got to do is to get a single. Then get another single, and another. Your fourth single is a run scored. You're more likely to strike out when you try for the big, out-of-the-park grand slam. Since baseball is a statistician's sport, let's look at some stats. In a recent Major League Baseball season:

- There were 165,360 total at bats.
- There were 132 grand slams.
- There were 4,620 home runs.
- And based on the overall batting average (.257), there were 42,498 hits.

From this data, we can say that about one in four at bats will result in a hit (which implies 3 out of 4 attempts went for naught), while about one in 36 at bats will result in a homerun. Only one in 1,253 at bats results in a grand slam! This means that statistically it's better to work your way around the bases one single at a time.

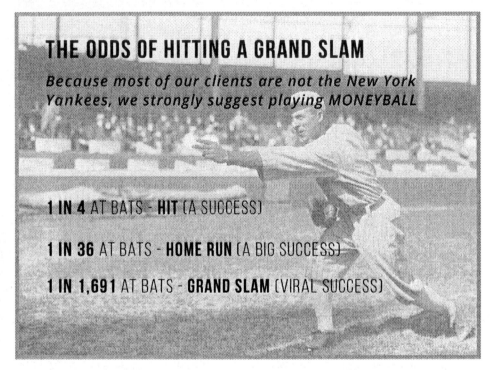

Figure 18: MLB at bat statistics

I'm not asking you to lower the standard on your content. If you're going to work your way around the bases, so to speak, the key is *to actually get the single* and then keep getting them. This means you consistently produce and distribute useful, engaging content that's targeted to your audience. If you get a grand slam, sweet! A good coach would tell you to celebrate that grand slam, and then get back to hitting singles – don't base your whole content marketing strategy around grand slams.

Why Story Telling is Important

So, what exactly is *compelling* content? Essentially, "compelling" translates on the Internet to mean "shareworthy." This is a term we use in the industry to mean that it appeals to an audience and inspires them to share it with their network. From your market research, you have a pretty good idea of what kind of content already interests your target audience. You know what they're sharing, what gets "liked" and what they link to. You know if they are into a particular media form – maybe videos are hot with your audience, or maybe they love lists. That's where you should begin, because it compels them to engage and share with their peers.

People love stories. When we share our lives with one another, we do it through stories. We meet over coffee to talk about what happened to us at work; we call our friend up to tell a story about our crazy party last night. Compelling stories persuade us and have the power to change our deeply-held beliefs. To really engage your audience, deliver stories that they want to read, watch or hear – stories they want to be a part of and will enjoy so much that they will be inspired to share them.

Storytelling has been around for as long as *homo sapiens* have existed, but the way we tell stories has evolved dramatically throughout the course of time, from painting the walls of caves, to the written word, music, theater, to digital communication on the Internet. Today we have the ability to share our stories with the largest audience ever. In the form of online videos, blog posts, and social media networks, we have the power to reach a population that storytellers before could never fathom. Even though the audience is bigger than ever, and despite the many changes in the way we tell stories, some of the fundamentals have remained unchanged.

The best stories relate to people of any age or culture, speaking to that mysterious thing that makes us "human." Humans know it when they see it. As marketers, we constantly tell stories to our audiences, particularly through our content, all the while trying to connect with that mystery. But what makes a story truly exceptional, even when the subject matter isn't the most interesting? Here are some compelling storytelling techniques that will enhance your content marketing efforts:

- **Remember the Essentials:** It may seem obvious, but don't skip out on the essential parts of storytelling. Think about it – without memorable characters, what good is a great plot line? Similarly, if you have an interesting story full of peaks and valleys, but no conclusion, people will just be confused and unsatisfied with your story. Make sure to include each basic element of storytelling in your storyboard, blog post or other content project.

- **Dissect Your Favorite Stories:** Your favorite stories are your favorites for a reason. Pull apart your favorite stories and find out why you *really* like them. Is it the plot line or the characters? Does the story teach a lesson that resonates with you? It may be easy to see why you love certain movies or novels, but applying that question to business may be more difficult. Think of your favorite YouTube videos or blog posts – why do you like them so much? Why do you return to your favorite site to read articles? Apply your findings to your own story.

- **Learn From the Masters:** Study successful storytellers including fiction and non-fiction writers, playwrights, directors, actors and even storytellers in your industry. Find out what inspired them to tell their stories. Read their histories and explore their processes. Borrow what you can from their methodology, patterns and idiosyncrasies. These people are successful storytellers for a reason, so see what you can learn about their methods and apply them to your own content projects.

- **Discover Different Media:** Storytelling comes in many forms – articles, novels, movies, blog posts, videos presentations and more. Don't be afraid to dabble in different media – getting out of you comfort zone is the best way to improve and expand your content portfolio. Be sure to research your target audience to find which medium it prefers. Also consider which medium works best for the story you are trying to tell. If your story has lots of dialogue, perhaps a video would be best. If the story is a narrative, the written word may be better. Check out tools like Prezi, Tiki-Toki, Canva and Visual.ly that are transforming the way we present information, data and stories.

- **Fascinate Your Audience:** Working to fascinate your audience may not be an easy feat, depending on what industry you're in.

But if you do fascinate them, they will surely remember your story and your brand. To tap into your audience's fascinations, consider working in one of the seven fascination triggers. These triggers, as described by branding expert Sally Hogshead[6], include: power, lust, mystique, alarm, prestige, vice and trust. She explains, "By mastering the triggers, your ideas become more memorable."

- **Be Honest:** Whether you are telling the story of your brand or telling a story about your industry, it is extremely important to tell the truth. If there is anything to be learned from the Internet, it's this: If you aren't truthful, people will find out. And once one person knows, everyone will know. The last thing you want is to be known as dishonest and lose credibility. While some degree of enthusiasm is permitted in marketing and in business, it's not a good idea to embellish your stories just to earn the interest of your audience. That kind of attention is short-lived and it is not a sustainable approach to marketing.

- **Keep the Audience's Interests in Mind:** Think about what is interesting to your audience as consumers and work that storyline. Tell the story for your audience, and always keep their interests in mind throughout the creative process. Your content should not only spike the interest of your audience, but offer something valuable to them within the story. Whether it's adding knowledge or simply for entertainment, you must offer something interesting to your audience.

- **Show Your Personality:** Sometimes brands are afraid of letting their personality show for fear of being labeled a certain way. The fact is, people connect with other people, and even more so with other people who are similar to themselves in some way. If your story doesn't divulge something personal or unfamiliar about your brand or business, your story could end up being boring. People don't spend time with boring stories – they quickly move on to something that is compelling and engaging. Don't let your story get skipped over. Share your personality and individuality with your audience.

---

6 http://www.howtofascinate.com/

Overall, there are many techniques to telling a memorable story. Most importantly, be true to your brand and tell a story that you are proud of, that can be repeated for many years to come. One of the fundamental goals of content marketing, and really of all marketing, is to create a fan base that will spread your stories for free, lowering your marketing expenses. Content that appeals to our social nature is ideal for storytelling, so find the stories about your employees, your company, your services and your products and tell them!

You Have a Blog Right? – RIGHT?!

The word "blog" is a blend of the words "web" and "log"; therefore, it's a place, either on your website or as a standalone site that gets updated frequently, like a log or journal. Blogs are platforms that enable regular communication with followers and visitors. For business applications, blogs should focus on the needs of your customers and the industry in general.

To be honest, when I was putting this book together, I thought I could have skipped having a section encouraging you to have a blog on your domain by now. I would have expected that everyone knew about blogs and made use of them. But I keep running into so many businesses and organizations of all types that do not have an active blog on their website. So, I'll keep preaching about the need to have a blog *on your website*, not hosted somewhere else.

As long as the blog is located on your website or domain, all the content that gets generated on the blog becomes new pages for your site. Blog content can be everything from text to video to podcasts to infographics (we will dive into the different types of content later in the chapter). All the content in a blog is searchable and can be archived, and every post has potential for coming up in the search engine results page. Once the blog is up and running, it can be a source of content that can be repurposed for other applications, too. Practically any kind of content can be posted on the blog.

If you still need to be convinced to have a blog on your site, look at these statistics from HubSpot:

- **Websites that have blogs get twice as many inbound links as websites without blogs.**

- **Sites with blogs will get about 400% more indexed pages and will see a more than 50% increase in traffic over websites that lack a blog.**

These stats alone tell you that a blog is pretty important to your content marketing strategy from a traffic and SEO perspective. The bottom line is that having a blog on your website provides you with a very easy-to-use platform to publish content on a routine basis, which gets the attention of search engines and gives people content that they can engage with. I'm calling it an "easy-to-use" platform because once your blog is set up, you don't really have to interact with your webmaster to add new pages. Your company has already given you permission to blog, so you just log into the management tool to submit posts.

Ideally, visitors find your blog so interesting that they will be compelled to follow, comment, and share your posts. Additionally, your visitors love User Generated Content (UGC); they love to interact with the ideas posted on blogs, and it creates a community atmosphere on your website. Search engines love UGC, too, which is another reason search engines like blogs.

16 Examples of Content for Your Business

You can certainly create a killer blog or an amazing podcast as the cornerstone of your content. But it's more efficient and effective in the long term (and necessary for larger organizations) to take a broader view – to create content that can come to life in various formats, across many different platforms, and that can address multiple audiences.

Please note: Each content option has merit of its own and should be judged separately on its value to your content marketing strategy. I do not recommend tackling all of them unless you have significant resources available. Pick only the ones that you feel confident in and will allow you to do a stellar job.

Press Releases

What are they?

Typically, a news release or press release is a written communication directed at the news media for the purpose of announcing a newsworthy piece of information. For your business, "newsworthy" doesn't have to mean headlining in *The New York Times*. This means announcing events or products relative to the activities in your business. These releases go out to the online press, but if they happen to be really good, they may get picked up by the big news outlets. The communication needs to be presented in a professional way and is usually very concise for business announcements.

How are they valuable?

Press release marketing will help expand your brand and exposure by targeting those that are interested in your industry's services. Many websites have RSS feeds,[7] which grab news releases off the press wires so that content will keep flowing on their site and will keep their viewers up on the latest news in their area of interest. RSS feeds scan the press wires looking for certain keywords. If your press release has keywords that these feeds are looking for, your news will spread. There are websites that you may never have heard of looking for content that you have. Say, for example, a Ford Mustang hobbyist website has a RSS feed that's set to collect any news coming off the wires that has the words "Ford" and "Mustang" in it. So it monitors PR Wire, and if it sees a post with those terms, the post gets re-posted on the feed.

In addition to expanding your potential customer base, press releases can help you gain backlinks by embedding links back to your site within your release. If that content gets picked up and reposted elsewhere on the Internet, that's more links back to your site.

For a small fee, a press release service will issue your announcement to the press wires in hopes that Google, Yahoo!, Bing or the AP wire service

---

7 http://www.whatisrss.com/

picks it up. And that actually happens more often than you might think. If you get approved ahead of time, Yahoo! News and Google News, for example, say, "You've got news? Great! We'll post it, keep it coming." If nobody clicks on it, normally it's gone by the end of the day (if not a lot sooner), but if it gets read and passed around, then it moves up to their hotlists, and that's what you really want – traffic and exposure from the hotlist.

More than likely, for day-to-day news released on the online press wires, there won't be anyone on the press side to edit the article. So whatever you write will hit the online press in the form you submit it. For this reason, you might consider finding a freelance journalist to write the actual press release for you. That way you can be sure that it conforms to press standards. Here's the basic information you'll need to provide the writer or follow for yourself:

- **Headline**: Incorporate your primary keyword phrase in the headline of your press release, and keep it at or under 10 words. The headline should be catchy and act as a lead-in to the article.

- **Summary**: Provide a short summary of the announcement (10 to 20 words) highlighting the press release's main subject.

- **Optimize**: You want to optimize each press release for keywords, because these get picked up by RSS feeds. Try to fit two or three keyword phrases into the body of the announcement, with the most important keywords in the title.

- **Add Links**: Be sure to include the URL(s) you'd like to link to in the press release.

- **A Quote**: A press release should include a quote from a person in your company. Be sure to include their name and title.

For this content type, people often hesitate and ask, "What do I write about? What do I have to announce that's important enough for a press release?" Actually, you'd be surprised at how much newsworthy activity is happening around your business. You can issue a press release on just about anything that's happening with your company. Here is a list of ideas to get you started:

- A new employee has joined your staff.
- An individual in your business will serve in a leadership position for a charitable organization.
- Recognition of the company, product or executives by a publication.
- A statement of position regarding a local, regional, or national issue.
- Announcing the results of research or surveys you have conducted.
- Making public statements on future business trends or conditions.
- Announcing that you've reached a major milestone.
- Forming a new strategic partnership or alliance.
- Expanding or renovating the business.
- Announcing free information available on your website.
- Sponsoring a workshop or seminar.
- Celebrating an anniversary.

I suggest you incorporate press releases into your editorial calendar so that you produce them on a regular basis, targeting at least one per month. The bottom line is that you can write press releases about your company, your products, your employees, your customers, community activities, and even your marketing efforts!

Top Lists

What are they?

Top Lists are arguably the most popular form of content on blogs today. I get asked all the time if this type of content is still worth creating since it seems somewhat overused, and my answer is always a resounding, "Yes!" The effectiveness of this type of headline and content has been long proven, even before the internet – so you shouldn't worry about it just being a trend that will eventually die out – people love Top Lists! I believe it is because we all love it when someone else has done the research for us, summarized it, and has made it easily digestible. Top Lists work due to the nature of the attention-grabbing power of the headline. Any headline that lists a number of details, secrets, categories, or tips will work because it makes it very clear what the reader can expect when clicking on the article. Additionally, these types of posts and articles are perfect for building your authority and demonstrating that you are the expert in the field.

How are they valuable?

In today's fast-paced society where it seems you can't get more than 3 minutes of someone's attention online, it's pretty obvious why people love this type of content. Popular sites like BuzzFeed and Reddit have changed the game of Top Lists for content (see Figure 19 on page 66). Their lists go viral on a daily basis. Top Lists can be awesome tools for reaching your set content marketing goals for a variety of reasons:

- **Lists are easily browse-able:** Readers can easily skim the piece and still obtain the exact information they're looking for. Like it or not – you don't have much time to capture the audience's attention online. That's what makes this type of content so effective.

- **Lists are digestible:** By grouping information for your audience in a list format, you are already doing a good amount of the work for them. People like to organize things to digest information and visualize different concepts.

- **Lists can quickly attract attention:** One of the goals for your content should be to generate interaction and comments from your readers – and lists are great for that. Even if the reader would put your Top 10 list in a different order, they might include their opinion, comment, like, and share your post. Think about when you are on social media, how many times do you see a shared BuzzFeed article on your Facebook or Twitter feed?

It's important to remember that numbers in the Top List headlines tend to drive higher response and activity. There are many reasons for this, including the fact that a specific number (even if it's a round number like

10) implies comprehensiveness and expertise and will drive higher email response rates.[8] The list format can also be used in different types of media, for example, a Top 10 Video can be just as effective just as a Top 10 written article.

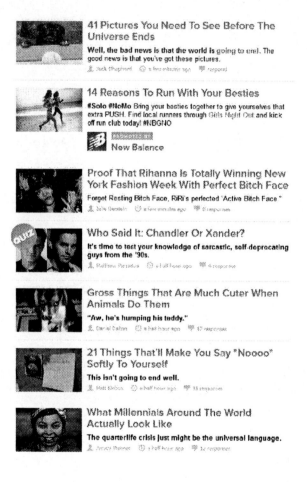

Figure 19: BuzzFeed top list posts

---

8 http://www.jcr-admin.org/files/pressPDFs/120313164431_Isaac_Article.pdf

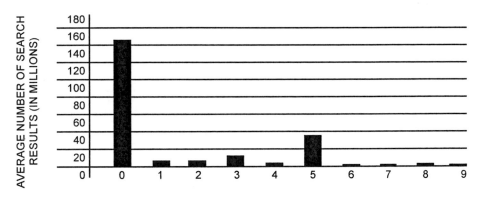

Figure 20: Rankings for what number works best for top list posts

Curation

What is it?

Thanks to the Internet, we live in a content-rich world. It's mind-boggling to think of the number of content pieces at our fingertips. From images to video to text, the sea of web pages is vast. We, as users of the Internet, constantly seek to find ways to make sense of all of it, to get as much useful and relevant content as we can, while at the same time filtering out the stuff we don't care about. Some websites use algorithmic search functions to aggregate content from all over the Internet and organize it by topic, thus making it more accessible to users. Sites like Google News do just this.

Curation is similar to aggregation, except that the content is reviewed, or filtered, by a human editor rather than (or at least in addition to) an algorithm. Having humans review the content before it gets posted increases the assurance that it has maximum relevance to the audience. I will use "curation" to represent both terms for this section.

How is it valuable?

Curation is an excellent way to demonstrate your industry knowledge, positioning your company as a thought leader. Through curation, you can take the best and most relevant content in your industry and present it in a crisp, easy to consume format. The value to your customers that comes from curation will be attributed to your brand, lending you an air of authority in your industry.

There are many ways to curate content on your site. You can make curated content appear occasionally on your site, say as a blog post. In a case like that, you would have an exceptional piece of content that you wanted your blog followers to know about, so you'd post a summary of the content, give a reason why it's so great, and a link to the full content, citing the source. Using curation as a supplement to your original content is the least demanding way to curate, and can be very beneficial to you. Your audience will see you as a contemporary organization with a finger to the wind in your industry.

You need at least one editor working to review content to ensure that the curated content is adding excellence to your site. The editor will either draft summaries of the content or they will work with a writer. You can get employees in your company to participate in the curation effort by having each one serve as a content trawler. By setting a standard for the quality of the content you want to curate, you will help your content trawlers to keep the bar high. They can search for any kind of content – blogs, video, white papers, and so on. Use the content ideas in this chapter to help define what kind of content you're looking for.

With additional effort from an editorial perspective, you can also develop an entire section of your site as a curated news center. An editor, or team of editors, would manage the content, ensuring that it was frequently updated and always high-quality. For a section like this, you would likely incorporate a mix of curated and original content. Your curation page would serve as an intelligence hub for visitors to keep current on industry news and trends. This kind of page could draw huge numbers of links and get significant traffic by delivering tons of fresh content.

There are plenty of software programs that you can acquire which will help you aggregate content. A few popular programs are: Curata, Curationsoft, Trap.it and Uberflip. These kinds of programs reduce the burden on the human effort to search for content by providing a slush pile of content that's organized and ready for the editor to work through. At the end of the day, the editor selects the content that appears on the page.

I would argue that curation can be one of the easiest ways to put content on your site, especially when you curate for a blog post. Using an RSS feed, you can find content and sift through it to pull out the content you want to summarize and curate. This kind of curation has a very natural feel to your followers, and encourages them to tune in regularly because of the value it adds to their industry knowledge. Quite often, the people or posts mentioned in your wrap-up will link to it, Tweet about it or otherwise help to promote it.

Since curation is the act of taking someone else's content and putting it on your site, you don't want to violate copyrights or plagiarize. The right way to curate is to summarize the page you're curating and link to it. In the summary make it clear how the article relates to your industry and the value it has to your audience.

Always remember to follow the guidelines of fair use. According to the copyright act of 1976, when determining whether or not the use of a work in a particular case is fair use, the following four factors must be considered:

- The purpose and character of the use, including whether such use is of a commercial nature or is for nonprofit educational purposes;
- The nature of the copyrighted work;
- The amount and substantiality of the portion used in relation to the copyrighted work as a whole; and
- The effect of the use upon the potential market for or value of the copyrighted work.

- To make fair use of the content, you will need to:
- Summarize the work
- Cite the author/original source
- Encourage your audience to visit the original work

Copyright issues can get sticky, so if your company has a legal staff, you should check with them on how to curate according to your company's policy. We suggest you check out www.copyright.gov for further copyright information in the United States.

In the end, curation on a small scale can actually be a huge time-saver, that is, when you supplement your original content with curated content. As discussed in the previous step, if you're struggling for ideas for your blog, you can opt to curate content for that post as a way to shake off the writer's block. Another great idea would be to use curation as a regular supplement to your content, such as a "What's happening industry wide?" feature. By curating content, you'll keep fresh content on your site while passing along the value of your aggregation and editing efforts to your visitors. That's an added value that they'll attribute to your brand.

Pricing & Costs

What are they?

Internet users search for pricing information all the time, regardless of product or service. Price comparison is often straightforward and easy when the products are on Amazon or other ecommerce platforms where they show the prices. On the other hand, it's much more challenging for the consumer when the content is for pricing on things like in-ground pools, custom machinery, software development, consulting services, etc. If you can create content that *addresses* the pricing questions of your product or service (even when you may not be able to give an exact answer), you can offer an enormous help to your customers. Just think how many times you have gone online investigating a product or service and have become frustrated over not being able to find pricing information? You conduct searches like "how much is *X*?" or "what is the cost for *Y*?" and no one is addressing your question. More than likely, this happens in your industry too, and you can provide the answer to the question your prospects are searching for.

How are they valuable?

One of my favorite content marketing success stories comes from my friend, and fellow content evangelist Marcus Sheridan, owner of River Pools and author for TheSalesLion[9] blog. River Pools was not only able to survive, but experience a boom, throughout the recent major recession. Marcus has since worked to spread the word about his content marketing achievements and how other companies can find the same success he did.

> **"I started River Pools with two partners in 2001, and when the housing market collapsed in 2008, we were in big trouble. That's when we discovered content marketing and decided to be the best teachers in the world about our business — which was inground fiberglass swimming pools. This decision saved our company."**
>
> **– Marcus Sheridan (@TheSalesLion)**

Marcus examined frequently asked questions from his customers and noticed that his competitors were failing to answer these simple inquiries. So, he simply wrote a blog post titled, "How much does a fiberglass pool cost?"

River Pools blogged consistently, writing at least two blog posts per week. Marcus used his blog to educate many potential customers. Before his new content marketing approach, many people would call his company, asking for pool information that he could answer with his content. By educating many potential customers at once through his blog, River Pools could now accurately funnel people through the sales cycle, while saving valuable time and resources.

---

9 http://www.thesaleslion.com/

Marcus used questions from potential clients and existing customers as inspiration for blog posts. The company prioritized each question it received, making sure to address each and every question. They then took it a step further by correctly optimizing the content for long-tail keywords so it would be found easily in search.

The blog post, "How much does a fiberglass pool cost" has now been tracked and measured over time – it's received 20,359 page views and 84 inbound links,[10] the highest numbers for both categories in River Pools' blogging history and generated over 3 million dollars in sales! Today, River Pool's website gets more traffic than any other pool company site in the world. The company is thriving, and Marcus has now expanded his business to include providing social media coaching for other businesses.

River Pools' success can happen to any company. What set Marcus apart from his competitors was that he publicly answered questions that no one else was answering online. Keep this in mind when creating price and cost content; don't be afraid to offer this information to your audience. This is your chance to be the trusted expert. If you don't offer the information on your blog, searchers will likely find it somewhere else, and the sale will likely go to the business that has the answers.

Comparisons & Reviews

What are they?

Shoppers spend a lot of time comparing products. Why not help them out? By adding a product comparison to your description, your page will become even more useful to visitors than the standard product page. As a result, your visitors will be more likely to return to your site to shop because they can get research information consolidated on your page. They'll not only see your page as a product source but also as a researching tool. Check out Amazon.com, Nashbar.com, and Zappos.com for examples of some excellent product comparison features.

---

10 http://cdn2.hubspot.net/hub/53/file-13221811-pdf/docs/ebooks/hubspot-ebook_river-pools-blogging-case-study.pdf

People look for comparisons and reviews before they commit to buy. When people search to buy something, they want as much information as they can get, and they want to be able to compare multiple options. For many people, the easiest way to compare the pros and cons of different products is to have a list of all the top products along with prices, reviews, features, and more, right in front of them on one page.

If you can provide that kind of detailed information for the user, they will be much more likely to do their analysis and make their buying decision via your website. A product comparison or service review can be a priceless bit of content, and as a result, it can quickly convert browsers into buyers.

Before you can create a quality comparison or review of a product or service for your audience, it's absolutely vital to do the research and speak as an authoritative expert on the best products available in your niche industry. Readers are smart. They have other outlets for information if they feel they're being misled or aren't receiving enough valuable information.

How are they valuable?

As mentioned previously, Amazon.com is a great place to review potential products. Reading buyer reviews can give you a great sense of what customers actually think of the product, and allow you to spot red-flags or triumphs for your products or competitors.

For example, Vanessa is looking for a new DSLR camera for her photography company. She notices that Nikon and Canon are the two most popular brands available, but can't decide on which camera would work best for her employees. Vanessa had begun her research with a simple search, "Canon vs. Nikon." There had been many reviews from buyers that owned different models of each brand, and she was able to narrow her decision down to two cameras. The review and comparison online had mentioned the picture quality that each camera provided was similar; however, the reviews revealed that Canon's interface was much more user friendly for novice photographers. Because Vanessa is hiring new photographers for her studio, this information is what ultimately leads her to choose the Canon. Her decision is not based on price or picture quality, but rather because the reviews and comparisons told her something she could trust and use for her business.

You need to do this research for your own niche. Like photography enthusiasts looking for a new camera, people are searching for more than price comparisons. They want to know what one product has to offer over another. This is information that you can provide to your customers and/or audience. If you carry competing products, such as photography equipment, you should have no problem posting comparisons. If you truly believe your products or services are better than your competition, consider creating content that demonstrates it.

Think about it. When do people get the most involved in content? During a debate! Any topic people disagree on will get more viewers. This is a theory that withstands the test of time. For example: Republican vs. Democrat, Mac vs. PC, Coke vs. Pepsi. Matt Siltala's popular infographic, *Evolution of the Electric Guitar,* which includes a Guitar Hero controller, featured below, is a great example of the complexity of a good debate.

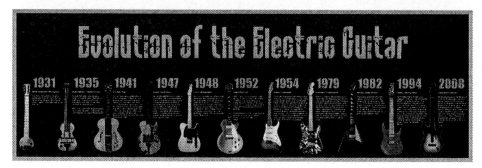

Figure 21: Evolution of the Electric Guitar infographic

Comparisons or Reviews are some of the best types of content for a blog, too. If done correctly, they are easily found in the SERPs and can be extremely useful to your readers. Comparisons can also be a great conversation starter for people reviewing your products, providing great user engagement and comments. The goal of a review is not simply to say whether you liked or didn't like something, but rather to educate others about the product and whether or not they should buy it.

Resource Pages
What are they?

At its most basic, a resource page consists of a selection of articles or content that is based around a certain topic (see Figure 22 on page 76). Ideally that topic will be one that generates a lot of search activity or that answers a common question. A resource page has a very select topical focus, and the articles included are the best of what the niche has to offer. Many bloggers tend to overlook the benefits of a resource page simply because they are unfamiliar with them, or scared that the outbound links will direct the audience away from their site. I would argue that this common misconception is holding a lot of bloggers back from providing a fantastic source of content. Resource pages are exactly that – a resource. As such, they reinforce your standing as a trusted expert in your industry. Even if they click away from your page, they'll come back to your brand because you provide them with valuable resources.

So now that we've talked about what a resource page is – and why your blog-site needs one – let's talk about how to begin creating one. There are a few basic steps that are easy to implement, and easy to remember.

- **Choose a topic for your resource page:** It should be a subject that has a large search potential and provides information that your audience is searching for.

- **Select credible sources:** Select articles or content that will offer only the very best content, whether it comes from your blog or from other sources. Resource pages that are of high quality are more likely to be shared throughout the community.

- **Offer more than just links:** As you compile your page, remember to include more than just the titles of the articles you have selected, and the links to the internal pages. You want to include something on each article to catch your reader's attention, it may be a short summary of that article or a pertinent quote from the body of the page.

If your resource page is lengthy (e.g. FAQs that contain thousands of words), you might want to consider adding quick links at the top of the page that will serve as a table of contents. This will benefit your readers and add value to the piece.

Figure 22: An example of a resource page

How are they valuable?

Don't be afraid to list lots of excellent resources for your customers, even if they happen to be your competitors (although you might keep that to a minimum). Yes they may click on a link and leave your site, but remember, the only way they can do that is to be on your website reading these resources to begin with. So you already won – that excellent resource page brought them to your website! A resource page brings several benefits to bloggers:

- Resource pages can actually increase the time spent for visitors.
- If it contains quality, informative content, readers will be encouraged to move around your website to see what you're all about.
- It can establish a company's expertise on a specific topic, allowing for the opportunity to network with others in your field.
- Perhaps one of the best benefits – it's excellent link attraction.

As a high value page that features only the best content available, it has greater potential to be shared, engaged with, and rank higher in the SERPs. A good resource page will get a lot of attention, readers love to bookmark and share resource pages. This offers you the chance to include call to actions or lead generation forms that can increase your site's conversion rate. Bottom line – resource lists are capable of getting lots of traffic and generating natural backlinks for your site.

Interviews

What are they?

This is one of my favorite types of content. Here, we're talking about interviewing industry experts to find out how they tackle specific issues in their industry, and what tools they use to solve their problems. You can ask them their opinion on industry trends, or to give a market outlook. The possibilities are limitless. It doesn't hurt to ask the same questions of different interviewees in order to gain multiple perspectives, so long as you avoid a template question-and-answer format. The main idea for an interview is to have a feel of real curiosity and investigation.

There are a number of ways to incorporate interviews as content on your site. They can be short, or they can be intensive. Depending on what your interviewee is willing and able to do, you could go big and interview a panel, or you would have a longer, more in-depth conversation with an individual. Typically, however, time is precious for your interviewee, so conversations should be concise, getting answers to a handful of specific questions.

You have three different media choices for conducting an interview:

1.   Text-based
2.   Audio
3.   Video

With text-based interviews, you will send a customized email with 10 to 15 questions for the industry expert you would like to interview. Ask the interviewee to answer eight or so. Then, post the text of the interview, add a bio and a headshot, and there's your interview. Email interviews are by far the easiest interview to obtain.

Likewise, you can contact your interviewee and ask for a phone interview for audio. Again, the interview should be about eight questions, netting you maybe 10 or more minutes worth of audio. For video, you have the option of doing a webcam interview, if the interviewee is up for it, or you can snag them at a conference for an impromptu interview. Video interviews should generally stay short to keep the attention of the viewer.

How are they valuable?

By having frequent conversations with other experts in your industry, you rank yourself among the top experts, and you show that you are connected to the cutting edge in your field. Interviews demonstrate that you're hungry to stay on top of the industry. They make fantastic blog posts and can generate traffic to your site, especially when you interview bigger names. Just by association, interviews rank you among the experts. As they say, you are the company that you keep.

Try to do regular interviews and tie them to your editorial calendar so that you can be sure to keep the content rolling. To find an interviewee, occasionally we at Vertical Measures have to do some research online to see who has been speaking at conferences in order to find experts and their expertise. Other times, we go to experts who are better known. When you've identified someone you'd like to interview, first ask them if they would be willing to be interviewed. If they say yes, let them pick and choose which of your questions they'd like to answer. Out of the 40 or more interviews we've requested, we have only had one individual turn us down, and only a couple have been late. The reason is: They want the exposure as well! Interviews are mutually beneficial. I get requests for interviews periodically, and I never turn them down. It's branding for our company, so if I can meet the deadline, why would I say no?

Video interviews are a dynamic format that works well as content. I go to conferences frequently, and I see people walking around with video cameras. They might grab me or another speaker from the conference, pull us aside, and do a quick one-or two-minute hallway interview. Right there is content for their site. If they conduct several interviews, they now have plenty of content for posting later on their website, helping them meet their content goals.

Another way to optimize your interview content is to transcribe audio (including the audio portion of your videos) to text. Using transcription software (such as SpeakerText, Speechpad or Rev) , this is extremely easy. By posting audio or video with their text transcriptions on the same page, you can optimize the whole content piece for search engines.

The fact is that interviews are easy. What I mean is that they have one of the highest ROI's because the investment is so low and the payoff is usually pretty good. If you can conduct one interview per week, at the end of a year, you'll have 52 interviews that you can package into an eBook, yet another brand new piece of content. Interviews offer major potential for repurposing.

The toughest part of conducting an interview – and most of the time investment – is actually coming up with the questions and finding the person to interview. I've found that by rotating topics monthly on the editorial calendar, it eases the strain of coming up with questions, because the topic itself steers the questions. For email interviews, it's only possible to have the interview if you send the questions ahead of time; however, for other interviews (live, audio, video, or text via chat) you absolutely must have your questions ready ahead of time. I recommend that you never walk into an interview and try to "wing it." Always be ready. If you're at a conference and conducting a hallway interview with a panelist, you'd better have a cue card of questions ready to go, should they agree to the interview.

Round Ups

What are they?

If you want to generate buzz for your brand and network with some leading industry experts, there is no better way than to use Round Ups. This form of content gathers several industry experts around a single subject of your choosing and allows them to give their insight. Your Round Up topic needs to be enticing enough for featured experts so they can get excited about contributing and be proud to share it with their own audiences. It should be useful and valuable for your readers so they can walk away with good tips from trusted leaders in the field. The strategy is very simple – present the knowledge of other industry experts and tap into their audience or network.

How are they valuable?

They are often really useful pieces of content on their own, but by their nature they tend to get shared a lot by the people that were included. Round Up posts are another great way to drive traffic to your website and increase brand awareness. They can actually boost the visibility of your blog because this content gets shared by both your audience and the audience of each expert you include in your content.

Round Up posts are an amazing way to start or strengthen relationships with other experts and industry leaders. Everybody appreciates an opportunity to be featured! Simply put, people are flattered when you choose to feature them. It's good practice to reach out to people you already know in the industry as well as people you'd like to get to know. A high-quality Round Up can lead to more backlinks and future opportunities. Featured experts usually treat it as a form PR and will be happy to link a Round Up from their websites.

This may sound simple, but it generally boils down to good karma. If you've got traffic coming to your blog, it's nice to send it someone's way. This ethical practice can go both ways – if someone contacts you to participate in a round up or collaborative post for *their* blog, you can still reap the benefits. When you promote their content, you're reinforcing that your brand knows what's important and what type of content people like to share and engage with.

Round Ups reinforce your brand as an expert in the industry. They allow you to collaborate with other leaders and work to provide the best possible content for users. They establish you as an expert and a curator of awesome content and information. Use this content to introduce your readers to helpful, useful information, no matter what niche your industry is in.

What Makes A Great Infographic? 8 Experts Weigh In

What Makes A Great Infographic? 8 Experts Weigh In

Arnie Kuenn on March 12, 2013 at 9:00 am

As you may have noticed, using infographics for content marketing is an incredibly popular tactic right now. Infographics are being used to illustrate a range of different information, including new employee announcement, data visualization, humor and education.

However, with the widespread use of infographics in marketing increasing every day, there is growing concern about maintaining infographic quality. Some believe that infographic marketing will go the way of article marketing if we begin to sacrifice content quality and placement. Thus, this post will focus on advice from experts on what they think makes a truly great infographic.

Figure 23: A Roundup post with infographic experts

Infographics

What are they?

An infographic is a graphic that conveys a visual representation of information using images and words. They are a great way to capture a variety of pieces of information and communicate them in an interesting and condensed format. Infographics often make use of charts and graphs, but they can also include pictures or maps. The possibilities with infographics are nearly endless. When it comes to content on the Internet, infographics are hot stuff right now. Everybody seems to love them because they're easy and fast to read, and are perfect for passing around via social media.

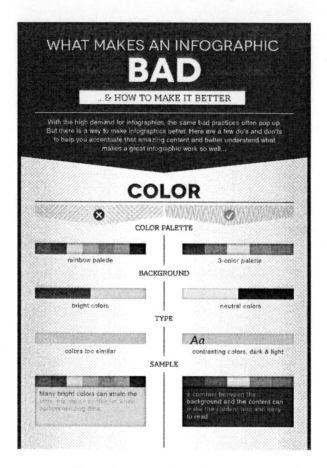

Figure 24: An infographic example

How are they valuable?

Most people would prefer to look at a picture quickly, rather than to read a whole article, especially in the middle of a busy day. Time is valuable, and infographics save quite a bit of time. Because of their appeal, infographics are a great way to drive traffic and, especially, links to your website, which is one of the biggest benefits they offer. When someone finds an infographic that they think is really cool, they will link to it from their page, embed it on their site, or post it on their blog. When someone grabs the content to post on their website, they credit the page they got it from with a link. Usually, that's seen as a fair exchange, basically giving credit where credit is due. The infographic benefits the person who grabs it because it's content that will interest their viewers, and the backlink drives traffic to the source's page. It serves you well to create your own infographics so that you can generate natural backlinks and traffic from them. Infographics make excellent blog posts, and they have that ever-tantalizing possibility of going viral.

It's not as hard as you might imagine to develop an infographic. All you need to do is identify a concept and supporting data, then ship it off to a graphic designer. They will find a clever way to present the data in an easy-to-read format. Any graphic designer with at least one foot in the 21st Century will know what an infographic is and how to work with you on it. But a graphic designer can't do everything for you. They can develop a color scheme and some of the visual elements, but you'll need to provide them some important details to get them started.

It's your job to come up with the basic concept for the infographic. This is usually a simple idea that will in some way end up becoming the title of the infographic. Make a list of the information you want to convey, and settle on the clearest, most concise way to express the data.

Some websites have actually been so successful with infographics that they've built entire libraries of them. One of our clients built out a whole subsection on their site devoted exclusively to the infographics they've created. Anyone who wants a financial infographic can go there and grab one. The stipulation with grabbing one is, of course, that you have to link back to their site. Their page is getting all kinds of juice from that campaign. In fact, there are websites that are devoted solely to compiling infographics from all over the web, and this is sustainable because of the high demand for infographics.

Frankly, I don't recommend that you nab infographics from other sources.

Instead, we always recommend to our clients that they commission all their infographics. By generating your own, you have the right to all the traffic, citations and backlinks. On top of that, the content of the infographic should be the kind of information that demonstrates *your* inside understanding of the market or industry your business is in. Fundamentally, there's nothing wrong with posting someone else's infographic on your site, but if you can go the extra mile and generate your own, you're going to be much better off.

Videos

What are they?

With the rise of YouTube, where average people upload their own videos for mass consumption, low-budget video has become completely acceptable. So, you can paint yourself as the authority using just a handheld video camera or even your phone. Short two-to five-minute videos are best because viewers tend to have short attention spans for online video content. Within those constraints, video can be used for anything – videos can be educational or entertaining. The only limit is the imagination.

Think about videos you've seen on the Internet that would never meet quality standards for television production or advertising but have made a point that you nodded your head to. Maybe your favorite blogger is sitting at a bistro in San Francisco and is leaning into a video camera that's propped on the table and he's discussing a fantastic strategy for your industry. The quality and film angle would never say "professional" in other media outlets, but it's great online. The benefit of this is that the users feel like they're right there with you, getting a personal lesson. In fact, video that gets momentum and goes viral tends to be filmed on the spur of the moment.

How are they valuable?

Videos can turn a blasé content idea into a winner, drawing traffic to your website. You could produce step-by-step text content with handy illustrations, and it could be great stuff. But by taking that idea to a video, the content can come alive and become dynamic. In fact, by taking a day or two to go through all of your products and create five-minute videos for each one, you'll spend minimal time and effort to create a huge amount of content that can boost your traffic tremendously. You can even supplement your video content on your site by setting up a YouTube channel for all your videos, expanding your opportunity to be found in search.

There are many places to post video. Everyone knows YouTube, but there's also Vimeo, Slideshare, and other sites, and this gives you the ability to post your videos on multiple channels. If you optimize your videos and get people to talk about them, they can do well in search, directing traffic to your website as a result.

While professional video production can be expensive, do-it-yourself camera work is very low-cost. To start, encourage your staff to shoot videos and get everyone thinking, "How can this be videoed and how can it become content?" Don't be timid. You're going to have to get in front of the camera. This may be easier said than done, but you have to get over it if you're going to do video. Maybe someone in your office has a great presence on the camera, so they become a bit of an office celebrity. If your group gets used to having a camera around, they'll quickly relax and act natural. Take the camera to where work gets done and find ways to make video content. Do you have a loading dock? How about an interview with your distribution manager right there? Don't forget the hardhats! You can film conferences, whiteboard presentations, and even lunch in your break room. Informal video content gives you a ton of options.

To create videos, you don't necessarily need a video camera. If you have a great PowerPoint presentation, you can narrate it and post it as video. Anyone should be able to do that. I recently did three hour-long training courses for the Content Marketing Institute, and that's exactly what we did. We created a PowerPoint presentation, I came in on a Saturday, knowing it would be quiet, and sat and narrated each one using the record feature in PowerPoint. Now the videos are presented as part of an online course. This is something that's often missed – you don't have to shoot live action video just to get a video made.

Figure 25: A video example: "Why Visual Content is So Important"

Of all of the content that's out there, videos are the most likely to go big-time viral. Everyone that gets into video wants to make the one that hits it out of the park and gets millions of views. However, it's pretty much proven that the content that tends to go viral was rarely intended to do so. Viral video is like a lighting strike. It just happens.

While you can't force a video to take off, you can develop quality video content that has appeal. Being of quality means it offers some kind of real value to the viewer; it's not just noise. It shows your industry knowledge and experience, capturing your brand within that context. In the pursuit of creative video, occasionally you're going to create one that you review and realize is junk; so you don't post it. But try again, and the next time you'll get something you really like. The key to success is to keep loose; don't be stiff. Video is a medium that can be taken too seriously, but really works best when the atmosphere is relaxed and fun. By establishing a standard for the quality of your content and having fun at the same time, you will improve your chances of creating video that will increase your traffic, generate leads, and maybe, just maybe, skyrocket to viral.

Webinars

What are they?

Webinars are web-based seminars, live presentations where users remotely engage in the presentation from their desktops. These are fantastic ways to bring together customers from anywhere on the planet. The limitations on participation are only a matter of user access to the Internet at the time your webinar takes place. To manage the connectivity and presentation, you can use a webinar service, such as GoToMeeting.com, On24.com, or Webex.com.

Figure 26: A webinar with Arnie & Steve Wozniak

Usually PowerPoint is used for the video display, though anything that you can display on your computer monitor can be displayed on the webinar. Because webinars are interactive, anyone who has joined the webinar can interact with questions or even tag-team the presentation. When we host webinars, we also record them, and then post the recording to our site for more content.[11] In essence, webinars are videos, but because of their valuable content, it's common for people to get over their short video threshold and watch them for up to an hour.

---

11 http://www.verticalmeasures.com/webinars/

How are they valuable?

Yet another tool for showing your industry knowledge, webinars are excellent ways to directly engage customers, and potential customers, with solutions to your industry's toughest problems. Through a webinar, you have an extended time with your audience, which gives you the ability to show your leadership and depth of knowledge.

Anyone can do a webinar on any subject, and I'm a little baffled that businesses don't do webinars more often. Webinars aren't just for business executives. You might be surprised to discover that there's a wide range of people out there willing to attend them. For example, REI hosts a number of webinars, with topics on choosing boots to choosing tents.

Depending on how in depth you go with the subject matter, webinars don't take long to prepare, either. Generally, you put together a PowerPoint and walk through it online. From your PowerPoint, you can link out to other sites or other content that you've created on the topic.

Webinars tend to range from 30 minutes up to an hour. Because people are there for the education and the webinar happens live, people will engage for a longer period than they would for many other kinds of content. Remember to leave time for a question-and-answer session at the end. Here's another cool thing about webinars: as people interact with the content that's being presented, you can capture all that activity when you record the session. That human interaction is another way to show your ability to contribute solutions to your customers in a direct way.

Because webinars require registration to participate, you can acquire the name and email of all participants, which you can add to your eNewsletter list, as well as your contact list for leads. The real challenge with hosting a webinar is that you need people to show up in order to have some level of success. This means that you will need to use promotion tools – Twitter, Facebook, news releases, you name it – to get the message out that you have a webinar coming up. You've got to push it. When you host webinars on a regular basis, you help establish a set of returning participants. If they like what they're getting, and they know exactly when the next one will be, it's much easier for them to come back.

Podcasts

What are they?

A podcast is basically a non-streaming webcast, in audio or video form. Podcasts are typically downloaded through web syndication via a Podcatcher. The Podcatcher is a software client that downloads podcasts and can manage the transfer of files to a portable media player. iTunes is by far the most popular Podcatcher, but there are many services that can catch podcasts. Audiences typically subscribe to a podcast channel, so whenever you publish a new podcast, it gets distributed to all the subscribers, automatically.

How are they valuable?

Since podcasts can be either audio or video, they are great ways to publish those kinds of media and to effortlessly distribute them to subscribers. The popular term "podcast," as opposed to "webcast," came about with the invention of the iPod, so podcasts are often associated with audio syndication. But technology for handheld devices is constantly evolving and iPods, mobile phones, and other multimedia devices can handle video without any trouble, which wasn't the case when podcasts were first introduced. Podcasts have evolved with the device technology and now include video. So, you can make use of the syndication power of podcasts by syndicating the videos you produce, as well.

Many radio news outlets, for example, make use of podcasts as a way to distribute their news, sometimes even parsing it out by topic (music, politics, business, etc.). Podcasts are a huge distribution channel, so it can help with building your brand, image, and authority. Because Podcasts can be forwarded, they, too, have the potential to go viral.

Many people continue to use podcasts for audio. Don't discount the value of audio in favor of video — audio can fill a niche and connect with your followers in a way that video cannot do. For example, they can download their latest podcast and listen to the newest audio files while commuting or working out at the gym.

What's great about audio is that you can use it to turn your blog posts into podcasts. You could record someone reading your text blog post into a microphone if you want a human narrator. Or you can use a dictation software tool to automatically read the text to an audio file. Dictating blog posts, for example, is a great way to make them more accessible. The files can be repurposed to a podcast for an additional distribution opportunity. Podcasts are a great way to distribute your email interviews, too. Any audio you produce for your webpages should be podcasted. For a minimum of effort, you get the huge bonus of expanded distribution of your content.

Product Pages

What are they?

If your company is an e-commerce site, you probably have tons of content that serves a very utilitarian purpose – to describe each one of your products. Every single product gets its 15 minutes of fame on a page of its own. If your product descriptions appear like the bulk of descriptions out there, they were probably set up just to get the job done. "The job" is to showcase your product in such a way that consumers know what they would get if they add it to their shopping cart. Many times, that means giving a product name, a graphic image, and a price, and often the image, description, and price come straight from the manufacturer, having nothing unique about them. So, why would anyone want to link to or engage with your product pages? They wouldn't unless you give them reasons to do so, say, by providing information they cannot find anywhere else, for example, or by giving them an opportunity to discuss the product.

How are they valuable?

Utilitarian product descriptions are helpful for customers in the act of shopping or price comparison, but they don't often get shared or even inspire your visitors to purchase. You can change that! By sprucing up your product descriptions, you can make them work much more to your advantage. Through original content and some personalized attention, you can make your content catchy and link-worthy. Product descriptions, if done well, can be a fantastic way to draw traffic to your site – and away from your competitors. Here are the general components of a typical product description that are fodder for creativity:

- Title/Description
- Images
- User Generated Content
- Product Comparisons
- Statistics

The title and description are the main text of the product description. This is where you have some flexibility to get really creative and even as companies like Woot[12] have done with their product descriptions, get attention and become a phenomenon. Primarily, you have to keep your keyword research in mind for the product, especially the title. If people are searching for the product exactly by name, you may not have as much room to modify the title. The description, on the other hand, is a great place to get creative. Enthusiastic content that has personality can engage visitors and lead them to link to your page. It's similar to having an enthusiastic salesperson in a store. When you walk in and the salesperson demonstrates knowledge of, and interest in, the products, you will be much more likely to make a purchase than in a store where the salesperson remains behind the counter and lets the product sell itself.

Why use one dull photo when you can have multiple, interactive photos? Get users to click on the photos and view the product from different angles. Try taking your own photos of the product from new and interesting perspectives. In an image search, the same exact photo for a product can come up multiple times for different sites. Be the unique photo in the results. Heck, don't stop there, be the unique video in the search results!

---

12 http://www.woot.com/

If you provide a place for users to comment on your products, you will then offer a fantastic opportunity to do two things: First, you'll get user-generated content on your page, which search engines love. Second, you'll facilitate users helping one another decide on their product. User comments, even negative ones, can be very useful. If the product description fails to describe the actual product in a user-friendly way, you'll hear about it in the reviews. It's a great place to get feedback on how you're presenting your product. You can get creative with your comments section by using forms to get directed feedback from your users. You can ask questions like, "How did you use this product?" or "Would you recommend this to your friends?" There are many possibilities for user comments that can make your website useful to users. Look around the Internet at other product user reviews that you might be able to replicate.

Thanks to social media, people have become hyper-conscious of trends and trending activity in the world around them. A number of e-commerce sites are now adding statistical information with the product descriptions to show how the product is trending. Do people primarily buy this product in the summer? Is it big in California? Perhaps show the top five cities to buy this product. A really great statistic to show is which other products appealed to the people who bought this product, and link to those product pages on your site.

The goal with developing great product description pages is to take your potential customers away from utility and toward exciting and engaging. Make them more useful, more helpful, and more interesting than the typical product description. That way, people will want to share the experience they had on your site with others.

Case Studies

What are they?

Broadly, case studies are research reports that isolate a group, event, or individual for in-depth analysis. The way to use case studies in a content marketing strategy is to consider a particular success your organization has had with a customer. The case study would analyze your customer's situation, their problem, and your solution, detailing how it led to your customer's success. They can vary in length and form, from a brief paragraph to a full report. A case study could include graphics and charts, and even video testimony, in addition to text. Ideally, a case study should provide short examples of work that your company has done for your customers, showing the success of the project.

How are they valuable?

Case studies are very good for touting your results, showing precisely how others have succeeded because they've worked with you, complete with tangible examples of your expertise. Case studies have a number of applications, ranging from blog posts, to inclusion in an eNewsletter, to a section on your website devoted to case studies – or you could repurpose the case study for all three places!

A great place to post case studies is the "about us" section of your website, or you could offer three or four brief case studies on a page that is linked to from your "about us" section. This is where potential customers will go to find out who they're about to do business with. If you provide case, they will give your potential customers a great chance to see your success stories. Case studies work especially well when they are quick and easy to read.

The main challenge with case studies is actually getting your client to cooperate with you. You need information from them before you can create the case study. Sometimes, it can become difficult tracking your clients' successes. Depending on your client, it can take some effort to get them to provide you with the information you need to create the study.

Let me offer an example from my business. One of our clients has a school that trains golfers to become golf pros for work at golf courses. Our client wanted to put together some case studies on students who went through their course, showing their success after graduation. One of the students actually went on to build golf clubs; others have become pros at prestigious golf courses. The graduate who built the golf-club manufacturing business was obviously proud of his success and was glad to be included in the case study. He cooperated knowing that it would also be exposure for his product. But for many students it was hard to keep track of them as they moved to various locations and took different career paths.

Fortunately, though, we have found that our clients often don't have trouble developing case studies because they tend to know when their clients have achieved successful results in a relatively short period of time. As with the golf-club manufacturer, it can be easy to develop a case study when it also offers a chance to give your client some positive exposure. For this reason, case studies can be some of the easier content to develop and post to your website, and they can offer some very good benefits.

Whitepapers

What are they?

Normally about 10 to 20 pages in length, a white paper is an authoritative document used to educate readers or help them make decisions. Sometimes, white papers are considered research reports or technical briefs. All white papers deal with issues that require in-depth explanation and argue the benefits of a particular technology, product, or policy to solve a problem. Business white papers can take the following forms:

- **Business-benefits:** Makes a business case for a certain technology or methodology.

- **Technical:** Describes how a certain technology works.

- **Hybrid:** Combines high-level business benefits with technical details in a single document.

Depending on the solution you have to offer, you can create a white paper as a standalone document, or you can present a series. If the content is rich enough, a series might be a good idea, but because of their length, this can be difficult. Many times larger companies will publish a white-paper series on each of the various technologies they've been developing. For example, Cisco might do a white-paper series on wireless routers, with each document outlining one of the routers they develop. A white paper series is a strong way to demonstrate your authority on a topic. In fact, you might even turn them into an eBook or even a webinar series, but you don't need to aim for a series to have a successful white paper. Standalone white papers are very strong examples of your industry expertise and require a fraction of the time investment to develop.

How are they valuable?

White papers serve to promote your company's solutions or technologies in response to vital issues that your customers face. These kinds of documents are perfect for demonstrating thought leadership on issues vital to your business. Your customers are often looking for the solutions your white paper can offer, and because of this they work really well online because electronic distribution is so easy and inexpensive.

The best way to make use of a white paper for your content marketing strategy is to put it on a page on your site and promote it. You can also set it up so that when someone goes to get your white paper, they have to give you a name and email address in exchange, making it a great lead generator. Your link could say something like, "If you would like our free white paper on *such and such topic*, all we ask is that you give us your name and email address." People tend to be more than willing to do this, seeing it as a fair trade. If they don't like the email correspondence you send them, they can unsubscribe.

The other advantage with white papers is that if they're done well and offer real value, they often get passed around. They can become a quasi-viral marketing tool, demonstrating that you're the expert and promoting your brand. When a white paper offers customers a valuable solution, your customers tend to spread the word, whether by linking to it on their blog, sending it by email, or just handing the printed version to their office-mate.

The challenge with white papers is the same as with a lot of content production: yes, they paint you as the expert, they can go viral, they can get generate leads, but they require effort to create. To get value out of a 10-to 20-page document, you have to commit yourself to the bigger picture. If you can dedicate the hours required to write a white paper, it could turn out to be a relatively small investment that gets you leads and reinforces your brand in a big way. It just takes the initial effort. For example, we spent several hours creating a white paper on The Beginner's Guide to Content Promotion, and now it gets downloaded regularly.

Free Guides

What are they?

People who know me know that white papers and free guides are my absolute favorite content marketing projects to produce. These short or long PDF documents often contain interesting graphics and are chock full of useful information. When executed well, a free guide can generate a large number of leads by placing content behind a lead capture form and requiring users to fill out information before gaining access.

It's easy to research your competitor's free guides, try search commands (filetype:pdf + an industry keyword) and you'll see all the free guides available. This is helpful when brainstorming and conducting a competitive review. The best plan is to know what else is out there so you know what you're up against later in the promotion phase.

Free guides offer your target audiences a robust piece of information that will help establish your brand as a trusted authority in the industry. Placing this quality content behind a lead capture will allow you to further engage with potential leads and build a relationship by answering their questions. But I just love it when our clients ask us to produce how-to guides or buyer guides. To us, a guide is normally a 10–12 page document that helps someone learn about a product, service, an industry, or a market. So it might help you choose your next TV or maybe even your next career.

How are they valuable?

Yale Appliance, a Boston-based appliance store with an e-commerce website, utilized content marketing to generate an amazing amount of traffic to their site. Their expertly crafted free guides allowed them to build up their email-marketing list, thus improving their conversion rates and increasing their overall revenue. Yale Appliance creates free guides for each blog category.[13] These free guides were developed to help consumers make a buying decision. They provide all the necessary information so that their readers can make a smart choice on their next appliance purchase.

Figure 27: Yale Appliance's "Buying Guides"

Each free guide is featured on its own landing page and is gated behind a lead capture form. The free guides require an entry of name, email address and ZIP code for download. This does not deter the readers from accessing the free guide because the information offered is so valuable. The form also includes a check box for email subscription, so not only are free guides a great resource for the consumer, they are helping expand the company's email marketing list as well.

Yale often publishes blog content optimized with less-competitive, long-tail keywords that assist visitors in all stages of the sales funnel. In addition

13 http://blog.yaleappliance.com/resource-center

to blog content, Yale produces buying guides, email content, videos and even recipes. Together, this content has made a great impact on the business, positively affecting their bottom line.

As a result of content marketing, Yale's traffic has more than tripled annually (from 40,000 visitors to 150,000) and leads have grown from 800 to 2300 monthly.[14] Even more impressive, revenue is up by 40% since 2009. By providing informational and educational content, Yale can showcase their industry knowledge while building trust with consumers, which often results in a relationship that transcends the first appliance purchase.

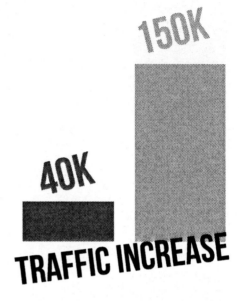

There are three distinct reasons why I just love the free guide concept:

Figure 28: Yale Appliance Results

1. They're great lead generators. All you need to do is put a little lead capture form in front of that content. Maybe just ask for somebody's name and email address to get this free download. Or if it's a really spectacular piece of content, you can ask a few more qualifying questions. But either way you're building your contact list and you're building your leads.

2. They tend to attract links. We've got example after example in which these kinds of pieces of content have generated dozens if not hundreds of backlinks. Why? Because, it's exactly what a webmaster or a blogger is willing to divert their traffic and their customers to, and fabulous piece of content.

3. Free Guides have a really nice, hopefully long lifespan. They become the

---

14 http://marketingland.com/how-a-boston-appliance-store-grew-its-business-through-content-marketing-61106

perfect evergreen content. We've got a few cases where we've built free guides for our clients five or six years ago, and we've only had to freshen them up once or twice along the way. But they're sitting out there just generating leads, and ultimately revenue and links for their websites well after they were originally created.

An investment of maybe $1,000, $2,000, or even $5,000 can have an almost immediate payback, and after that it sits there, quietly working for you. It's generating those leads, links and hopefully revenue for your business, and that's why I love free guides (and whitepapers).

Conceptualizing and Drafting

Once you have come to a consensus on an idea to pursue, it's time to conceptualize the piece and develop a draft. This is a great time to turn to your editorial calendar and review deadlines for the first draft, edit phase, and launch. With the timetable established, you can then allocate adequate resources to meet your deadlines, and determine if your staff can manage the task or if you'll need to outsource the activity to a writer or graphic designer.

Moving into conceptualization, you'll need to determine the lead person on the project, who will either create the piece or oversee the creative talent you've outsourced. The lead on the project will:

1. Determine the media form to express your idea
2. Draft or mock up the idea to see how it will work
3. Share the idea for feedback
4. Revise, if necessary, and complete

Going into conceptualization, you may already know how you'd like to express your idea. The drafting and mockup phase will make it clear if the idea works.

At this point there are two basic paths: you can do the work in-house or you can outsource the talent. Most businesses outsource the creative talent to some extent, depending on the skill level required. For a blog post, you can probably handle that in-house, but an infographic takes graphic design skills that often are best sought through a professional graphic designer.

The best way to get a sense of how your idea can work for your goal is to keep current on the kind of content that's already successful online. Familiarity with the environment will really help you as you join in the conversation. Encourage the people in your company who will be developing content to keep current on the trends in your industry. The more familiar your team is with existing online content, the better your chances will be for creating engaging content. (This might be a good time to address those of you from small businesses reading this. You might not always have a team of people to delegate to; often in a small business, one or two people might have to handle all of the roles being discussed here. Sometimes, for example, the brainstorming even extends to friends and family or just a simple business lunch.)

As you draft, keep the length of the piece appropriate for the kind of content you're developing. Know the standard. Blogs are a bit looser, but the trend over the last few years is longer and longer content – and it's been proven to work. You should target blog posts with 1,000 words or more, and always include a couple of optimized images. If you plan to post a video to your YouTube channel, then you need to ensure that the length of the video conforms to their restrictions.

As you draft content, ensure everything you produce avoids a negative spin. When you have so much freedom to deliver content, there can be a temptation to get snarky or sarcastic, especially if you're trying to put out a humorous piece. If you want to position yourself as an expert, you can't let yourself fall into negativity and risk losing the respect of your customers. Keep your content professional and retain an air of sensitivity to your subject. For example, I once came across a blog post that an insurance company wrote, discussing retirees in Florida. The gist was, "Stay off the roads because senior citizens are going to cause accidents." The content was related to the insurance industry, but in an attempt to be funny they put a spin on it that would have probably offended a large group of people. And these people are potential customers! It should go without saying that it's a bad move to offend some of the very people you are trying to engage.

For this reason, I'm big into the idea of communication within your organization on the creative element. Collaboration in the drafting phase helps catch subject matter that might go astray of your standards. Ultimately, using collective energy, the content will be enriched. Try to pass the concept or draft around the whole creative team so that each person can give a little more information or add comments for revision. By the time it's made the rounds, you will have a solid piece that has the team's stamp of approval. The team doesn't have to consist of all marketing pros; it could include people from IT, the warehouse, or service departments, for example. You can bounce ideas off industry people, too. This can be a great way to build networking relationships that can play out in other content areas, like interviews. While you're at it, return the favor, and offer to help them out; everyone can use a helping hand when it comes to creating content.

For some content, you might be shipping it out to a professional writer, say if you're creating an article or a press release. If you go that route, you may still want to workshop your idea before you send the summary to the writer. Likewise, if you're working with a graphic designer for images, like infographics, it will be a good idea to refine your idea with a team before you hand off the project. That way you have the most refined idea coming out of your company that will fit in with the overall body of your online content.

Edit and Launch

After the draft is finished, give the content a final edit. Even if you receive an article or blog post from a professional writer, I suggest that you edit every piece of content to be sure it's the highest quality before it gets posted. You'll ensure that it truly represents your idea and content goal. The editing phase is your last chance to review the piece before launch. When you edit, remember that this represents your brand, so it should be as crisp and clear as possible.

Before you go live with any content, make sure to check for grammar, spelling, and mechanics of style. This is a quick check that someone other than the author should do. Often writers will get entrenched in creating, so when it comes time to check for mistakes, they might not be able to see the forest for the trees. Even if you have outsourced to a writer, it's best to review the content in detail before launch. Keep in mind that even professionals can make mistakes, too! For small businesses with limited resources for content production, try hiring an intern from a local university to do your editing. In fact, interns are great sources of inspiration for content, and they often provide a kind of energy that can only be found in college students — you may want to consider keeping an intern on board as part of your content development team.

This is also your last chance to intercept "salesy" content. We've been saying this throughout the book, but it's very important. Content marketing shouldn't come across as advertising or be all about you. Content should focus on your customers. If the final draft has an advertising feel, it might need one more round of tweaking to weed out any blatant sales pitches.

When you're ready to launch, make a concerted effort to meet your deadlines and keep on track with your schedule. Content marketing hinges on frequent postings of fresh material. Once you launch new content on your site, remember to distribute it across as many relevant channels as possible, and start promoting right away. Most importantly, do not delay launch over little details. Just like software products, it is often better to get it out there when it's 98% finished and edit later — if it ever becomes necessary. Remember, "Done is better than perfect."

> **I cannot tell you how many times I have seen that last 2% cost a business a small fortune because it's sitting waiting for approvals rather than generating leads like it was meant to do.**

Steps 5 and 6 will explain the best ways to do both promotion and distribution. Your pages will get the most attention when you proactively work to get them in front of people. For this reason, you should consider promotion and distribution part and parcel with launch.

Repurpose Your Content

Repurposing is a fantastic way to capitalize on a successful piece of content, or to take a fabulous idea that may not be so hot in its current form and work to improve it. After your content audit in Step 1, you'll likely discover some repurposing opportunities, but keep a look out for ways to repurpose your content throughout the strategy and maximize the idea's potential.

Starting with the goals for your content, seek out other avenues to use the piece to reach a wider audience. If the content currently reaches the demographic you've targeted, you may be able to repurpose it for distribution on a different channel that attracts a similar demographic. For example, if your YouTube video is successful, the same video could have a good chance of success on Vimeo, since video sites tend to attract a similar demographic. This same strategy can be employed for images. If your images posted to Pinterest are getting traffic, you could consider posting them to an image-sharing site, like Flickr. Channels that work well for Business-to-Business (B2B) marketing, like LinkedIn and SlideShare, tend to share demographics, as well. If your content is successful on one B2B channel, chances are good that it will be successful on different one. When you post content to any channel, make sure to create descriptions that include a link to the originator site (i.e. your website) to draw traffic to your pages. Don't just post the content and leave – always optimize to direct traffic to your site!

In addition to repurposing for multiple distribution channels,[15] some content can translate to multiple media forms. You can often migrate one kind of content to another form with minimal effort. For example, imagine you have a blog post that was a big hit and attracted a lot of attention. Your company is really active on SlideShare, so why not take this success and reach a new audience with it? Summarize the blog post into to a slideshow and post it on SlideShare with a link to your original source on your site.

---

15 http://www.verticalmeasures.com/content-marketing-2/content-repurposing-how-to-lower-marketing-costs-and-expand-audience-reach/

Take it a step further and turn that slideshow into a video and distribute to those channels!

Many ideas are flexible, meaning that, with a little creativity, you can reuse them in different forms. As you set out to create a piece of content, keep in mind the other ways that it can be repurposed to extend the value of your content strategy.

Get Inspired!

Be on the lookout for content. Inspiration is all around you. You engage with staff, friends, customers and industry partners *all the time*. Turn those experiences into content that lines up with your overall game plan.

Make sure you have tools on hand that will allow you to create content at a moment's notice. By having a digital camera and a digital video recorder on hand in your office, or in your bag when you travel to industry conferences and events, you can be ready to capture activity that might lead to publishable content.

Figure 29: ALS Ice Bucket Challenge

The greatest value to having digital cameras on hand is that they can provide content from a single event that can be repurposed for multiple channels. Here's an example. A couple of people from your staff go to a big industry-wide conference in Chicago, packing their brand new iPhones. From that single event they generate the following content:

- Summary of the conference for your blog
- A "top 10 new things I learned from the conference" list, also for the blog
- Photos of the event with interactions between your staff and the attendees posted in the blog articles, to your Pinterest account and other photo-sharing channels
- Video interviews of some key attendees, posted to your blog and your video-sharing accounts like YouTube

And there could be more content that gets generated, too. It has a lot to do with how your business creatively responds to the world it's engaged in, as well as having tools available to help record it.

Make it fun!

When we talk about great content, we're talking about content that has *genuine* appeal. Many content marketers pump out content just because they know that they need to without considering the audience, and the result is a lot of stale and boring pages. If content lacks originality, it ends up blending in and simply adds to the noise.

While I've given you a big list of content ideas in this chapter, this isn't the end of the possibilities. Keep researching the content your competition and industry are producing to get ideas for other forms. The main purpose for a list like this is to generate ideas when you're brainstorming for adding content to your website. This is a go-to guide that can inspire your next project.

The best advice I can offer is this: Be willing to have fun making content. When you loosen up and have fun, you can tap a lot of creativity and end up with entertaining content. If the content turns out to be weak or fails to be funny, then you don't have to post it. No matter what, encourage people to create content. You'll eventually end up with some gems.

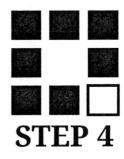

OPTIMIZATION
Critical for Your Online Marketing Success

Want to know the secret to optimizing content for search and social media? Solve people's problems. Help them accomplish their tasks. By focusing your efforts there, you'll build long-term value that does well in search and social media regardless of the way ranking algorithms evolve. On top of that, you also truly connect with visitors who come to your site, resulting in more return visits, conversions, and lifetime loyal customers. As I discussed in the previous steps, there are all kinds of data that uncover what people search for. Take advantage of that data to ensure that you provide quality content that matches your audience's needs.

Creating content is only half the battle. You have to make sure that your site architecture allows search engines to crawl and index it effectively, that you leverage awareness efforts for greater visibility, and you use web analytics data to determine what works so that you can make effective adjustments. However, if you lose focus on solving your audience's problems, the reset of your effort won't matter much.

Today's SEO Landscape

Search Engine Optimization (SEO) is the process of making content web friendly for search engines. SEO facilitates the crawling of the search engine bot through your pages, helping to make the essence of your content clear to the search engine algorithm. When done correctly, your content will be recognized as highly relevant and will likely rank high in the search results. This chapter covers a lot of optimization detail that is critical for your online marketing success. I recommend you read through it once to get an understanding of what you need to be aware of, then return to it as necessary as an SEO resource when working through your content marketing strategy.

Let me start by clarifying that search engine optimization is *not* an exact science. Search engine algorithms are proprietary, so we can't know exactly how they work. Instead, SEO is based on theories that have been carefully researched and tested across the Internet. Therefore, it's *not* guaranteed that optimized content will automatically rank higher or more frequently in search. However, by following optimization best practices, you will greatly increase your content's chances to beat the competition.

SEO can seem too technical for some people, so it often gets written off as the webmaster's responsibility, or at least the territory of people with computer science degrees. I'm willing to bet, however, that you could look at a web page right now and identify whether or not it's following good SEO practices without ever looking at a line of programming code. That's because optimization practices not only work for the search engines; they also make the page readable and clear to humans. Search engines reward content in the search results for being clear and user-friendly, so optimization is about making content exactly that. Certainly, you should ensure that your webmaster understands SEO, but your web content creators need to understand optimization, too. This means they should understand some of the technical stuff – so that every content creation effort includes optimization, rather than leaving it as an afterthought.

Optimizing Your Content

First things first, you can't avoid working with code for some of your SEO. You should know how to see the code behind your web page and be able to identify some basic aspects of it. Hypertext Markup Language, or HTML, is the fundamental coding language for the World Wide Web. Over the years many languages have been built on top of it, but HTML typically forms the framework for most web pages. Within the code lies background information that not only tells your browser how to display the page but identifies key aspects of the page's relevance to the search engine bot.

You can display the code for any web page by going to your browser and opting to see it. For Google Chrome, you can use the shortcut Control-U. For Firefox, go to "view" and then "page source." Every browser allows you to see the source code. For most browsers, like Google Chrome, Firefox and Explorer, the code will be displayed in a separate window so that you can compare the code and the displayed web content side by side.

Web pages are divided like most paper documents; they have a header, a body, and a footer. In terms of the coding, the information will contain "metadata." It's considered *meta* because it's data *about* your page, and most of it never displays on the page itself. This is code that bots consider important, so you've got to consider it important, too!

Let me de-mystify code a little bit. HTML is actually pretty simple to read for the casual user. It's built on tags that define the contents within them. HTML tags are command words set off by angle brackets. Generally speaking, there is an opening tag and a closing tag (identified with a slash). The text between the tags is defined by the tags. For **example**, to indicate that the word "example" should appear in bold, the code would read like this: <bold>example</bold>. Knowing this little bit about how to interpret HTML will enable you to take a quick look at your own code to ensure that it's optimized. You need to know the names of some of the basic tags and what they do, but once you know them, you're on your way. If you see a tag in your code that you don't recognize, just Google it – the answers are all out there. If you would like to know even more about HTML, check out http://www.html-reference.com/.

The sexiness of your page's coding, believe it or not, actually matters to search engines. Inefficient, poorly written code can slow down the load time for your page. Search engines measure the time it takes to load a page and actually penalizes pages with excessive load times. So do humans, who have short attention spans and won't tolerate slow-loading pages either.

You can speed up your page-load time by allocating to a separate file certain aspects of coding like JavaScript and other scripting, or Cascading Style Sheets (CSS) and inline style data. (Entire books are written on that subject.) Making your code crisp and concise can reduce bounce rates[16] and improve your rankings.

Optimization is about making your content understood by the search engine bots. Right now, search engines can't follow or index certain non-text-based site navigation, such as JavaScript, Flash, or even pure images. While this kind of coding can offer a cool experience for your visitors, it won't do much to help your page rankings. When a search engine bot crawls your page, it needs to be encouraged to explore your pages. If it can't follow the navigation, then it won't be able to completely explore your site unless you have created a comprehensive sitemap.[17] It's best to avoid non-text-based navigation as much as possible and instead use text-based navigation to help your pages be found. Navigation should be natural and clear, allowing visitors to find their way through your content and not miss out on critical information. Search engines generally do not consider keywords used in navigation, so there is no reason to try to fit them in unless they would be there naturally.

Search Engine Optimization: Understanding the Algorithm

Crawling

As you produce your remarkable content, you need to be certain that it is optimized for search engines. In our business, when we say, "You need to create great content every time," we mean not only great for the human audience but also for the search algorithm that will be reading and analyzing the content as well. Search engine bots crawl nearly every single page on the Internet and store the information that they find on their servers. From there, the search engine breaks down the data that it finds and begins

---

16 http://en.wikipedia.org/wiki/Bounce_rate

17 http://en.wikipedia.org/wiki/Site_map

to derive relevance from it.

Your goal is to have the bot crawl every page of your site. To facilitate this, your website's architecture needs to be optimized as much as the individual pages. A key aspect of optimizing your site's architecture is having a clean sitemap. Search engine bots use the sitemap to understand and recognize the pages on your site, following the map and indexing the content. A good sitemap will aid the search engine to crawl every piece of content on your site. According to Google's website, "Sitemaps are particularly helpful if:

- Your site has dynamic content.
- Your site has pages that aren't easily discovered by Googlebot during the crawl process – for example, pages featuring rich video or images.
- Your site is new and has few links to it. (Googlebot crawls the web by following links from one page to another, so if your site isn't well linked, it may be hard for [Google] to discover it.)
- Your site has a large archive of pages that are not well linked to each other, or are not linked at all."[18]

Make sure that you have your NoIndex/No Follow set up correctly. This will prevent the crawl bots from crawling unnecessary pages or even an entire site. To prevent all robots from indexing a page on your site, place the following meta tag into the <head> section of your page:

<meta name="robots" content="noindex">

To allow other robots to index the page on your site, preventing only Google's robots from indexing the page:

<meta name="googlebot" content="noindex">

When Google crawls the noindex meta tag on a page, it will completely drop the unwanted page from their search results, even if other pages link to it. Other search engines such as Bing, however, may interpret this directive differently. As a result, a link to the page can still appear in their search

18 http://www.google.com/support/webmasters/bin/answer.py?answer=156184

results. By ensuring that your webmaster understands the value of a crisp architecture and a well-organized sitemap, you will make your pages more accessible to humans and bots alike, and you'll encourage the crawler to explore every page on your website.

Be *very* careful with "NoIndex/NoFollow" tags. Our firm still finds sites that have accidently blocked important pages, and every once in a while we see an entire site accidently blocked Needless to say, this kind of error can be devastating to your promotion efforts.

Duplicate Content

It's critical that you regularly audit your entire website for duplicate content. Matt Cutts, head of Google's Webspam Team, has noted that certain kinds of duplicate content, such as a Terms of Service page, will not be penalized, as long as the content is not inherently spammy or obvious keyword stuffing. There are various ways to identify duplicate content and remove it from your website.

95% of all duplicate content is unintentional.[19] Since Panda and Hummingbird, it's rare to find a website that intentionally duplicates their content, mostly because it does nothing but demote a website's rankings. The remaining 5% of duplicate content, the intentional stuff, happens a number of different ways. A franchise might open up a store in a new geographic region and replicate the neighboring franchise site's content as filler, for example. This is intentionally duplicating one site's content for another, but isn't malicious. In fact, the vast majority of duplicate content issues are quite innocent and unintentional. Regardless, unidentified duplicate content can wreak havoc on your site's rankings if Google gets confused and decides not to display the duplicate pages in its search results. Google does not give you the benefit of the doubt in most cases when well-intentioned webmasters and business owners are simply trying to do their job and publish their content on the Web.

---

19 http://www.verticalmeasures.com/search-optimization/what-is-unintentional-duplicate-content/

Unintentional duplicate content can come in a variety of forms, including duplicate secure HTTPS pages, development or staging server sites, URL parameters, or heavy CMS templates. On top of that, if you have a blog, tagged pages can really create a problem because they end up cannibalizing keywords; in other words, if Google becomes confused over which page to rank for certain keywords because all the pages look the same, Google will drop the ranking. If you have pages that are duplicates, each one of these titles competes for the other page's keywords. Your pages should work harmoniously with your content marketing strategy; the last thing you need is to have pages creating discord, damaging your efforts.

So how do you rid your site of unintentional duplicate content? First off, you have to *identify* the duplicate content, and there are a number of tools that can help:

Moz Crawler: The Crawl Test tool sends out their very own crawler (identified as RogerBot) to crawl the links on a given URL. Crawling each link on that URL, the bot crawls up to 3,000 pages and emails you a CSV report with data on each found URL.[20]

Screaming Frog: The Screaming Frog SEO Spider is a small desktop program you can install locally on your PC, Mac or Linux machine which crawls websites' links, images, CSS, script and apps from an SEO perspective. It fetches key onsite elements for SEO, presents them in tabs by type and allows you to filter for common SEO issues, or slice and dice the data how you see fit by exporting into Excel.[21]

Once you identify duplicate URLs and duplicate content, then you can use a number of things to clean up your pages. Tools such as:

Robots Meta Tag: It's a header level directive that sends a very strong signal to Google that the bots follow every time. That's the Noindex, Nofollow tag that we discussed previously.

---

20 http://moz.com/help/pro/crawl-test
21 http://www.screamingfrog.co.uk/seo-spider/

rel=canonical: Although it's not a header level directive, it's still a signal for search engines including Bing and Yahoo.

URL parameters in Webmaster Tools: This is more of an advanced feature, but you can use this to tell Google bots which parameters you don't want them to count in their index.

404 errors or 301 redirects: You can manually redirect old addresses to your preferred destination or create automatic redirects to send your visitor to the most relevant URL.

It's important to recognize that most forms of unintentional duplicate content do negatively affect rankings and traffic. A thorough site audit can help identify any form of duplicate content you might have, and you can take specific actions to remove the duplicate content and URLs from Google's index through the use these methods and tools. I always say, if you confuse Google, you'll almost always lose. So keep it crisp and clean: don't make work for yourself by leaving duplicate content on your sit.

Indexing

Google organizes the content it has crawled on its indexing servers. These servers work like the index in a book, by organizing all the information on the web by keyword so that it can be brought back up in a particular query. When a query is submitted to Google, the keyword runs through the indexing servers and matches it to all the available content.

Google pays attention to how sites change from one round of indexing to the next. If a site has frequent updates, then Google will increase the frequency that it crawls and indexes the site. Google interprets frequent updates to a site as more relevant than a site that has stagnant content, meaning that frequently updated websites tend to have more pages in the index thus will have more pages appearing in the search results.

Conversely, if Google feels you are not updating your website, feels your content is thin, or senses there is something spammy going on, it will start to remove your pages from its index. This means that your website needs to have new content posted to your site frequently in order to encourage frequent crawling and up-to-the-minute indexing.

Keywords and Rankings

The Google search appliance uses two primary factors when analyzing an indexed page for relevance and ranking: PageRank and understanding the relevance and value of your content. PageRank is Google's key feature. It's what made Google, Google. The mechanics behind PageRank is driven by the network of links to and from websites. In fact, Google boasts of knowing the entire link structure of the web. By understanding the link structure of the web, Google can track this network of links and backlinks to determine relevance of a given page. This means that a major aspect to ranking well in search is to get links to your site.

Google clearly states that the content itself is, in a way, *understood* by the algorithm, and therefore you can't really trick it. This is because it factors in the page content together with link structures. Therefore, the best plan is to include your target keywords *naturally* within the body text and strategically within the metadata.

In other words, create your content for humans, *not* algorithms.

Google's algorithm works to deliver real content in the search results, weeding out the junk. The fact is, if Google returned garbage results, it would drive users to other search engines, so Google's highest priority is to be sure that the junk stays out. This is good for the searcher, since the searcher relies on Google to bring back only relevant content. Ultimately, this is also better for you, the website owner, because you are forced to put together useful content. Useful content is best for your brand and will find you the most success in the long term.

Optimizing Your Pages for the Web

In their book *Audience, Relevance, and Search,* James Matthewson, *et al,*[22] offer a guiding philosophy that addresses the way you ought to approach your content in the context of SEO. They state: "Writing for search engines approximates writing for people. Your pages should work for a human first – that is, a human should be able to understand your content and derive meaning from it relative to the search query that was performed. If that can happen, it will work for the search engine, too.

When you create metadata for your pages, it should also be recognizable and relevant to a human looking for content relative to the keywords in your metadata. Your content's metadata is part of the larger framework for your content and will help boost the content's relevance in search. It follows, then, that content development should include an optimization plan to be sure that all content is optimized at the outset.

Optimizing metadata is a matter of knowing who you are targeting for each page and the appropriate messaging. If your business has an SEO and a content specialist managing content creation and launch, those two will need to be in close communication (sometimes they might even be the same person). You can ensure that your pages will always be optimized by instituting a plan that governs the handoff of the new page from the content specialist to the optimization specialist for launch. That way everyone knows who's in charge of the process and can rest assured that it's being implemented properly.

By nurturing your content through SEO, you will do yourself a huge favor. Ignore SEO, and your awesome content ideas will have less chance of being found in search. You don't want to miss the opportunity for your content to pack a full punch. If you include optimization as part of your content development process, rather than as a separate round of work, you can be sure that the details, like optimizing the title, body and metadata, don't become an afterthought. This will lead to more naturally optimized content and ultimately more efficient output.

---

22 James Matthewson, et al, *Audience, Relevance, and Search*

The header of your page is set apart in the code by the tag <Head>. The metadata within the header gives a huge amount of information about the page to the bots. The metadata also provides information about the page that appears in the browser and in the SERP, which searchers will see but may not consciously recognize as page content.

Figure 30: Optimization for meta description, title, and URL

The page title tag is set off by the tag <title> and it serves a number of purposes. It usually states what the page is about and is viewable to users in a number of places. In the search engine results, and on many social networks, the title appears as the link for the website. It also appears at the top of the browser when you are viewing the page. If your browser is tabbed, it will be the name of the tab for the page being viewed. Therefore, it serves a meaningful purpose for humans as the identifier for your page's content. It also has significance to search engines. Optimize your title tags like this:

- Title tags should contain at least one keyword phrase related to the page's optimized content. The closer to the beginning of the title, the better
- Make certain that the title is no more than 55 characters long.
- Be strategic. Don't repeat titles. It takes effort, but **each page needs to have a unique title**.
- And for your visitors' sake, as much as for the search engine, titles should match the content of the page.

Next, you have the meta description. The meta description is one single tag (rather than text sectioned off between tags). The tag for *example description* is formatted: <meta name="description" content="example description"/>. The meta description typically would be viewed by the user in the search results as the descriptor text about the result.

For the humans viewing the search results, this description is hugely important and should make it quite clear what visitors will find when they click to your content.

Therefore, avoid generic descriptors, such as, "Welcome to our home page." The description should include your keywords without resorting to keyword-stuffed descriptions. A good description is a complete sentence that concisely states the purpose of the page content. It's your opportunity to "sell" the individual on clicking through to your page. Search engines limit the amount of real estate they give to descriptions in the SERPs, which is normally about 125 characters. Anything more than that length is usually cut off.

The meta keywords tag is not very important these days, but we still recommend adding two or three keyword phrases in this field rather than leave it blank, or delete the tag altogether. The tag for *example keyword* is formatted: <meta name="keywords" content="example keyword"/>. Use commas to separate keyword phrases. This tag does not get displayed for human visitors, so it does not necessarily have to be meaningful to a human visitor.

One last word: meta tag optimization is no place to get lazy. Often, people spend a lot of time creating awesome content, then they go to upload it and suddenly remember that they need to optimize. Anxious to post, they blast through the last optimization step, giving it very little thought or even skipping it altogether. But it happens to be a step that needs your close attention. Remember, the description and title meta tags will feed into the search results and other really important places like social media sites, describing the results that the searcher can expect to find. These tags are critical to search engine indexing. You don't want to sell short your fantastic web content by letting SEO slip through the cracks. The two tools mentioned above, Moz Crawler and Screaming Frog, can help you identify any optimization issues.

Optimizing the Page Body

The page body is the page content that displays as the web page. The page body is, of course, written and designed for people first and search engines second. Naturally, you should provide content that *people* want to read. Organize the page content in a way that is clear and natural for humans to engage and, especially, share. Natural links (links that other people create out of interest in the content) are the ultimate SEO boost. You won't get natural links if your content is badly organized, sloppy, or redundant.

Fitting Keywords Into Your Content

Keyword usage has totally changed over the last few years, please do not compromise the quality of your content in order to squeeze in more keywords. If a keyword is used once or twice in a great piece of content, generally that is all you need. People search keywords because they want information related to the keywords; they have no tolerance for a page that optimizes a keyword but delivers unrelated content. This will get you nothing but a huge bounce rate and lowered rankings.

Remember that the user experience should always come first, and excessive keyword density is a thing of the past. You'll not only hurt your reputation as a brand, you'll also seriously damage your online reputation as an expert if you deliver valueless, irrelevant content. The idea is to give people the good stuff. If you do, you'll be rewarded by Google with good rankings and by humans with shares and natural links.

Headers Tags in the Body

Just like in a word processor, HTML allows you to manipulate the text by creating headings, bold text, and colors. The tags that control fonts get a close inspection by the search engine bots.

The page headings are tagged <H1>, <H2>, etc., with H1 as the top level heading. Search engines pay close attention to the H1 tag, and less to the subsequent heading tags. Here's how to use them:

- Each page should have **only one H1 tag**. (If you need to have headings for multiple sections on a page, use H2 or H3.)
- H1 tags should be located at the top of your page content above any other heading tags.
- If possible, put your important keywords into your H1 tag.
- Above all, the H1 tag should serve as the content's title, communicating what the page is about.

Links in Your Content

The way that you handle links within your page content is an important part of SEO. Most importantly, make it clear to your visitors where a link will take them. Don't surprise them! Bots are programmed to look for the same kinds of clarity that humans want. Search engines prefer to see links in your content.

Fundamentally, you are free to color your links any way you want, but it's recommended that you make it obvious they are links. A link's color should be different from the main text. Most people expect links to be colored blue and be underlined, so you might want to keep that in mind as you set up your style sheet. Remember, there's no shame using the default font style if users will be able to engage the page with ease.

The actual text that is linked (the text that's colored differently and underlined) is called the "anchor text." Because you've set the link apart by color and an underline, it naturally draws the reader's eye. The words that are highlighted, then, can be a very good clue to the content that you are linking to. You should use terms that make an effort to communicate where the link is going and avoid sending your visitor to a page that they aren't expecting. On that note, it should go without saying, then, that all of your links should be functioning properly. Broken links look sloppy and give the impression that you've forgotten about the page. Not only do your users dislike broken links, but search engines frown upon them, too. Below is a great tool to use to help identify any broken links on a page.

Link Sleuth: Xenu's Link Sleuth is a handy, free app that will let you check that there are no broken links on your website.[23]

An internal link is a link to other pages on your own site. Internal links are as good for you as they are for search engines; they are clues to your website's relevance. By using internal links, you encourage your visitors to engage your content on multiple levels, and you demonstrate your depth of knowledge as an expert in your industry. When you use **internal** links, avoid generic anchor text, such as "click here" or "more." It's a tempting way to link because it's fast and easy to say, "Want to read more? Click here." But search engines want to see relevance in the anchor text *when it's on your own web pages*. The best way to ensure relevance is to make sure that the anchor text for those links closely aligns with the title of the page it links to, whether it is a page on your site or a page on another website.

Above all, links should direct users to pages that are relevant to the content that they are currently engaging. Your goal should be to keep them engaged. Directing users away from the topic at hand is a surefire way to lose their attention.

Optimizing Images for Search

Images are perhaps the most commonly used vertical search type. Because they get searched so frequently, the images on your website need to be optimized. Images can appear in the main search results if Google determines that image results are relevant to a particular search. Your image could appear, even when your other content pages don't. This gives your content more chances for competing in search. In fact, it's common for an image in a blog post to bring thousands of visitors to that page based on people finding the image when doing an image search. We've had that happen for our company's image content many times. Our Facebook "selfie" image brought more than 10,000 visitors to our blog post where the image was used (see Figure 31 on page 122).

---

23 http://xenus-link-sleuth.en.softonic.com/

Figure 31: The Vertical Measures company selfie

Because search engines can't derive complete meaning from images, they rely on the context of the page on which the images reside as well as the meta tags for the image. These clues help the search engine to understand the image's contextual meaning and its relevance in search.

The metadata for images includes source (i.e. file location and name), alt, and title tags. For best results in search, all of these tags should be used and optimized for your images.

Alt tags serve as alternate text to describe the image when the image is not available. If there's an error loading the source image, the alternate text will display. For text-reading software, alt tags are read aloud so that images can be understood by the listener. Though it isn't as common today, users with slower Internet connections may turn off image loading so that they can peruse the web faster, and the alt tag lets them know what image was supposed to be displayed.

The image title tag is similar to the alt tag, but it displays when the mouse scrolls over the image. The title will help the visitor to understand the context of the image, and therefore it should describe it accurately and with detail.

A good alt tag is a simple, keyword-rich phrase that adequately describes the image. The image title tag should be keyword-rich but it should also give a better sense of the context of the image. Not only should your alt and title tags be keyword-rich, but the filename for your image should also contain the keyword that you're optimizing. The alt and title tags are imbedded within the image source code as follows: <img src="pepper-oni_pizza.jpg" alt="pepperoni pizza" title="pepperoni pizza with proper distribution of pepperonis">. All of the information contained in the tags provides clues that search engines use to understand exactly what the image on the page really is.

ALT: "Pepperoni Pizza"

Figure 32: ALT text

As with all the content you produce, try to provide as best a user experience on the page as you can. This means that you will need to consider how the images will help the user engage your page. Offering high quality images is not only good for your user experience, but they will also help them retain quality when they are displayed as thumbnails in the search results – and in social media.

It's always advantageous to use on your website unique images that attract interest and encourage links. For eCommerce sites, make an effort to generate your own product images rather than use images provided by manufacturers. This can help your images stand out among the results, and can make them appealing enough to get links. If you create your own unique images, you may want to specify that others are free to use them in exchange for a citation or link back to your website. This way, your content gets circulated and you are able to build links back to your source pages.

Remember, if you use images from other sources on your site, be sure that you have permission to use them. You don't want to set yourself up for a copyright-infringement issue.

Optimizing Videos for Search

Creating and publishing video on today's Internet is so easy and popular that its value to marketers can't be ignored. Video has exploded on the Internet because of sites like YouTube, Vimeo, and Facebook that have enabled casual users to upload their videos, create channels for their content, and encourage user comments. Paired with the boom in video recording technology, like cell phones, working with video can be a snap. The Internet video phenomenon has made it much easier for anyone, including marketers, to use video for communication. Video does not have to be professionally produced in a studio to be interesting, fun, or even go viral. It only needs to be compelling.

When a video gets big time views, you want all the benefits, like traffic and links, coming to your site rather than going offsite to YouTube or other video-sharing sites. On the other hand, YouTube gets so much viewership that it can offer you the opportunity to get much more exposure. A successful video on YouTube can lead traffic back to your website; however, the burst of activity around a successful video generally remains with the hosting site, so, ideally, you would want to host the video on your site and simultaneously post it to sites like YouTube to maximize traffic.

For simultaneous launch, you can save yourself some hassle by first posting your video to a video-hosting site and then embedding the video onto your webpage. Most video-hosting sites provide an embed code that you can paste into your webpage's HTML, allowing visitors to play the video from your page. Post the video to YouTube and, when it goes live, grab the embed code and post it to your site. That way, you make use of your video posted on YouTube but publish it on your website. You should also create and optimize branded channels for your business on YouTube, Vimeo and others. This way you can increase your brand recognition and leverage your successful videos to promote your other content.

Video optimization is similar to optimization of images. Here are some tips to keep in mind for video:

Make sure your video title is keyword-rich, but give it some pizzazz.

Drab titles that appear to viewers as only keyword-conscious will lead them to believe that the video itself is just marketing propaganda. By using an interesting title, you draw viewers in and make your effort seem more natural.

For the video's description, make sure it clearly represents the content of the video and contains your keyword phrase. Lead the description with a link to the most relevant page on your website, that way it will ensure that it displays so that users can easily click on it.

As with images, when posting video to your site, be sure to optimize the description and title tags.

Likewise, optimize the video filename and URL in the same way that you would with images. Make sure they incorporate your target keywords.

Figure 33: Optimized video with Jay Baer

When you're in video production, keep in mind the following tips; they will help the humans who watch your videos, giving your videos a better chance of going viral:

During production of your video, consider lighting, camera angles, and audio. Viewers are tolerant of amateur video online, but you should aim to make your content as viewable as possible and to give your production a level of quality that supports your professional image. If you are doing an interview, use a tripod to keep the camera steady. Run a test to make sure that the lighting works well and doesn't blur the subject of the video. Be sure that the audio is being picked up by the microphone and that the room doesn't distort the sound or create an echo.

When you select a thumbnail for your video, take an image that's going to intrigue viewers and lead them to click on your video. Your audience will likely find your video within a queue of suggested videos, or when as a share on social media, so the thumbnail should be both interesting as well as make it clear what the video is about.

Keep in mind copyright if you use music for the background in your video. You'll either have to get permission from copyright holders to use their music, select royalty-free music (from providers like GarageBand), or generate your own original music.

Encourage user comments and ratings for your video. Search engines keep track of user-generated content and favor videos that have it.

Allow other websites to embed your video in exchange for a link back to your site. Also, encourage sharing of the video by adding social media share buttons, such as the Facebook "Like" button or the Twitter "Tweet This" button.

Optimizing for News Sites

You might not be a journalist proper, but you may still produce industry-related news all the time, whether it be through your blog or other means. If that's the case, then you want to be recognized as a new source in your industry. And while it may be a great time to jump into online news, it will take effort to get news content to rank in search. Therefore, you've got to know how to optimize news-oriented content.

If you've been building a follower base, make sure to get your news to your followers first and foremost. By setting up an RSS feed, you can publish news content to your followers the instant it's created. Many RSS followers want to read the entire article from the feed, so if you can do it practically, it's best to send the complete article through the feed rather than a summary. Include a link to your page content to enable users to navigate back to your site.

If you publish an RSS feed, then your key focus will be to grow your following. By placing an RSS feed button by your content, you will make it easy for people to start following you. Social media applications like Google+, LinkedIn, Twitter and Facebook are also great ways to share your news, making it easy for others to pass it along, and encouraging more people to join your network of followers.

To publish news content that ranks among mainstream news sites, you'll need each article that you produce to exist on a static URL, meaning, that every article you produce will be listed on a separate page, rather than having multiple articles compiled on a single page. In order to have your website's news feed included in Google News, you'll need to submit your blog or press release sections directly to Google News. They will review your content, and once it's approved, they will start including your content in their news feed. Google News has specific requirements for adding news sites to their pages.[24] To routinely appear in news feeds, you should produce newsworthy content on a frequent basis. And whenever you think about regular production of fresh content, you should automatically think of the editorial calendar. It's the best way to stay organized and on schedule with content production.

News articles should be optimized for keywords in the same way that you would optimize other content. The body of the article should have your keywords included, but the article should not run the risk of appearing to be keyword-optimized.

Article headlines should be interesting and grab your readers' attention. Sometimes, you won't be able to get the keyword you want into the headline. Be sure, then, that you've optimized the meta data (title, description, and keywords) for the keywords you want to isolate. By including the keywords that you want to rank for in the title tags, you greatly increase your

---

24 http://www.google.com/support/news_pub/bin/topic.py?topic=8909

chances to get ranked for that keyword.

Take advantage of news aggregators like Google News and Yahoo! News and submit your stories to them. They publish fresh news at the top of these sites on a continual basis, so when you submit a story, you'll temporarily rank at No. 1 simply because you've written an optimized article. This doesn't last for a long time, especially for competitive search terms, because new postings will immediately rank on top, but you have a great chance to get your content found when it sits at the top of the rankings. Optimizing your content for hot-trending keywords is a great way for your news to get picked up by social media users and get shared.

Optimizing for Local Search

Google Maps, Bing Maps, and even local search and review sites like Yelp. com provide vertical searches for businesses based on their geographic location. Not only do many search engines use vertical search for localized results and directory information, but search engines have begun to emphasize local search results in the main results data, as well. Certain product searches will return vendor location suggestions in the area near the searcher. If a searcher enters a location into the query, they will get results relative to the location specified. Even if location is not specified in the search query, the search engine can often determine where the searcher is physically located, and if the query is appropriate for local search, it will return localized results. This means that if your product or service has an application for localized search, you need to optimize for it.

Figure 34: Mixed local results for "Scottsdale, Arizona"

When optimizing your content for local search, you should follow many of the same SEO steps as you would for other pages on your site, like keyword use in meta tags and H1 tags. The key to success is targeting geo-specific keywords. Just as you would do for all your other target keywords, research geo-specific keywords that you can target, as well. By way of example: "Miami-Dade" vs. "Miami, FL" vs. "Dade County."

Ensure that your full physical address appears on your website's pages. If your business has multiple locations, you should dedicate at least one page on your site for each location. This is better than listing all your locations on a single page because you can optimize all the on-page SEO elements for each location. You want your pages at the top of the search engine results when your keywords are paired with location. For example, say you own a chain of cycle shops in south Florida. You want to be found when someone searches "bike rental Miami." Here are some tips to help make that happen:

- Each local-search-optimized page should include tons of relevant details about your business, including an exact address, hours of operation, maps, and directions.

- Get user-generated content (ratings, comments, reviews) on your pages that are optimized for geo-specific search. This will help raise the awareness of those pages with search engines.

- Get listed in local focused directories. But be particular with this and only request a listing on human-edited directories as these tend to be more trusted by search engines. A great example is Best of the Web's Regional Directory.[25]

Optimizing for Social Media

While it is important to pay attention to onsite SEO, your offsite social media presence should be optimized as well. When your business chooses to create one or more social media profiles, each one should be optimized for that network's user experience. Social Media Optimization (SMO)

---

25 http://botw.org/top/Regional/United_States/

generally refers to the social aspect of marketing strategies and is typically applied in two ways. First is the promotion angle, in which marketers take advantage of the power of social media to promote their content and their brand. This book focuses on the promotion angle in Step 5. Right now, we're going to explore the second angle, which is to optimize branded social media profiles to increase their search rankings.

Social media gives you more places to post your content and to link back to your website. Setting up profiles and encouraging prominent people within your organization to engage with social media on behalf of your business is a great way to evangelize your brand.

Anyone can set up a business profile and start engaging followers. Just as onsite SEO can be forgotten or overlooked, social profiles can fall victim to the same kind of neglect. At the very minimum, if your profiles aren't optimized, you'll miss out on some great ways to communicate with your followers and promote your business. At worst, you run the risk of having a generic looking and easily forgettable profile. Instead, this is an opportunity to make your profiles stand out. To get your social media profiles rocking:

Make sure your keywords are in your profile, especially for sites like Facebook and LinkedIn. This will help your profile rank higher in search, whether it be searches within the social site or on search engines like Bing. Just as with SEO, you don't want to overdo it with keywords. Find ways to get your keywords into your profile naturally. Summary sections and About Me sections are especially great places to describe your business using the keywords you want to optimize for.

Take advantage of websites that allow you to customize the color schemes and backgrounds. Use clean, appealing themes that complement the layout of your profile. Avoid busy backgrounds or obnoxious schemes that detract from the content. Sites like Twitter and Slideshare allow for graphic optimization.

Above and beyond the background, be sure to customize the profile banner, if the site allows you to do so. This is an opportunity to make your profile shine. Some profiles can be customized to such an extent that they start to look like an entirely new website and less like a channel on a social media site. In the banner, incorporate your brand logo and your slogan. Sites like Google+, Facebook and Twitter give you the opportunity to make fantastic profiles.

Don't forget to give your profile a face. Nothing is more uncool than encountering a profile that uses a generic, two-tone silhouetted bust – or auto-generated cartoon character – to go with the name. Don't be that profile! Nearly every social media site allows you to put a face or logo to the name. Sites like LinkedIn, Facebook, SlideShare, and Twitter rely on the profile image to attribute visual uniqueness to the content within the profile.

Link to your website. Nearly every profile allows you to do this, and some allow multiple links, so don't forget to add them. A great second link would be to your blog.

Facebook is great for communicating your status updates to your followers, but it has a number of other features that can get overlooked. Make sure you offer rich information about your business. Facebook has an events option for posting events that you will host or be otherwise involved in; it has discussion boards, video and photo boxes, and many more. You can control which boxes appear on your profile. Some business profiles fail to take advantage of the possibilities that Facebook offers and thus fail to make their profile a destination. They might get liked and updates might appear on their followers' pages, but their followers may never come back to their page for more interaction. By creating an engaging profile, you encourage more return visits and user engagement.

Video sites offer multiple formats for displaying your playlist and organizing your content. Consider how the available options can keep users on your channel. For example, you can feature your coolest related videos in your playlists. You can boost UGC by openly inviting users to comment on your channel.

For any channel that gives you the option, display the subscriber list. It's always good for people viewing social media to feel like they are part of an active community. Showing other members of the community is a great way to encourage that sensibility.

Optimizing for Mobile

As I mentioned earlier on in the book, mobile content cannot be ignored. A huge volume of internet content is now viewed via smartphones, tablets, etc. You don't need to redesign your entire website or create an expensive mobile app in order to provide content for mobile users. Instead, consider using the mobile tools already at your disposal, such as Instagram or Vine. These networks allow you to use their format and create any type of content you want under their guidelines, and are both great for creating engaging, visual content that's easy to consume and share to with others. You can make optimizing your content for mobile as easy as cutting your videos to fit within Instagram's 15 second timeslot, or Vine's 7 second clips.

Depending on your market, you could miss a huge untapped audience if your content is not optimized and distributed for mobile users. Today, mobile devices can access the internet from anywhere in the world, which has made them the go-to tool for just about everything online.

Your audience should be able to use their mobile devices to read your blog posts, or shop for your products, etc. You can ensure your content is as approachable and user-friendly as the rest of your optimized website by keeping it organized, up-to-date, relevant, and easy to read. These bedrock principles will make your content user friendly and mobile friendly – you can't use a website redesign as a way to get around them.

You might be tempted to assume that because people are on their phones, they have a shortened attention span for your content. While that might be true to a certain degree, some recent studies have shown that long-form content (such as entire TV shows or movies) is just as popular and heavily viewed on mobile devices as on wired devices. This is true for full- length articles, resource pages, and video content – your audience will stay to the end if the content is available and useful. A survey of 50,000 users found that 65% of mobile video viewers preferred watching full movies and TV episodes over briefer stuff (music videos, movie clips) on their phones.[26] In another survey, 8 in 10 people said they would watch TV shows on their phones if the shows were available for mobile devices; another 88% said they would watch full-length movies.[27]

Mobile users might be willing to spend a lot of time on their phone, but they will typically make quick selections on what content catches their eye. If you want to get mobile users to open and read your articles, focus on creating highly engaging headlines. Spend time brainstorming the best possible headline that will draw the audience in for more information. An excellent headline can even help you attract bored readers who may be browsing just to find any interesting piece of content that comes along. If you consistently offer compelling headlines, and follow them up with great content, you will build trust with your readers that you're a source of insider knowledge, interesting information, or even that you're willing to be there to satisfy their occasional boredom.

On Facebook, people share images more than any other kind of content. Photos on Facebook receive 53% more likes, 104% more comments, and 84% more click-through rates than the average post.[28] With mobile, your company's graphics or behind the scenes photos often hold even more merit in your follower's feed. This form of content is great for user engagement, but keep in mind these details, if you want your images on mobile to get shared:

- Are your fonts and text easy to read?
- Is the photo the correct size?
- Will it be visually pleasing?

To optimize for mobile, evaluate the content your audience actually

---

26 http://advanced-television.com/2013/10/30/65-prefer-to-watch-movies-or-tv-shows-over-shorter-content-on-mobile/

27 http://www.marketingcharts.com/wp/online/us-mobile-video-viewers-happy-to-watch-long-form-content-37763/

28 http://blog.kissmetrics.com/more-likes-on-facebook/

engages with, and respond with stuff that they can digest easily, whether they're sitting at the computer in the office, or catching a train on the way to a sports game.

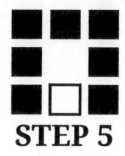

STEP 5

CONTENT PROMOTION
Put the "Marketing" In Content Marketing

Promotion is about communicating the value of your content to the people who will be able to share it with their own networks. By proactively finding ways to spread your content outside of your immediate sphere of followers, you can draw a wider audience to your site and grow your own base of followers. Developing quality content is only half the battle. The other half is all about getting maximum exposure for that content. You could have the best content in the world, but it will only be as good as your ability to make it visible.

Now is a good time to discuss the difference between content *promotion* and content *distribution*. Although they are similar and sometimes work together, I generally view promotion as talking about, sharing, or incentivizing a dialogue about content that exists on your own website. Distribution, on the other hand, is the effort of taking your content and publishing it on various channels off your website. For example, if you have a video on your site, and you link to it from Facebook, that's promotion, but you could also publish the video content directly on YouTube or Vimeo, which is considered distributing content. We will dive deeper into distribution in the next step. For now, we'll focus on promotion.

Up to this point in the strategy, we've spent a lot of time talking about the *content* part of content marketing, but once you've created that great webinar, blog post, or infographic, you want it to get some attention. It's time to put the *marketing* in content marketing, and that's where the power of social media really kicks in. By leveraging social media interactions, you can circulate your content and put your brand in front of potential customers. If you're paying attention to where your target audience hangs out online, you can interact with them there.

As I've said, traditional marketing through television, radio and even print is interruption-driven, whereas content marketing engages your customers with stuff they're *already* interested in, providing them with creative solutions to their problems. This makes the social web the ideal place to promote your business as the source of information that your customers are looking for.

Promotion is the work of announcing what you have to offer and ensuring that it gets distributed to the people that you want to see it. Many times, this is a matter of sharing media within a network of relationships that you've established and nurtured. Every business will have a distinctive approach to how it promotes its content, based on the specific industry and unique customer profiles. Small businesses with smaller staffs may not be able to manage a major social media campaign. In many cases, you'll need to pick and choose what kinds of social media channels you have the time to work with. There are a number of possibilities to choose from, including: blogging, commenting on blogs, participating in discussion groups, and posting status updates on social networking profiles.

How to Use Social Media Interactions for Earned Content Promotion

Having progressed through the previous steps, you should be able to identify how your competition uses social media. The best thing about social media is that you can more or less spy on your competitors because their content is all out in the open. So, if your competition has 3,000 people interested in a subject, you might want to start targeting some of those people. You may not be on their radar right now, but they are interested in your industry and they could be your potential customers in the future.

If you see your competitors' activity isn't getting much traction, it may mean one of two things. One, that your audience simply isn't active on that particular social media outlet, or two, that your competition is doing a poor job of engaging this audience. Given that over 67% of the American population use social media today,[29] it's likely that there is a big opportunity to become an authority in your market. If, on the other hand, you see lots of activity, you can be assured they've struck a chord with a network that you should get in on, as well.

What channels have they been using? How many friends do they have on Facebook? How many followers do they have on Twitter? Maybe your competitors are working in blogs and forums. If not, why not? Are there any niche forums out there that have audiences that might be interested in your work? Check out the media and bloggers that normally write about your industry. Make friends with these bloggers. Then pitch your content to them to see if they will promote it on their site! Remember, you aren't "giving your content away" so they can capitalize on it on their blog; rather, you're hoping that a link within the content directs readers back to your website for more information.

The greatest value in social media is, of course, that it's social. This means that you have the opportunity to engage customers in a way that wasn't possible for marketers in the past. A key executive in your business can post an update via Twitter and interact directly with potential customers, industry experts, and any other followers. This kind of engagement adds a sense of familiarity and comfort to your brand image. By engaging through interesting, conversational content, you can keep your brand in front of customers so that when they're ready to look for products in your market, they'll think of you.

Anytime you create totally awesome web content, don't let it sit on your site waiting for searchers to find it – get a buzz going! By promoting your work, you generate interest in your content, and when people find interesting stuff, they naturally share it through social media, or link to it from their websites.

---

29 http://www.mediabistro.com/alltwitter/social-media-america_b56131

I think it's important to dispel the myth of viral content. I want to make it clear that your goal in promoting your content is to spread your content in an active way, rather than focusing on every piece going viral. The phenomenon of viral content is still anomalous in relationship to the total content on the web. If your content does happen to go viral, it will have achieved web marketing nirvana. It's not something you can make happen. The very nature of "viral marketing" has everything to do with the unpredictable nature of mass social obsession, which you have no control over. It has to surprise us. So, don't try to make every content piece a big hit. Rather, focus on making every piece interesting, engaging and useful. Keep in mind the baseball analogy from Step 3.

Social media is absolutely critical for content promotion. As you grow your social networks, you foster relationships with the people who will share your cool stuff when you ask them. To keep social networks engaged, you have to know how each social network operates and understand the rules of engagement.

Facebook

Facebook is sort of like the Beatles for the Internet, no matter how old it gets, everybody seems to like it. Facebook allows you to share an assortment of content with friends and followers – such as blog posts, images, articles, video, etc. Users comment on and "like" each other's status which will in turn show up on their friends' News Feeds. On their profile, users can see all the activity within their network, so if you are posting awesome content that gets a lot of "likes" and shares the audience it can reach is virtually unending.

At the time of my first book, Facebook had just over 500 million users worldwide. Today, the number has skyrocketed to about 1.3 billion users worldwide; 50% of those users, according to Facebook, are online at any given time sharing 1 million links every 20 minutes![30] Primarily, the site is about networking with friends, and the average user has about 130 friends.

---

30 http://www.statisticbrain.com/facebook-statistics/

Beyond the networking of friends, the site has had a huge amount of success with platform applications. Ranging from games, to contests, to promotions targeted to the user's profile, Facebook claims that more than 70% of its users engage with the variety of applications.

The newest version of Facebook is designed to accept a huge amount of personal information. Beyond gender and age, it captures the real interests of its users as they "like" pages. Facebook also allows entities other than private individuals to create a page and share content. "Public Profiles" are pages for public entities, businesses, non-profits, and brands. Public profiles keep their followers informed on news about their page. Every time a public page posts new content, its friends get an update into their feed. Similarly, Interest pages capture human interest topics and create followings based on those interests. When a user likes one of these pages, all the friends of that user see the like and can like it, too. This gives these pages the possibility of going viral, as friends of friends like them, causing the page to gain momentum and spread exponentially throughout the Facebook community.

Additionally, when a user likes a page, they make their profile data available to the page creator, so many interest pages are created in order to capture marketing data on the users who select them. Because of the volume of activity on Facebook, it's a great place to gauge how people think about topics, how they perceive your product, and what they learn based on the questions they tend to ask. The newest Facebook update gave link posts a larger, clickable area to attract visitors and drive them to offsite content. Post your great content on Facebook to drive people to your website. This is easily accomplished by copying and pasting your optimized offsite URL, and pressing Enter. You will notice that the content's H1 Tag, description, and associated image has been taken from your URL and placed in the Status update bar (see Figure 35 on page 141).

Facebook gives you a chance not only to showcase engaging articles, images and videos, but it also gives you a way to foster a two-way conversation with your audience. Ask your friends and followers to share their thoughts and feedback on your content, products and services, or topics in the industry. Suddenly, you have a great opportunity to listen to your customers and improve your strategy based on their response. You can then post fresh content that shows you took *their* feedback and worked to solve *their* issues. This is a great way to build customer loyalty and prove that your followers' views and opinions matter to the brand.

Figure 35: A Facebook post that pulls in the featured image and meta information

You can also share exclusive discounts, promotions, or information through your Facebook posts to encourage followers to act fast! Depending on your industry, try offering special deals or discounts to your followers to keep them interested. Even if they do not immediately buy or use your service, they will keep your brand in mind and search for your brand in the future. As you gain new followers or clients, reward them by providing exclusive information about your industry. For example, promote an in-depth Free Guide through Facebook and get those new followers further down the sales funnel.

So how do you actually attract new followers? First, all your posts should be timely and trustworthy. To better manage your time, schedule your posts well in advance and plan for upcoming holiday events and special deals within your industry. Scheduling Facebook posts is easy:

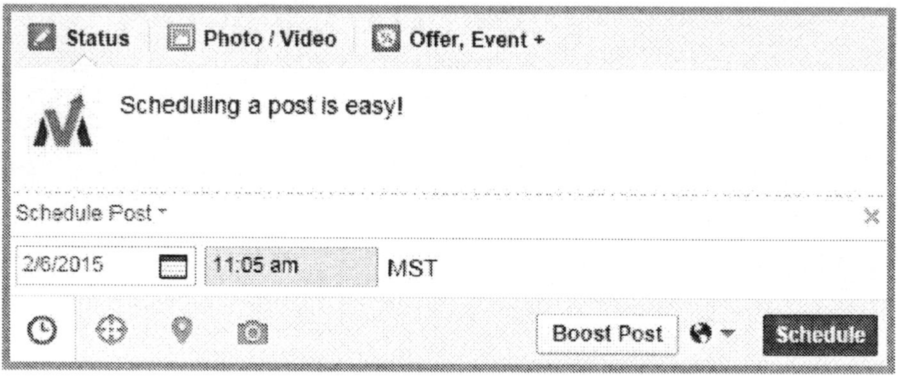

Figure 36: Scheduling a Facebook post

After you've scheduled a post, you can manage your scheduled posts by going to the top of your Page and choosing Edit Page and then selecting Use Activity Log. This might sound obvious, but the Internet isn't actually a 24/7 operation! Be sure to schedule your posts when your fans are actually online. Posting updates in the middle of the night will do nothing to promote your content; although it might give some of your insomniac followers something to do. You can find out when the majority of your fans are online by visiting your Page Insights and going to the posts tab.

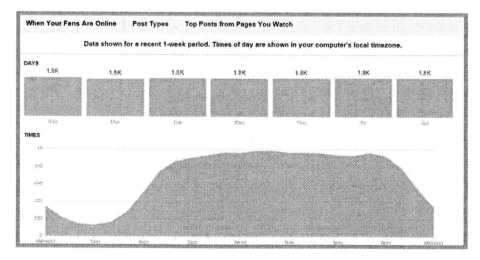

Figure 37: Facebook Insights

Twitter

Twitter is a self-proclaimed "information engine." That moniker alone should tell you that it can be an awesome platform for promoting your content and subsequently your business. The primary application for Twitter is to keep your followers informed about the cool products and services that your business can provide. The secondary application is to actively engage the phenomenon of crowd-sourcing. By meeting the needs of individual users head-on, you can actively promote your content to the potential customers who are looking for answers.

To make the most of Twitter, it's imperative to build a following. Your Twitter handle should appear on every page of your site – of course, this rule goes for all the social media channels you use. If your page visitors like the content they find on your pages, they should be able to follow you in a heartbeat.

No one should have to search for your handle.

Don't limit your handle to only your web pages. Put it on your email signature line and put it on your blog. Everyone who sees your content should be able to start following you and should know what they're in for when they do. Keep in mind that page visitors may be reluctant to follow you if they don't know what you'll be tweeting. If you make it clear what to expect – "Follow us for coupons and specials only available to our followers" or "We tweet tons of insider advice – follow us!" – you will be more likely to get followers who are truly interested in your content.

Your content pages, with your handle, can attract followers, but to build a following proactively, you can do yourself a big favor by catching the attention of influential Twitter users and getting them to follow you. The rule of thumb for gaining someone's following is to follow them first. Many Twitter users will return the favor. You can contact a person directly and suggest they follow you, but be sure you have a compelling reason for them to accept. If they are showing interest in your niche industry, let them know that your tweets will benefit them.

Promotion begins with your followers. When you develop new content, tweet it. Your followers will be *expecting* it. Similar to Facebook sharing, if you tweet your content, your followers can retweet it, bringing traffic to your pages and expanding your brand recognition. Some third-party applications like TweetDeck and HootSuite can help you schedule tweets so that you don't bombard your audience over a short period of time. This can be a life-saver with a promotion push that needs frequent attention. When you set up your blog's RSS feed, add it to your Twitter feed, too. Every time your blog has new content, your Twitter followers will know about it. Of course, you should promote your own content, products and services. I happen to be a big fan of just being yourself and tweeting about your personal interests too, this way you give people the opportunity to know the person or people behind your brand.

Figure 38: Promoted Tweet

At the end of the day, social media is about making and maintaining connections. This means that if your followers tweet at you, you should make an effort to respond in a timely way. As your following grows, it will be more challenging to respond to all tweets. Be sure to check in to see who's tweeted at you or mentioned you, and make an effort to respond. Tweet-Deck or HootSuite will add functionality to help manage your Twitter account and keep you connected to your followers. For example, you can set up lists by keyword so that you can track and engage in conversations that are happening in real time.

Google+

Although Google+ is not as popular as Facebook or Twitter, it sets itself apart by heavily emphasizing Search Engine Optimization (SEO). Google+ allows you to embed links directly to your profile page, allowing you to increase the visibility of your content and website once more people join your circles, or click and engage with your link.

Be sure to start joining or creating respected and relevant circles in Google+. With these social circles, bloggers are able to place followers within certain groups. When posting content, look for a small check box that says, "Also Send Email to this Circle?" (see Figure 39 on page 146)

Be careful not to check that box for every post (thereby spamming people who are not interested), or when posting to your key influencers circle. Using the email feature at the right time can mean that other key influencers will see your blog post, +1 the content, and reach a bigger audience. When you use this feature, you will ensure that people in your Circle receive an alert in their inboxes that you shared a post with them.

By making use of Circles, you will keep your followers from feeling spammed by information that may not interest them. This can actually be helpful depending on your industry; for example, if you are an ecommerce site selling various products in different categories, you can tailor your posts so that they are delivered to the most relevant target audience.

As of now, the Circles on Google+ are very straightforward, if a person is interested in something related to your industry, they will be motivated to join your community. This gives your brand another opportunity to interact and have direct conversations with members of your Circles. As always, once a level of trust has been established, your relationship with the follower will eventually drive sales.

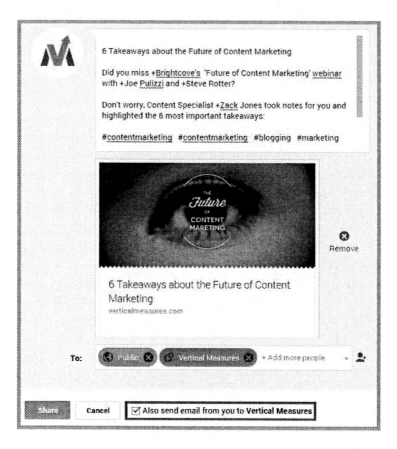

Figure 39: Send an email update to a Google+ circle

If it turns out that you are in a very niche industry and unable to find a related Google+ community (which would be unusual), you can create your own! Setting up a new Community or Circle is fairly simple, just follow the steps provided by Google in their help section.

Once you've created a new Community, open it up for new members and blog about it, post that awesome content from your website and get people talking. You can even promote your Google+ profile on your Facebook and Twitter page, and give followers a new venue to engage with industry enthusiasts. Many industry experts use Google+ to provide answers to these smaller, specific audiences. If you discover that your industry tends to have a low influence on Google+, this is your chance step in and prove that your brand or service is an authoritative expert and thought-leader in the industry. If your brand has a blog for more in-depth reading, point your followers towards your blog posts for answers to their questions.

Figure 40: Google+ Circles

Google+ is a melting pot of influential leaders and casual audiences. Your brand must engage with individuals leading the field, as well as those looking for more information, which you can provide in the form of your content. When you share insights about your industry and spark engaging conversations or topics, you will solidify your relationship not only with potential customers, but with industry experts, as well.

LinkedIn

LinkedIn is established as the premier social networking site, devoted solely to professionals. It is said that LinkedIn's 277 million members include an executive from every Fortune 500 company. There is no other social networking site where you have a greater chance of being able to interact with an influential decision-maker. LinkedIn remains the best social networking site to market your business-to-business (B2B) products and services because of this special demographic. Even for business-to-consumer (B2C) companies, LinkedIn is important. Not only are wealthy consumers members of LinkedIn, but even B2C companies have B2B marketing activities through distributors, agents, and strategic alliances. Imagine all your key management staff for sales, marketing, and business development contributing to LinkedIn in some, or all, of the following ways. It has the potential to offer you a powerful opportunity to obtain mindshare and thought leadership, which could ultimately generate revenue for your business.

Promotion on LinkedIn begins with ensuring that your company can be found in the LinkedIn Companies directory, a database comprised of primarily user-generated information. LinkedIn Companies is quickly becoming a free, alternative source of company information. Should someone search for a company with your expertise, you want to ensure that you are found and that your best information is on display for potential customers. You can do so by optimizing your company profile so that it's in sync with your company website. Use the "specialties" section to add any keywords that you want your company to be found under but that aren't represented in your description.

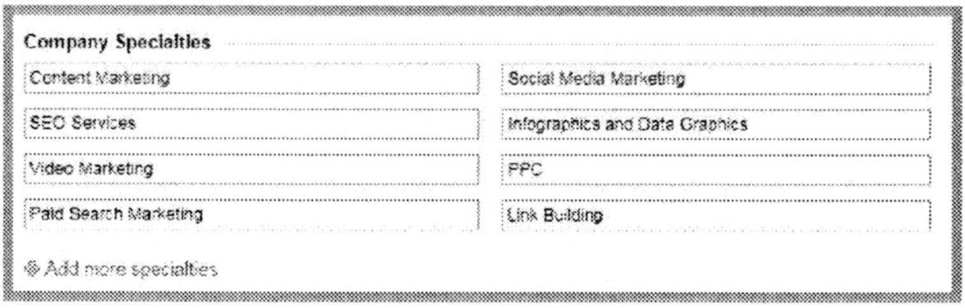

Company Specialties	
Content Marketing	Social Media Marketing
SEO Services	Infographics and Data Graphics
Video Marketing	PPC
Paid Search Marketing	Link Building
⊕ Add more specialties	

Figure 41: LinkedIn specialities

Be sure to choose the most appropriate Main Company Industry section because this is a field that may be used in a search to find your company. LinkedIn gives you the opportunity to enter up to five physical locations, so make sure you take advantage of this. Add your corporate blog's RSS feed to show your latest blog entries. If your company has a Twitter account, make sure you include your username to include your latest tweets on this page as well.

Remember, with LinkedIn, every employee is a sales person. Since LinkedIn is a social networking platform, many searchers look for those with expertise by doing a keyword search under "People." Every employee representing your company on LinkedIn increases your chances that your company will be found indirectly. The more connected your employees' networks are, the easier it will be for people to find them.

Just as tweets can be a powerful way of sharing your knowledge, so can the LinkedIn Status Update. While only your LinkedIn connections will see your status update in their network updates, you can display your status update for public visibility so that anyone who views your profile can see what you have been saying.

> **Obviously, LinkedIn is not Twitter and therefore it is not about quantity of updates, but quality.**

Aim for one update a day on information that you find compelling, new relevant content you have to offer, or noteworthy news about your company that might be interesting to your target demographic.

Similar to Google+, creating a LinkedIn Group is surprisingly simple, as is indicated by the sheer number of groups that exist. That being said, there is one very important thing to consider that will make or break your group – your LinkedIn Group name. No LinkedIn user wants to be sold to; therefore, the name of your group should NOT be the name of your vinyl record store, instead try something like "Classic Rock and Roll Headquarters."

Once you've started a LinkedIn Group, what's next? Groups are all about promotion, start by introducing your community to relevant professionals in your own LinkedIn network. You have an advantage if your employees are already established users with LinkedIn connections. Of course, your employees should only introduce your group to individuals in your target demographic and who would find the group valuable; otherwise, a generic introduction to your LinkedIn Group could be perceived as spam.

Once you've built up the group, you can deliver content to the group, but other members can post to the group, too. Social media marketing works through relevance, so it's important to keep your group relevant by actively managing and keeping irrelevant information out. By keeping the standard as high as possible, the group will get the most value from it. To be at the forefront of your targeted audience and to be found by them, there are usually multiple LinkedIn Groups where you can participate outside of your own. LinkedIn allows you to join up to 50 groups, so why don't you and your employees join the maximum if there are enough relevant groups to be found? This can only help you and your business be found on LinkedIn.

Don't know where to start when joining a new group? Check out the "Most Popular Discussions" section and check out how many comments it has. You can make a quick splash by adding a relevant and thought-provoking comment to the discussion. If anyone who has already commented still subscribes to receive follow-up comments by email, your comment could go out by email to hundreds or possibly thousands of people.

Because there are so many things your business could be doing on LinkedIn, marketing your business there can take some time. It will require a little sweat equity before you can say, "We landed this account because of LinkedIn!" Like any other social media marketing effort, becoming an active and contributing user on LinkedIn will undoubtedly help your marketing efforts and assist your company in gaining thought leadership, which can ultimately contribute to greater business in the future. Just be sure to measure your results against your time and effort invested to be certain you understand the actual ROI.

Pinterest

Pinterest offers perhaps the most unique experience among all social media platforms. If your company has not factored Pinterest into the content marketing strategy, you could be missing out on a huge chunk of traffic. At over 70 million users, this image-sharing platform can work superbly for many business niches. Pinterest is most popular among culinary arts, fashion, lifestyle accessories, travel destinations, decorations, and even real estate buffs. As with any content marketing effort, you must identify your target audience if you're going to be successful. 80% of Pinterest users are women aged between 25 and 55. Even so, there's plenty of room for your brand to market towards male Pinterest users, as well.

Pinterest is social, so be social! Remember to engage with fellow pinners, and re-pin interesting content that relates to your company. You can even comment on pins to help build relationships within the community. Link your Pinterest profile to your other social media sites to give your brand a better chance at keeping visitors active.

In 2013, Curalate's data science team studied[31] over half a million images and analyzed 30 characteristics for each image and compiled a detailed analysis of what makes a successful Pinterest post. Here are the top three takeaways:

Post content that stands out: It might seem obvious that unique images get repinned more frequently than images that blend into a branded website. Do not fall into the same style and type of image – take risks and get creative!

Colorful images improve your content: The study found that images with multiple dominant colors were repinned more than three times more than images with a single dominant color. Although branding guidelines are important when creating content, do not become a hostage to them.

---

31 http://curalate.tumblr.com/post/75811710390/beautify-your-content-8-image-features-that-shine-on

Do not include people's faces: This might not always be true with other social networks, but images on Pinterest that do not show people's faces are repinned 23% more than images that do have faces in them.

To optimize your Pinterest account, these are some other best practices you can follow to optimize your profile and promote your content:

Create captivating descriptions: When you pin your content, write interesting descriptions that encourage people to take a look and click the repin button. Longer descriptions actually lead to more repins.

Categorize your boards: Make it easier for people to find your pinboards and your pins by taking the time to identify the categories your boards belong in.

Use your keyword phrases: Use keywords in your pin titles and descriptions so that it's easier for people to find your pins when visiters use the search feature.

Include a Pin It button on your website: Make it easy for Pinterest users to pin content from your website. Be sure the Pin It button is installed correctly and visible on all pages of your website.

In another interesting study,[32] Fannit suggests the best times to publish content on Pinterest to get the most engagement. As with most social media, it's good to be active when your audience is active:

Saturday's are best: Try to pin your content on Saturday mornings to get the highest number of repins. Research shows that Pinterest users are most likely to repin content that has been pinned on Saturday mornings.

Afternoon and evening: To get the most repins, Pin content between 2:00 p.m. and 4:00 p.m. or 8:00 p.m. and 11:00 p.m. Pinterest users are most likely to repin your content in the afternoon and evening.

Remember to track your analytics, such as sources of traffic, most engag-

---

32 http://fannit.com/social-media-infographic-when-are-the-best-times-to-post/

ing content, keyword performance, and lead conversion. Pinterest provides analytics once you're verified your website. If you repin other content, return the favor and credit the source of your image. Pin Search is a nifty function of Google Chrome that will help you discover the origin of the image. You can find this extension in the Chrome webstore.[33]

Instagram

Instagram is the tenth largest mobile app reaching one out of four smartphone owners, both iOS and Android.[34] Instagram has 150 million monthly active users who post and share 55 million images or videos per day! Instagram is no stranger to brand engagement, with over 70% of top brands using it. Roughly one out of five brands posts once a day. From a content creation perspective, this means you should be able to find success by posting once per day to be in the top quarter of the most active Instagram brands.

In case you haven't heard – those #hashtags are actually important. In fact, over 80% of Instagram posts by top brands include at least one hashtag. As with most of life, moderation is best. Use related hashtags for content discovery but don't overdo it. Like other platforms, use 1 to 3 hashtags to expand content discovery.

Instagram offers a unique set of custom filters, enabling users to enhance their photos or video. Users can edit their photos by adjusting: brightness, contrast, warmth, saturation, highlights, shadows, and sharpness. Vignettes and tilt shift can also be added.

Curalate, a visual web marketing firm, did a review of approximately 8 million photos on Instagram. They found the following characteristics garnered more likes on Instagram:[35]

---

33 https://chrome.google.com/webstore/category/extensions

34 http://www.comscore.com/Insights/Press_Releases/2013/12/comScore_Reports_
October_2013_US_Smartphone_Subscriber_Market_Share

35 http://curalate.tumblr.com/post/68079619904/study-6-image-qualities-which-may-
drive-more-likes-on

- Blue is the winning color
- Images with a high amount of background
- High level of lightness
- Single dominate color
- Low saturation
- Highly textured

The Instagram video feature offers capabilities that social media market-ers will want to note. Instagram Video offers up to 15 seconds of video recording, giving you an opportunity to showcase the best of your content in a compressed format. This video offers a ton of possibilities:

Short clips of your product demo: That simple how-to video on ty-ing a fishing line knot would be perfect content for Instagram followers. Instagram videos give you the chance to answer your customers' questions quickly and efficiently.

Create a visual portfolio of your work: As long as you don't violate any confidentiality clauses, Instagram can be great to show off work you've done for recent clients, and give your potential customers an inside look into your services. A great example of this would be a coffee shop show-casing the skill of their baristas, and their unique cappuccino designs.

The Instagram video feature is housed within the existing Instagram app, making it immediately accessible to all users who update the app. However, one of the most important benefits of Instagram is that videos play in-line on Facebook for desktop users. Like YouTube and Facebook videos, a Facebook user can click and watch the clip right within Facebook. Images can also be fluently posted with Twitter, Facebook and other social net-works to hit the largest audience possible.

Reddit

Reddit is a constantly growing content arena that shares and categorizes submitted content for a huge audience of active members (or Redditors). Reddit allows you to post video, audio, text and images. As users submit content they get Reddit Karma, good or bad, displayed next to their username as the community votes their content up or down. If a user posts irrelevant or advertorial content, they won't get karma for that post. The idea behind Reddit Karma is to reinforce that users want useful, interesting content on Reddit, rather than spam or ads.

Reddit users take their voting seriously! They will quickly vote down a piece of content if it's placed in the wrong category, or if it is overly advertorial in essence. This down-voting usually will be accompanied with colorful rants in the comments, so beware of violating the community rules. On the other hand, as the content gets recommended and voted up by Redditors, it will rise in popularity and can cause a major boost in traffic to your site.

Reddit uses generic categories, called Reddits, for content submission. There are user-generated categories, called Subreddits with categorized content into smaller niche areas. Thousands of subreddit categories have been created to date, ranging from War History to Computer Engineering to popular Memes. For every Reddit or Subreddit category, there are subcategories, which include:

- What's hot
- New
- Controversial
- Top

Content receiving positive votes moves to the "what's hot" category. "New" is for content that was recently submitted and needs votes. "Controversial" content is content that might be off-color or that has generated strong opinions or comments that others might find offensive. And lastly, "Top" features content items that have gained high scores. Going even further, users can sort this list by top scores for today, this week, this month, all time, or even this hour.

I mention all of these filters because there is an important point to be reinforced here. Regardless of what filters Redditors use to narrow their results, one thing will always remain the same: quality content will appear in any of the results filters.

You can discover content that gets the most engagement by browsing through the generic Reddits that have the most activity. Try using Subredditfinder.com to work your way down and search various Subreddits that relate to your industry. Subreddits make it easy to filter the content exclusively to your niche.

Once you know where to be active, you can begin engaging with Redditors in those categories that relate to your field, joining in discussions, and offering further information by linking back to your content. Reddit has one of the most active communities out there, if you contribute useful information and content, you achieve some impressive results through this platform.

StumbleUpon

StumbleUpon is a content discovery engine, emulating and greatly enhancing the way that people find content to bookmark in the first place. StumbleUpon starts by getting to know the user's personal interests. Initially, this comes from a short survey when the user creates a profile, but it grows in complexity as the user engages content through the service.

Users click the "stumble" button on the toolbar, which gives them a new web page to interact with. If they like what they've been offered, or "stumbled," they can give it a "thumbs up." If they don't, they can give it a "thumbs down" vote. If the user wants to bookmark the site, they can tag it. They can return to tagged sites for more content. The StumbleUpon algorithm includes a social network element, which takes into account content the user's network also has tagged and given a thumbs up. Content that is voted up by the people in the user's network will be more likely to appear in the next "stumble" for that user.

You get marketing data from StumbleUpon's massive bank of activity, you can view a number of different trending data:

- **"Recently Hot" tags:** These are the current trends that people are tagging. Drill down for more content under the tag.

- **"Most Popular All Time" tags:** These tags change less frequently but will change. To see what is gaining the most attention, look through these tags. Again, drill down for more content.

- **Stumbles by topic:** You can see what activity is happening by topic.

- **Top Rated websites:** These are the pages that are getting the most stumbles.

Using Paid Media to Boost Promotional Efforts

It can be difficult to accurately scale the successes and ROI on earned media promotion. Many companies turn to paid promotion on the same channels we discussed above. Traditionally this has meant paying per click; however, native advertising is quickly rising as a method for attracting eyeballs to a piece of content.

Google PPC (Adwords)

On Google's search results page there are sponsored links on the right-hand side and sometimes at the top of the page. These listings are generated through Google AdWords. Businesses bid on keyword phrases and links to appear higher up the page, giving their website maximum exposure. Utilizing Google PPC to promote your content will allow you to put your brand in front of customers at the moment they search for a product or service. With Google Adwords, you only pay when a customer clicks through your site (known as pay-per-click or PPC).

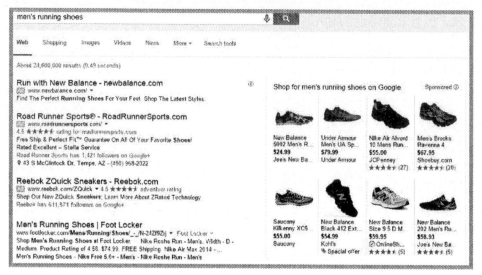

Figure 42: Paid search results at the top and side of the page

This type of paid advertising is a valuable way to gather steady traffic from related search results and other websites. Google PPC campaigns provide useful data that can help improve your content marketing strategy results. To start your Google PPC campaign, start by answering the following questions:

- Which parts of the country – or world – are most interested in your services?
- What are your most effective product or services that people search for?
- What type of content do you want to promote?

When you set up a Google AdWords account, you'll be asked if you want to place your ads on the Display Network. This is different from a sponsored link that appears on a search results page. If you chose to advertise on the Display Network it means your ad will be placed on related sites owned by Google and its partners.

For instance, Kathy Brewer runs a shipping company out of Wake Forest, her packaging and service ad might appear on a convention center website. The visitors to the site might be her target market, but they may just be looking for shipping advice when they visit the site. You have the option to manage your own display placement using Google's placement tool, or let Google decide where to place the ads for you.

Consider using automatic bidding if you're new to Google Adwords to keep the process as low maintenance as possible. You can also set a maximum cost-per-click (CPC) rate to prevent the system from spending more than you want per keyword. Keep in mind that your ad's position on the page is influenced by many factors including bid, click-through-rate, ad relevance, and landing page relevance. Improved ad copy and landing page experience has a major impact on your PPC campaign's performance so, as you become more skilled, the less your future PPC campaigns could cost.

> **"The biggest mistake many new advertisers make with their search marketing campaign is sending ad traffic to their homepage. To get the most ROI for your campaign, you will want to send your ad traffic to a page that is focused on conversions for the product or service you are advertising. Conversions can easily be lost if you send people to a generic homepage and make them have to search for the product or service you were advertising."**
>
> **– Kristi Hines (@kikolani)**

Remember, potential customers search for products and service information, so avoid using your company name in your ad title unless your goal is brand awareness. As your confidence grows, expand your campaigns by adding new ad groups from a wider variety of keyword phrases.

Bing PPC

The search alliance of Yahoo and Bing combined represent 30% of the U.S. online search market.[36] Bing not only serves its search results on

---

36 http://searchengineland.com/bing-hits-14-percent-google-and-yahoo-flat-comscore-76777

Yahoo!'s portal, it also has 14.1% search share itself.

Although Google is still the leader in search for North America, it would be a mistake to ignore Bing's influence. Many people have brushed aside Yahoo! and/or Bing in favor of Google, but there are some good reasons to consider taking full advantage of Bing PPC.

Overall, Bing PPC ads typically cost less than Google Adwords.[37] So with Bing PPC, you can pay the same amount or less and rank higher in the Bing or Yahoo! search results. The downside is that fewer people will see your ads on Bing because they compete with Google. Nonetheless, you have the opportunity to rank for a more competitive keyword phrase for a more cost effective pay per click rate on Bing PPC.

Another great benefit with Bing ads is that you can target your audience down to age and gender, allowing you to boost your cost-per-click bids for customers with your target age or gender. For example, you can have Bing increase your bid 10% if someone between the age of 25 and 34 is searching and by 20% if a woman is searching. (NOTE: Bing can only identify the age and gender of users who are signed into their Windows Live accounts and have included this information in their profiles).

Generally, Bing includes more sponsored ads at the top of the page than does Google. This means that with Bing there is greater opportunity for your PPC ad to appear at the top of the page. But it's important to highlight here that Bing PPC advertising is currently limited to certain countries. When signing up for Bing advertising in Microsoft adCenter, a prompt will direct you to select the country you live in from a drop-down menu. Your choices are:

- United States
- Singapore
- Canada
- United Kingdom

---

37 http://www.mediapost.com/publications/article/229197/advertisers-pay-45-on-average-more-per-click-on-g.html

The only language choices are English and French. Microsoft will likely expand its country and language options, but for the time being many people are not qualified for Bing advertising. Another upside: Bing's content network includes major sites like the Wall Street Journal, CNBC, and FOX Sports. If you want your ads to appear on any of these sites, advertise through Bing PPC.

Facebook Ads

There are three types of Paid Facebook ads: Sidebar, News Feed, and Mobile News Feed. Ad costs can be calculated on a cost-per-click or cost-per-impression basis, the choice is yours. The best bet is to test both options and see which delivers you the least expensive traffic and best results. Obviously, Mobile News Feed ads are specifically designed for display on mobile devices.

Your Facebook ad then goes into the Facebook ad auction. Within the ad auction, your ad competes against other related ads for the same targeted audience. The overall reach of that target audience is based on your competition and ad budget. For example, if your target audience is not within a competitive market, the amount you'll need to bid to reach them will be lower.

Figure 43: Optimizing a Facebook ad for clicks

Facebook offers superb targeting capabilities that will ensure your ad will be seen by the people within your target audience, or those who are most likely to engage with your content. There are 3 main targeting approaches:[38]

Demographic targeting: The most straightforward targeting strategy with Facebook ads is demographics: age, gender, location, etc., as well as the more specific demographic categories like sexual orientation, relationship status, workplace, and education level.

Precise targeting: This is where ad targeting gets fun. Precise targeting allows you to show your promoted content exclusively to people who have expressed interest in your subject matter. Interest targeting is based on a user's stated "likes" and interests, and allows advertisers to hone in on their optimal content audience.

Broad category targeting: Broad category targeting allows you to target your ads to Facebook users based on, essentially, the categories those users can be placed in. Some examples include people whose marital status indicates that they are engaged, people who are expecting a baby, small business owners, hold a particular political stance, etc.

The most important part of precise and broad category targeting is finding a balance. You need to show your Facebook ad to enough people that the click-through rate brings in enough readers to be worthwhile, but targeted enough to ensure that those readers are actually interested in your content.

Remember, always promote posts via Facebook's ad manager; this allows you to hyper-target your audience using Facebook's algorithm. Promote your content to three groups: Non-fans, friends of fans, and even your existing Facebook fans. This helps create new connections and reinforces your brand as an industry leader to existing customers.

Promoted Tweets

Promoted Tweets are similar to organic Tweets because they can be retweeted, replied to and favorited by anyone. Keep in mind that Twitter

---

38 http://contentmarketinginstitute.com/2013/10/amplify-content-strategy-social-media-advertising/

clearly identifies Promoted Tweets, so there will be no surprises to viewers. Promoted Tweets can include links to websites, hashtags and various content mediums. You can promote Tweets that were originally published organically. Only one Promoted Tweet will appear in a user's timeline at any given time and can appear in any of the following places:

- Home Timelines
- At the top of relevant search results
- Search results for Promoted Trends
- On Twitter's official desktop or mobile clients like TweetDeck, Twitter for iPhone and Twitter for Android, among others
- Syndicated to some third-party Twitter clients like HootSuite

Promoted Tweets allow you to Tweet to specific users, during specific moments, even to non-followers. Promoted Tweets can use these metrics to target the right audience for your content. The following is straight from Twitter:

- **Target by interests and gender:** We know where to find the guys, gals, fashionistas, gamers, foodies, activists, and whoever else you might want to reach.

- **Target by location and language:** Going local? Entering a new market? Target by country or metro area as well as language to connect with the right people.

- **Target by device:** Target specific mobile or desktop devices to catch up with people on-the-go or from the comfort of their living rooms.

- **Target by similarity to existing followers:** Your followers already love you. We'll help you find more just like them.

Similar to Facebook and Google, Twitter's pricing system is based on bidding. Start by setting the maximum amount you're willing to spend per follow or click, and Twitter will give you suggestions for what you should bid to optimize your campaign. Twitter provides useful tools that allow you to see how each of your tweets are performing. After a few days of running promoted tweets, be sure to check back to gauge how the campaign is working to improve your efforts.

LinkedIn Sponsored Updates

Similar to Facebook, LinkedIn created an ad unit that puts promoted content in the newsfeeds of followers, called LinkedIn Sponsored Updates. Here are a few tips for effectively using this feature (These tips are true not just for Sponsored Updates, but for any content you promote on Linked-In):[39]

- **Share content of high value only:** These include expert-level blog posts, eBooks, free guides or white papers. LinkedIn audiences generally prefer more substance in their content than a list or top tips blog post.

- **Make sure the content you share has a great image:** You can't upload your own image on LinkedIn. Instead, you are limited to choosing one of the images on the page you're sharing. Selecting an image on the shared page that will grab reader's attention is essential to successful LinkedIn promotion.

- **Don't forget to target LinkedIn groups:** While you can target based on location, title to industry, groups on LinkedIn get right to the heart of what people are most interested in, similar to a Facebook page "like."

LinkedIn Sponsored Updates consist of a headline, description (up to 75 characters), your name or company name, small image and a URL. Currently, you can specify which LinkedIn members view your ads by selecting targeting criteria such as job title, job function, industry, geography, age, gender, company name, etc. Like with Twitter and other social media networks that offer paid advertising, you set a maximum budget and only pay for the clicks or impressions that you receive.

---

39 http://contentmarketinginstitute.com/2013/10/amplify-content-strategy-social-media-advertising/

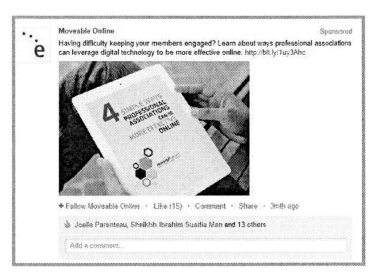

Figure 44: A Sponsored updated on LinkedIn

According to LinkedIn, the best-performing ads are relevant to the target audience and written with clear, compelling words.[40] LinkedIn suggests that you highlight special offers, unique benefits, white papers, free trials or demos to get people's attention. They recommend that you include strong call-to-action phrases like "Try," "Download," "Sign up" or "Request a Quote."

Reddit Sponsored Listings

As discussed earlier, Reddit hosts an influential and fair community of people that doesn't like force-fed advertisements or branded listings. So how can you leverage your promotional efforts and provide valuable content to Reddit users?

Let's start by diving deeper into Reddit's audience. Reddit is largely comprised of users between the ages of 18 and 34 who tend to be well educated. More than 50% of Reddit's community base has had at least some college education, while another 30% of users have a bachelor's degree or higher, they tend to make under $50k/year, and you can do best to target

---

40 http://mashable.com/2013/06/18/paid-content-marketing/

them when they're most active on Reddit.[41] Redditors tend to be more active midmornings and evenings.

Targeting the right people, and the best times to reach them, is the way to get lots of up-votes, and ultimately it will give you the most out of your advertising budget. Of course, getting them to engage with the content depends entirely on the quality of your content and whether or not you've posted it in the correct subreddit.

Much like the Ads on Google's SERPs, Reddit advertisements are annotated as "sponsored links" and appear at the top of each page:

Reddit's model allows marketers to service untargeted ads on all of Reddit, or to target specific subreddits that better relate to the service or product that is being sold. There is a manual review process at Reddit, so be sure to double check before you submit or you'll have to start the process all over again, which can cost you days. A "campaign" is defined on Reddit as having a start date, end date, the subreddit/area of Reddit you're going to advertise on and a daily budget. Each campaign can only target one subreddit, but you can run multiple campaigns, you'll just need to set them up one at a time.42

StumbleUpon Paid Discovery

StumbleUpon has an advertising program known as StumbleUpon Paid Discovery and offers some unique features (The following comes from StumbleUpon):

Spend ASAP or Spend Evenly: Advertisers now have the option to spend budgets as fast as possible, or pace evenly throughout the campaign.

Improved Templates: We've made it easier to create and use templates

---

41 http://www.ignitesocialmedia.com/social-media-stats/2012-social-network-analy-sis-report/

42 http://www.clickz.com/clickz/column/2306770/reddit-social-ads-for-the-more-so-cially-savvy

– save them for future campaigns and now either put in all or partial targeting based on desired results.

Similar Interests: To help advertisers optimize their campaign, we now recommend related interest categories based on what's been selected.

DMA Level Targeting: DMA level targeting groups several surrounding areas into one region and provides greater reach for local campaigns.

Multiple Locations: Advertisers can now target multiple locations with a single campaign.

Audience Estimator: We can project how many people can be reached based on the targeting criteria selected, so we'll provide feedback on whether it's too specific or too broad to fulfill campaign goals.[43]

Your content will be rewarded with more traffic from StumbleUpon users if the content is relevant to the community. When you advertise a link using the StumbleUpon Paid Discovery Tool, StumbleUpon displays your page when users browse through new websites in a particular category. If the content appeals to the users, you can get more votes and hence exponentially more traffic. To get started advertising on StumbleUpon, sign up with the Paid Discovery program. Like Reddit, when you submit a campaign, you have to wait for a StumbleUpon executive to approve the URL.

Once your campaign has launched, you will start to see visitors from the paid discovery tool. If visitors like your page and give it an up-vote, you will get the benefit of the vote with natural visitors, which doesn't cost you anything. Therefore, if your content is good stuff, it can sell itself on Stumbleupon.

---

43 http://www.stumbleupon.com/ads/blog/stumbleupon-paid-discovery-adds-new-advertising-features/

Outbrain: Amplify Your Content

Outbrain is a free widget that automatically provides related links to posts as users browse the Internet. Their primary value is the algorithm that understands the content the user has been interacting with and connects it to other related content that the user might be interested in. Outbrain also lets outside sites buy their way into the list of suggested related content. Those links are marked "Paid Distribution."

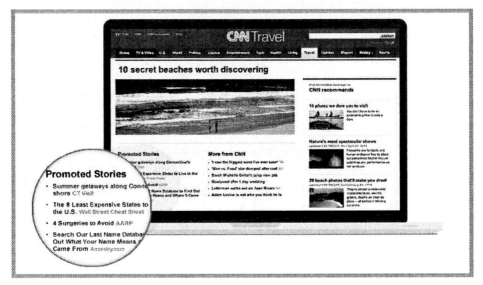

Figure 45: Promoted stories with Outbrain

Outbrain allows any brand to expand a relationship with their potential customers by providing valuable, informative, and appealing content. Similar to Facebook and Google AdWords, Outbrain Amplify offers a cost-per-click bidding system. They provide users with the ability to live test various headlines on the same content body, which can be a vital tool in the early stages of your content marketing strategy.

Outbrain's premium network of publishers helps ensure that you gain traffic from quality sources, as the algorithms behind their content discovery platform constantly work to find the most engaged audience for your content.[44]

---

44 http://lp.outbrain.com/search-vs-social-report/

You can find great success by using Outbrain to drive traffic to a piece of content, and then retargeting that person in Google's Display Network or via Facebook's Custom Audience retargeting. In this way, social, search, and discovery can work together nicely. With sophisticated metric analysis, Outbrain offers some great functionality that could be worth exploring as part of your content promotion strategy.

Outbrain categorizes your content, and displays it to readers based on their online behavior. For example, if you were reading about how to play the guitar, and then went to YouTube to watch a video on guitar songs for beginners, you might see a recommended link for guitar lessons from Marty Schwartz at GuitarJamz.com.

Outbrain also allows you to drive traffic to individual blog posts or articles, a blog feed, earned media and positive reviews, slideshows, video content and mobile-optimized content. Outbrain limits you to drive traffic to editorial content, not promotional content. Essentially, this means you can't drive to any page with a form fill or other means of generating leads or sales. So, your gated free guides will have to find promotion in other ways.

Press Releases and Media Outreach

It can seem daunting to start from scratch in a media outreach campaign, including blogger pitches. The plethora of media outlets on the Internet make it nearly impossible to keep track of who writes what and for which target demographic. Fortunately, there are public relations firms managing all of this data on media lists, and they can help you pinpoint your media target.

Companies like Vocus and Cision specialize in media outreach and have active databases that can help you target pitches and press releases. Media lists provide detailed information for a wide range of media outlets, including television, newspapers, magazines, and blogs. While these lists are comprehensive and include offline media, for the purpose of this book, we're focusing on the benefits of ties to online media outlets, specifically links and traffic.

When you want to make an announcement in the form of a press release, media lists can connect you with niche news outlets that might be more likely to pick up your release than some of the larger outlets. When your release gets picked up, you get the benefit of a link, brand exposure, and the possibility of traffic. It's worthwhile to pursue niche news media that might run an article on your release, creating a URL that links to you.

A media database can also give you an edge when you're developing content that you want to promote through blogger pitches. Media lists not only contain information on the outlet, but include contact points for each outlet. Knowing the blogger's name and contact information is a major advantage as you create your custom pitch.

When you develop a press release or a blogger pitch, keep in mind that a lot of journalists and bloggers like the fast approach. If the press release or the pitch contains enough information, they will often repurpose it with a few tweaks and post it up, rather than rewriting an entire article. So it's best to provide enough information in your pitch to make it easy for them to repurpose it.

For blogs, frame your pitch with the same information that a blogger would normally give when posting a piece of content. Namely, why would the audience like it? Briefly describe the value of the content to the blogger's readership – "This is a great top 10 list that gets us thinking about the healthy ways we should spend our time after work!"

News outlets and blogs are driven by similar motivations when it comes to picking up content to publish. They want content that will attract traffic to their site. When you pitch, your goal is to find an outlet that will benefit the most from the content you have to offer. That is, your content will most likely attract the visitors that they are looking to attract. As you work through media lists, keep in mind the kind of traffic that media outlets target. If the content you have to offer is likely to generate traffic to their site, they will be more likely to go with your pitch.

Blogger Engagement

By reaching out to bloggers who have a following and "pitching" your new content page to them, you can tap the network that they've already established. Each of the blogger's followers will get exposed to your expertise and may click through to your website. As you find bloggers who are focused on aspects of your industry, and by networking with them, you can offer solutions to the problems that their followers are experiencing.

The essence of blogger engagement is networking. By networking with bloggers, it's much easier to pitch your content, and even ask them to write a post for your content. Practically speaking, you build your network by searching for the bloggers with whom to network through media lists and Google blog search.

At the center of blogger engagement is commenting, which fosters relationship-building. Bloggers welcome good comments that are on topic with their posts because they enhance the quality of the blog and increase its favorability with search engines. This means that you can leverage blog commenting to your advantage in order to promote your web content and your brand, if you engage blogs in the right way. By engaging bloggers with great comments, you get the opportunity to:

- Reach out to potential customers who subscribe to those blogs by joining in the conversations they're having, demonstrating to the blogger and its readers that you are an expert in your field.
- Continue your promotion efforts by including a link back to your web pages if appropriate (but not all the time).
- Build partnerships with other bloggers, which can lead to further content promotion.

When you have a new piece of content to promote, seek out blog posts that your content can complement. If a blogger posts 20 great infographics in your industry, for example, you can respond with a comment saying, "Awesome post! These infographics are fantastic! I really like the third one using the timeline to demonstrate how fast things are changing in our business. Here's a link to one that we created that I think your readers will enjoy. Check it out." Then, link to one of your own infographics.

Make sure that your comment is thought out, on topic, and contributes to the conversation. Remember, your comments brand you among the other commenters, visitors, and bloggers. So, it's only to your advantage to take the time to make the comment count.

It takes some effort to find quality blog posts that you can comment on. You can start by commenting on the blogs that you subscribe to as an investment in your relationships with those bloggers. Eventually, however, you'll want to reach out beyond that circle, and you'll have to actively search out appropriate blog posts. Once you start interacting with bloggers through commenting, keep track of the individuals you're working with. Use a spreadsheet to track the blogger's name, website, etc. You may want to segment (by topic, niche, etc.), depending on what your engagement is like.

Over the long term, blogger engagement and forum participation will provide opportunities to foster robust industry relationships that you can leverage to promote your content. Keep in mind that, just as with any relationship, blogger partnerships require give and take. If a blogger in your network approaches you with a pitch for some content to include in your next post, try to accommodate the request. You proactively boost your favor with a blogger by linking to them in your content. When a blogger gets linked to, WordPress and similar blog platforms can alert them to the new link. Bloggers take note of links to their blog, and the prevailing culture is to return the favor at some point. You'll build a reputation as a friendly blogger and other bloggers will be more likely to do the same for you.

Forum Participation

Forums are the evolutionary descendants of chat rooms. They aren't necessarily as popular as other forms of social media interaction, but there are some avid users of Internet forums. Many industries have niche-related forums. It's worthwhile to dedicate some time and effort to participating in industry forums. Through forum participation, you can:

- Demonstrate your expertise by offering answers to participants' questions.

- Promote your content pages by linking to pages that might interest or benefit the group.

- As with other social media, it helps to develop relationships with other forum participants, who might be willing to promote your content in their networks, such as their blogs or other social media spaces.

Attract Links to Your Content

Up to now, we've talked about content marketing strategy primarily in terms of creating content that gets found in search and gains traction around the social Internet. Your objectives depend heavily on search engine rankings and exposure through links from other pages to your own. A major contributor to search engine rankings is the number of links to your website, and links from reputable sites help increase traffic to your site. Needless to say, links to your content provide a major benefit to your efforts. So you have to find a way to get people to link to your content.

I'm suggesting that you move away from the concept of link *building* and focus on link *attraction*. Link building has traditionally meant that you reach out to a website and offer to pay them to link to you. This often leads to bad practices and low-quality links. In fact, Google will penalize websites that both sell and buy links. The best alternative to paying for a link is generating linkworthy content.

On the other hand, if you generate awesome content and then promote it, you're going to attract natural links. In effect, if you develop really compelling material, links are bound to follow as the content gets shared. That's link attraction. It's really quite simple, and it serves as one more very strong case for taking care to publish *magnetic* content. The process of promoting and distributing your content gives you an edge in link earning because in those cases it's reaching a targeted audience that will be compelled to share your page by linking to it from their site.

Link attraction plays a vital role in making a link request, too. You won't attract a link without providing some kind of value to the site that you want to link to you. The right way to request a link is to target bloggers that are blogging on topics related to your industry. If your content can respond to the issues they address on their blogs, you can offer up your page as a solution. A link request that is targeted and customized will answer the question, "Why should I?" before the webmaster or blogger has a chance to ask.

The way I look at it, the right kind of link attraction is centered on creating excellent, quality content that has inherent value to the person linking to it (including their audience). The industry term for this kind of content is "linkworthy." I like to think of link building as a rewards program for your content. Do it right, and you'll get rewarded with relevant traffic driving links to your content.

High quality links are the right way – and the best way – to make your content rise in search engine rankings. Linkworthy content generally gets *more* links from a *variety* of different sources, which is enormously valuable to your rankings and overall success. The traffic generated by those links often attracts a better potential customer. Put in the effort to make your content rock, and the links will follow.

Developing Relationships, Building Partnerships

Like social networking sites, forums and blogs are community-centered media where content can be shared. Through active participation, you build trust and recognition with other members in those communities. If you earn a reputation as an upstanding member of the community, the other community members will be more likely to share your content and promote your products with their subscribers and followers. As you establish relationships through engagement, you'll have the opportunity to leverage those relationships to promote your content.

Leveraging social media for content promotion boils down to nurturing relationships within online communities and finding ways to put content in front of potential customers. For small businesses, the work of tending the social garden, so to speak, could seem like a fulltime job. A daily to-do list like the one below can appear excessively time-consuming:

- Updating one's social profile status
- Responding to comments
- Contributing to forum discussions
- Commenting on other blogs and building blogger relationships
- Bookmarking content to enhance your profile

How do people keep up? The answer is that much of this can be parceled throughout the week, adding up to only a relatively small time commitment each day. The key is being disciplined with your time. If you have to, block off specific hours for this work and stick to your schedule. The hardest part of social media is setting up a profile and optimizing it. Maintaining it and commenting can require a commitment of only an hour per day, depending on the level of engagement. This is a modest investment given the potential return. As you develop your social persona through various media outlets, you'll open up a variety of options for promoting your content. The more you can take on, the more opportunities for promotion you'll create.

Diving into social media may also require a shift in your perspective. Historically, social activity was seen as mutually exclusive with efficient work practices. Social media is no exception. (You mean my employees are going to be on Facebook all day?) The truth is that your employees can be excellent sources for branding and promotion. Your employees' social networks effectively expand your corporate reach, and you can leverage these networks for content promotion. To manage social media at work, it's good to have a company policy that covers how and why social media is useful to the company and how it's to be used on the job. Try to have a relaxed policy so that your employees can engage with their networks in a natural way.

The bottom line is that you need to use social media in some capacity to promote your content. Establish your baseline by identifying what social media you need in order to compete in your market. Here, again, research is critical. By knowing what your competitors are doing and what your target demographic uses, you can find out what you need to prioritize. You can then weigh that information against what you're capable of taking on. Because you can't afford *not* to engage in social media promotion, start by focusing on the channels from which you're able to derive the most value. Hone in on the communities that are really engaging with you and your industry.

Content marketing is all about trying, testing, and measuring results. Some businesses might find that their Facebook profile isn't getting a lot of traffic but that their Twitter channel is. So, they may want to focus on Twitter. There are many social media channels to work with, the key is to find options that are working and invest your promotional efforts there.

There are great opportunities, in the form of promotion, to put your content in the hands of potential customers. People love to share the content that appeals to them, and social media has simplified sharing. If you get your content in the hands of the right person, it can spread like wildfire. Through targeted pitches and social media interaction, you can increase your chances of landing your content in the spaces where that person is likely to be found.

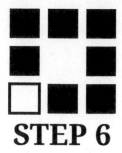

STEP 6

DISTRIBUTION
Give Your Content Wings

Distribution goes hand in hand with promotion, so naturally it follows as the next step. The difference between promotion and distribution is that promotion refers to the act of drawing attention to the content on *your* website, whereas distribution is about creating and posting pieces of content specifically designed for one of these other channels. Here, we will focus on how content distribution fits into your content marketing strategy. To be successful, you need to choose the distribution vehicles that will work best for your business; in other words, you'll distribute to the places where the vast majority of your audience hangs out. Take the time to research your audience, looking across the spectrum. There are many distribution channels out there and you can't use them all. You're broadcasting, so work with as many channels as you can safely manage to target your market. You can distribute content through:

- Social media
- RSS
- Content-sharing sites

In the last step, we covered the options for promotion in social media. Nearly all of them are designed to communicate to the audience that follows your brand. When you have a new piece of content, you can easily distribute it or promote it through these social media channels to your followers.

Not only will your target audience see the post and be drawn to it, but if they like the content, they can quickly pass it along to the people in their networks. It pays to nurture your own social networks and offer plenty of opportunities for people to sign up and follow your updates. Think of it this way: Your existing followers are already interested enough to want to know when your next piece of content comes out, so don't keep them waiting too long!

Really Simple Syndication, or RSS, feeds are another way to distribute your content to people who have asked to receive it. RSS is an awesome tool for blogs that instantly broadcasts any new content. "Feed catchers" receive the updates and alert the followers that new content is available for viewing. The best part about RSS distribution is that once you've set it up, you're good to go. The RSS feed will automatically distribute the content for you. We will get deeper into this later on in the chapter.

Given all of the distribution channels available out there, some of the best are content-sharing sites. These sites are designed for sharing specific types of content. For example, YouTube and Vimeo are video-sharing sites, and SlideShare is a slideshow-presentation sharing site. Most content-sharing sites offer users the ability to have branded profiles where all of your uploaded content is aggregated.

In this step, we will go into detail about how to distribute content through these channels to a network of followers and how to use an RSS feed on your site. Beyond distributing to social networks and followers, content can be distributed through publishers, video sites, and other kinds of sites looking for specific content. By distributing content on numerous properties, your business can claim more real estate online.

Finding the Right Distribution Channels for Your Content

At this point in the strategy you should have some awesome content on your website. It's great stuff, and you should be proud of it! Your content offers value to your audience and shows off your brand's industry expertise. So it's time to open up some channels where you can distribute your ideas and claim even more real estate online. Distribution channels add more opportunities to deliver content to potential customers and to link back to your products and services.

You'll need to strike a balance between promotion and distribution, between finding ways to put your web page content in the hands of potential customers and creating fresh content specifically to post on other websites where potential customers can find it. Again, the difference between promotion and distribution is that promotion is all about generating a buzz around your onsite content and in distribution you design content specifically to appear on third party websites. The secret to maximizing your ability to distribute your content is to diversify or repurpose it.

> **"You don't necessarily need to continually create more and more content. Instead, take some time to plan how you will promote your content, to get the most benefit out of each piece you create. At a minimum, try to utilize each piece of content across all of your owned and social media channels. Then, look into how you can incorporate often overlooked ways to extend your content reach, such as linking your content to appropriate product pages on your website or including a link to your content or blog in everyone's outgoing emails."**
>
> **–Heidi Cohen (@HeidiCohen)**

When you diversify your distribution channels, you give yourself the opportunity to fill the search results with your content. Your latest infographic on Slideshare or your article published on the Huffington Post might just outrank similar content on your own website. If you have a diverse distribution strategy and you target the right keywords, you could potentially fill the search results page with your content on many different sites!

RSS for News and Blog Feeds

RSS has been a part of the Internet for more than a decade. (In Internet terms, that's some decent longevity). As technology has improved over the years, RSS has evolved to keep up, but the basic idea has remained the same. There are millions of blogs and other providers of content on the web. Who has the time to go directly to every website and blog to check for new content? It makes more sense to have new content sent directly to readers so that they can check into one central location and read the new stuff at their leisure. As mobile devices have grown more sophisticated, and e-readers have hit the market, RSS has become the desired way for many people to keep up with news and blogs – anywhere and anytime.

So it goes without saying that RSS, and blog feeds, are awesome ways to distribute your fresh content to the masses. Not only does RSS deliver updated news to the subscribers who follow your feeds, but it can also be picked up by feed catchers, widgets, and other applications that aggregate RSS content by specific keywords. RSS ensures that your content will get to the people who want to receive it. The bonus with RSS distribution, thanks to aggregators, is that a person might be compelled to start following your blog if they find your great content in their aggregator inbox.

Figure 46: RSS icon

It's a no-brainer. If you have a blog, you should use an RSS feed. Most blog platforms such as WordPress or Blogger already have a feed capability built in. All you have to do is set up the feed and your blog will start transmitting. Encourage your site visitors to start following your feeds! Your blog should have an RSS feed icon to prompt RSS subscriptions. All your new content will flow through your feed so that it immediately gets distributed to your RSS subscribers. The best part is, once you've established an RSS feed, the maintenance is minimal. Your content goes out to your subscribers and to feed-catchers looking for your keywords. Just as fast as you can develop content, your RSS feed pumps it out.

RSS is great for getting content out there, but wouldn't it be great to have some analytics on how your RSS is working? Historically, it has been challenging to know much about subscribers and to find out what articles are catching their attention and which ones they skip over. Fortunately, online converters like Google's FeedBurner can provide you with analytics that can help shape the content you distribute through RSS. These analytics will help you determine which feeds are getting attention from subscribers, and who's clicking through to your site from a feed to get the whole article which can be enormously helpful as you plan future posts.

Video, Photo and Podcast Sharing Sites

You have plenty of opportunities to produce tons of audio, video, and image content for your site. Whether you're reporting your success at conferences by sharing photos, interviewing industry experts with video, or issuing audio versions of your content for those that prefer to listen, you should have some fantastic content in a variety of media formats. It only makes sense to open up a variety of distribution channels where you can post that content.

Once you've opened up these channels, you have an even greater incentive to continue producing content in these media forms. As you brainstorm for content to put on your site, think in terms of the channels you've opened offsite so that you can distribute it broadly. If you have a YouTube channel, think of content ideas that include video. When you have events, bring a camera to post photos to your image sharing accounts.

When you create customized, branded channels for showcasing your video, photo, and audio content, you add more opportunities for that content to be discovered in search. Create content experiences that can be posted on multiple channels. The more channels you can employ, the larger your footprint (see Figure 47 on page 183).

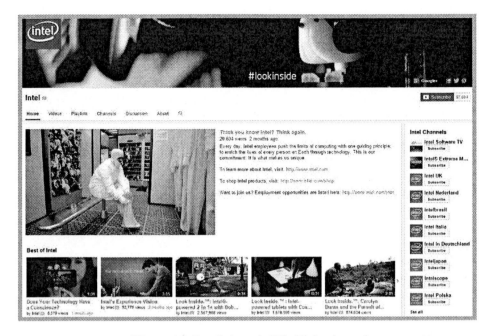

Figure 47: Intel's branded YouTube channel

Video is Booming

Video content is highly visible and easily digested. It's a great medium for communicating your thought leadership, and for demonstrating your expert know-how. Video is one of the most entertaining ways to connect to your audience, opening up the possibility for creative, fun content.

Your videos should appear not only on your site, but on sites like YouTube, Vimeo and DailyMotion, as well. Video is easily shareable, and for this reason you should make as much use of distribution channels as possible. Video channels add numerous opportunities for you to engage your audience – posting content to the channel is just the beginning.

YouTube

YouTube and Vimeo both offer the ability for users to create branded channels where you can upload your video content. If you haven't done so already, I recommend you set up branded channels for both sites. You can set up background images to show your brand logo, and coordinate the color theme to match your brand style. When you optimize the channel, make sure to link back to your website. Promote your video channels to gain followers. When you post new content to your channel, your followers will be alerted to it.

YouTube allows users to recommend content to their followers. Recommending is a form of promotion, and it's great for a few reasons. First, it's a fantastic way to network. By promoting other users' content, they may return the favor. Next, it keeps your channel on the radar for your followers. If you don't have any new video content of your own, you can provide other, useful content that your followers might be interested in, giving them the sense that new content is still flowing from your channel. As with any form of content promotion, if you keep the recommended content relevant to your audience, you reinforce your thought leadership in your industry.

Vimeo

Vimeo offers a group feature, similar to LinkedIn. The cool thing about groups is that you can often post new videos to a group without having to be a member of the group. If you have relevant content, search for groups by keyword and post your video to the group. Groups make for excellent targeted distribution. If you actively produce video, you should make use of Vimeo groups, both by joining groups and hosting your own.

If you host your own, the name of the group should not be your business's name; instead, use an industry-related, keyword-optimized name that will prompt interest in the group. As a group owner, you'll be responsible for moderating the content – so you'll need to remain active to keep it up to par, especially if you allow non-group members to post content. Vimeo also gives you the ability to categorize your content, so make sure you optimize for the relevant categories. Many searchers narrow the scope of their video searches by category. Without optimizing your category, you could be missed in these searches.

DailyMotion

DailyMotion is an open video-sharing site like Vimeo and YouTube. It's designed to be an entertainment hub for business content and user-generated web series. Dailymotion draws over 112 million unique monthly visitors and has accumulated over 2.5 billion video views worldwide. The France-based company offers 35 localized versions in 18 different languages. They have even released an app that encourages user-generated videos that can be shared through the standalone website or mobile. Because of the volume of traffic they receive, I recommend you take a look to see if your business would be a good match for their site.

Lastly, remember to repurpose your videos! Video is an excellent medium for repurposing; interviews to text or to audio, for example are great ways to get more mileage out of your video content. Likewise, if you have a great piece of text content, try having a dynamic person in your organization present it in video format. When you repurpose other media content to video, keep in mind that a natural effect is better: avoid having the presenter dictate the message into the camera. Make sure they *do something* to keep the video from being boring, even if that means they simply work at a whiteboard.

Distribution Possibilities for Images

If you've developed some cool, original photos or images, start sharing them! Photo and image sharing is a great way to keep people engaged with the excitement that's happening in and around your company or industry. Photo-sharing sites center on the concept of the photo album. Many users engage these sites to collect photos of their memories for the purpose of sharing them with the friends in their networks. For this reason, photos and images are extremely *shareable*. When you take advantage of photo-distribution channels, you not only raise the visibility of your content but also encourage it to be shared.

Photo sites offer dozens of ways to organize, optimize for search, and share images. When you distribute your content on these channels, take advantage of the options. Optimizing images might seem like extra work, but the payoff can be well worth the effort. Not only will you increase your opportunities to be found in search, but you'll also enliven the experience for the viewers:

Nearly every photo-sharing site makes it easy to publish photos to other social media sites like Facebook and Twitter. This can make it a snap to expand your distribution throughout your social media footprint. When you publish content to a photo site, use this feature to share the photos to your social media platforms, letting your networks know that you have new photo content available for viewing.

Most sites have a "places" tag linked to Google maps and other maps for photo albums. This is a fantastic way to add dimension to photos, especially when you bring them back from an event away from your headquarters. Say your staff attended a conference in Dallas and took photos of the experience. Optimizing the album for location will make it more engaging for users, and a search for your content by that city could bring up your images.

Make sure to use the description feature for each photo you publish. Make your description natural, but also be keyword-conscious. Descriptions are the critical information that search engines use for identifying relevance and can get your photos into the search results.

Sites like Flickr use category tags to aid searching. Make sure you optimize your images for tags. Category tags are another way to get images found in search by adding relevance.

We covered promoting content on Pinterest and Instagram in the previous step, but this time we are focusing on distributing images on those sites. Here are the best ways to take advantage of these social media channels to distribute your content to the largest audience possible.

Pinterest

As we discussed in the last step, incorporating a good headline and story description with your content can give you a better chance of capturing the audience's attention. While images will always be a critical component of a Pinterest post (pin), there are additional strategies to ensure that your content is viewed by a large audience. This is because Pinterest is trying to break away from its established platform concept of pinning exclusively visual content.

First off, distribute your content evenly. This is one of the biggest tips for Pinterest and it will help you gain followers, keeping them coming back for more. Be sure that your profile is filled with not only brand related boards, but also industry related boards from other contributors. This doesn't mean you can't have boards dedicated to your products or brand-related items. For example, Kyle's Sporting Goods Store can have a Pinterest board dedicated to men's sports clothing as well as a board for women's sports clothing; for these boards, Kyle only pins images of the clothes and various styles sold in his store. In addition to these specific boards, he also creates a board dedicated to broader topics that relate to sports culture where he pins both images of his brand and images from other contributors. These industry related, "culture-boards" can very easily mix both brand and non-brand related content very well; for instance, Kyle can use it to show off his store's apparel at a baseball game.

Figure 48: Baseball-themed Pinterest boards

One of the biggest goals with any social media platform is of course, recognition. Your company wants to reach as many people in your target audience as possible with content. When it comes to Pinterest, people should follow you, interact with your pins, and repin your content for others to see. In order to achieve success with Pinterest content distribution, try adding a small branded logo to the corner of all your pins. This is a small and subtle addition to your pins that can amplify your brand name tremendously. For example, when someone comes across this pin below on Toy Splash's page, the audience will be able to see the source right away. This encourages viewers to either begin following your pins, or to go check out your site for more information.

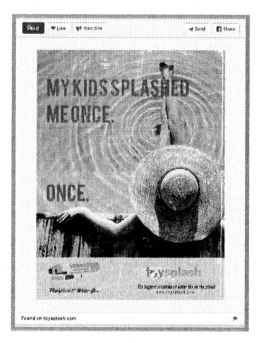

Figure 49: An example of a branded Pin

Another great way to expand your presence is to let other people on Pinterest do it for you. By adding On Hover Pin it buttons (beware these don't function on mobile browsers), and Pin it share buttons on all the images on your website you will encourage people to pin your content for you. This is a great additional source for spreading your content around Pinterest, and will also encourage visitors on your website to start following you on Pinterest for more content!

Pinterest recently unveiled Guided Search, which offers a way to add filters to the user's search, narrowing down their results to stuff in their niche interest. The feature uses topics and keyword parameters to hone in on a selection. In theory, this should make it easier for users to comb through pins to find information. But for brands, Guided Search makes it even more critical that you optimize your pins to make sure your content shows up during Guided Search. How do you accomplish this? Get specific. Each of your descriptions should accurately and thoroughly explain the details of the pin. Using the Kyle's Sporting Goods example, it's not just "Baseball Equipment" it's a "2.5 Inch Turf Cleat for Men." As Pinterest puts it, "Mention the most compelling and distinct parts of the pin in your description and you're more likely to surface your Pins when people get specific in searches."[45]

Instagram

A great example of Instagram-specific content is to leverage Photo Contests. Try using Facebook status updates to encourage your fans to enter your Instagram photo contest. The content is obviously going to depend on your industry niche, but businesses can host photo contests on Instagram using a trending hashtag that is related to your industry. Using our recent Pit Bull shelter example, the popular organization, www.dontbullymybreed.org has used Instagram hashtags such as #instapit, #dontbullymybreed, and #dogsofinstagram to give many shelters a chance to show off their loyal companions and help find a new loving home.

Your distribution efforts on Instagram will be most successful if you optimize your profile.

Instagram is great for giving a behind-the-scenes view of your company – try posting photos of your employees at work to show the personality of your workforce. These company photos can also be a way to celebrate staff and showcase their talents and how much they're valued (see Figure 50 on page 190).

---

45 http://businessblog.pinterest.com/post/69009812003/reaching-pinners-through-search

Figure 50: An Instagram from company Brit + Co. showing a staff event

Instagrammers can use a number of trending hashtags to join in a bigger part of the visual community, and your brand needs to join in on the fun with your awesome content! If you're at an event or conference that has created or designated a hashtag (something like #ContentMarketing-Works), add it to your photos so that other attendees or people interested in your field can find them. Iconosquare[46] is a great resource for discovering competitor trends or industry-related hashtags. Simply enter the brand name or hashtag into the search box and click Search.

You can track the relevance of your Instagram hashtags with TOTEMS.[47] This Instagram analytics platform provides metrics on hashtags including other contributors, type of content, and user engagement. Since Instagram released its video feature, companies from all industries have been taking a stab at creating their own unique, 15-second videos. While some brands are still learning how to use it effectively, others have excelled in making Instagram videos that are creative, informational, and fun.

---

46 http://iconosquare.com/

47 https://analytics.totems.co/

Imgur

Imgur often doesn't get the credit it deserves as a stand-alone success due to the fact that it hosts millions of images and GIFs on Reddit. But Imgur demands attention from content marketers – it brings in over 100 million unique visitors per month, which technically means it's bigger than Reddit[48] (which has about 73 million unique visitors each month)! What's really impressive is that just two short years previously, Imgur had no more than 30 million visitors a month. Today, those 100 million monthly unique visitors click on about 2 billion images a day,[49] making for a heck of a lot of this:

Figure 51: A popular internet meme

Imgur has become the main resource for users to post any of their photos onto Reddit, especially since Reddit banned Quickmeme back in June 2013. The site's subsections (imgur.com/r/pics, etc.) are tied directly to Reddit's. In order to share an image on the Imgur subsection, you have to first post it on the subreddit with the corresponding name, at which point it will be automatically added on Imgur if it reaches a certain popularity.

Imgur is not ony for Reddit users; in fact, when you see an image or GIF on a website like Buzzfeed or Reddit, chances are good that it was first

---

48 http://www.businessinsider.com/imgur-is-officially-bigger-than-reddit-2013-9

49 http://imgur.com/blog/2013/09/26/100-million-uniques-higher-upload-limits-and-https-support/

uploaded to Imgur. Due to the major influence it has had on websites across most niches, the company recently introduced it's first-ever analytics platform, Imgur Analytics. It's a place which allows users to track the lifecycle of successes and failures of uploaded images as they are distributed and shared online. This will enable your team to see where their images travel over time and better understand what image content tends to go viral in your industry. The platform now allows users to:

- Track total image views over time.
- Graph image views over time, filtered by date range and even by the hour.
- See top traffic referral sources (ex. Facebook, Reddit, Twitter) which aims to reveal the lifecycle of an image as it travels and is shared online.

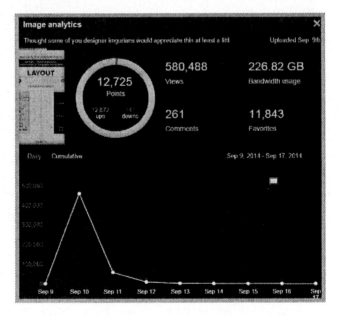

Figure 52: Imgur Analytics

Imgur Analytics also ties in with the company's new native advertising business model. This enables users to track image views during active campaigns as well as earned media views following paid campaigns to better gauge success. These tracking insights will help your team measure the overall successes and failures of each campaign.

To understand image popularity, Imgur has always logged how many views an image receives over time. Now, Imgur promises to look deeper into how images are shared and where they travel online, which will lead to a better understanding of what drives the popularity of content that "goes viral."

> **"Brands are tired of ineffective banner campaigns. Sites like Imgur present fresh alternatives to dated approaches, and our ability as a platform to help content go viral is a primary reason brands are attracted to us. Brands have already started to recognize the platform's potential as a vibrant, influential online community and as a distribution mechanism for viral content."**
>
> **– Alan Schaaf (@imgur)**

Flickr

Flickr is perfect for content distribution, its entire design is about creating unique visual content and sharing it. Flickr tends to do a better job of displaying images than free image blogs or other photo sharing sites. Their well-designed, user-friendly interface makes uploading and editing photos very easy. Another added benefit of Flickr is that you can edit your photos using a wide variety of editing tools: white balance, exposure, saturation, brightness, color balance, and contrast are just a few tools your team can use if professional editing software is not available. Add to that one terabyte of online storage, and it's enough to make your competition's head spin.

Flickr has many active users that take their community seriously. Selling your products on Flickr is strictly forbidden. Nonetheless, their community guidelines actually help businesses stay within the Flickr terms of service and safely use Flickr for content distribution. These community guidelines are very clear – "Flickr accounts are intended for members to share original photos and video that they themselves have created." For Pro Account holders, Flickr Statistics are designed to give your team insight into the ways that people find your content:

- Comments
- Tags
- Notes
- Favorites
- Added to gallery
- People
- Replies to your comments
- Adds you as a contact or to a photo
- Writes a testimonial
- Shares
- Keywords used on search engines when your photos come up
- Referrer

That last metric, "referrer," can be a little confusing. Flickr defines a referrer as, "another website that has linked to one of your Flickr pages. For example, if someone does a search for something on yahoo.com and one of your photos comes up, their click through from the Yahoo! search results page will count as a referrer. You'll also be able to see what they searched for in the stat about that referrer. When you look at your referrers, you can click through the link to visit the site itself to see where the link came from, and how your content is represented there. If that link doesn't work, you can also go to the base domain name and see what that site is about."

When looking at your site's statistics, it's important to note:

- Your own views of your own photos are not counted.
- Flickr tracks views and referrers when a page on flickr.com is loaded. They are unable to count views of your photos on external sites (like your blog).
- The "Search Engines" group of referrers counts traffic from most of the major search engines online, including Bing, Google, Yahoo!, MSN, and even Ask.com.

When using Flickr to distribute your great content, share interesting and original photos and videos that relate to your industry or brand. Upload unique, industry-related content rather than product photos or staged, advertorial content. Remember, with any of the distribution or promotion channels we have discussed in the last 2 steps, your goal should still be to build trust with your audience. With that said, posting photos that show off your organization's culture and personality will help you build relationships with your followers, gaining their loyalty. For example, sharing behind-the-scenes photos of your products or services within your organization can show your audience what you have to offer to the field, and how you are a leader in the industry.

Here are some examples of organizations using Flickr in neat ways:

- A home appliance shop owner shares photos of happy customers in his store.
- A winery shares behind-the-scenes action from their vineyard.
- A Pit Bull shelter shares video and pictures of their community volunteer event.

Figure 53: A Flickr page for a pit bull rescue organization

Flickr also offers video from their mobile app to be uploaded on the main site. Compared to Instagram that only lets its users show off a 15 second video, Flickr allots up to 30 seconds for their mobile video. And posting directly on the website allows for up to 3 minutes of video content.

Because you have more time available, you can use even more techniques per clip, and get creative with editing. There are fewer options for editing videos compared to images on Flickr; however, you can apply filters to a clip (similar to Instagram), as well as choose a segment or snippets of a video to publish online. With the current trend for short video (especially those found on Vine or Instagram), it makes sense to also include those videos on Flickr. You can also optimize your post and add full descriptions and titles for each video.

Podcasting: Your Own Private Radio Broadcast

People all over keep up on industry news via audio. If you deliver audio files to these listeners, you can capture an important niche audience. Typically, people listen to podcasts when it isn't possible to engage in other forms of media, like text and video. By providing your content in this format, you can make your content available to your potential customers even when they are away from their computer. Essentially, podcasting is an audio RSS feed from your site. When you set up a RSS feed for your audio, you are effectively broadcasting your audio file over the Internet. Anyone with a podcatcher that's set to search for your feed, or keywords in your feed, will download your file. But that's not the only way that people pick up podcasts. Many users go to podcast directories like iTunes and Podcast Alley to browse podcasts to download. You want to ensure that you've established accounts with these sites and set them up to receive your feed. This way, your feed will go not only to individuals with podcatchers but will also be available to anyone browsing the directory sites. To take full advantage of podcast distribution:

- When you set up the feed from your site, be sure that the metadata description of the episode is optimized for your target keywords. As always, the title should be natural for the human reader browsing directories, but it should contain keywords that will get it picked up by podcatchers searching for your term. Because most browsers use keywords to find podcasts to follow in directories, you need to optimize for them, too.

- For each directory you register with, you'll be able to give your podcast channel a title, description, and a link back to your web pages. The title should be optimized to be catchy but also express, at a glance, the nature of the content that you'll be providing. Your description should be short and meaty; you want to attract a listener at this point, so aim for both pragmatic and attention-getting.

- When you set up an account with podcast directories, you don't always have the opportunity to establish a branded channel, but with iTunes, you do. iTunes is the Mecca for podcasts, and it makes sense that they'd offer some great features there. If you're going to do podcasting, you can't afford to miss out on iTunes. To set up an account and a feed, iTunes requires an image as cover art (300 x 300 pixels). This is your chance to include your brand logo, and to splash some color onto the page.

- The medium attempts to mimic the idea of a radio broadcast, and for that reason podcasts are geared toward episodes; in fact, that's the term iTunes uses to describe each file. Your branded channel, then, will work well as an *industry news channel*. As such, this affords a unique opportunity to repurpose much of your content, especially your blog posts, to an audio format, while at the same time remaining within the scope of your channel description.

- Once you start transmitting podcasts, don't slow down. When you gain a following, they will expect regular content delivery. In fact, iTunes states that it favors podcasts that get frequent content updates and will reduce search rankings for podcasts that have not provided content in a while.

Presentation-Sharing Sites

For business-to-business, slideshows are the way to knock 'em dead with your expertise. Not only is this a way to diversify your distribution by posting your slideshow presentations, but you can also find creative ways to use presentation-sharing sites to distribute content beyond traditional slideshows. The fact is that slideshows are gaining popularity outside of B2B because they are a great way to move an audience through an idea thanks to easily digestible text and graphic images.

While the bulk of content shared on SlideShare, and similar sites, is still traditional presentations, I've seen some very creative slideshows that go beyond presentations. For example, travelogues are finding their way into the slideshow format. They work well because the traveler can post pictures from a trip and add text descriptions of the experience. Some have delivered eBooks, white papers and even product comparisons as slideshows. Sites like SlideShare offer functionality that can enhance the old-fashioned slideshow and turn it into an awesome distribution channel:

- Some sites enable you to add and synchronize audio to presentations to make them more dynamic.

- Some sites will allow you to convert presentations to video for uploading to video-sharing sites, making it simple to repurpose the same content in multiple formats.

- Users can comment on the slideshow.

- Text content is extracted and searchable on some sites, making keyword phrases within the presentation searchable.

- SlideShare has a widget for LinkedIn, putting your slides right on your LinkedIn profile.

The core message for distribution is: "Find ways to get it out there!" The more you capitalize on the multitude of online channels for distribution, the more you will put your great content in the hands of the potential customers who need it. Distribution is where you get to show your brand's ability to deliver industry wisdom. The more you create content for distribution, or repurpose content for distribution on multiple channels, the more your brand will show up in search, and the more opportunities you'll create for sharing. You have great content – get it out where it can be discovered!

STEP 7

LEAD NURTURE
Shepherding Prospects Through the Funnel

Lead nurture is one of the most important steps in this strategy because it capitalizes on all the work you've already done: you created great content, optimized it to be found online, promoted and distributed it to the right channels, and you've even gained leads. Real, live, and (hopefully) qualified leads!

Now is your chance to build a relationship with those leads, growing their loyalty to you, and if all goes well, one day win their business. Lead nurture can be defined as a process of engaging new and past leads through a series of correspondence and ongoing engagement that is targeted to your prospects based on their behavior, interests, or activity, with the end goal of gaining their business.

Let's break it down a bit more:

- At its core, lead nurture is **the creation of trust** between you and your potential customers.

- According to Gleanster Research, 50% of leads are qualified but not yet ready to buy.[50] Think about that for a second - *Half* of all

---

50 http://www.gleanster.com/report/measuring-the-impact-of-lead-nurturing-on-the-sales-pipeline

the people that come through your digital door are the people you want to be working with. They just aren't ready yet.

- When they *are* finally ready to commit to a product or service, who will they think of? *It should be you.* Lead nurture is your chance to differentiate yourself, win their loyalty, and get them ready to buy…from *you*!

- People buy from people they like.

- People buy from people they trust.

In Internet marketing, you create trust by offering content that people will find relevant, interesting, and above all – *useful.* Therefore, the question is: How are you creating useful content that encourages relationships based on trust and loyalty?

The Importance of Lead Nurture

Your goal with any lead nurturing effort should be to guide your prospects on a journey from hesitation to commitment, from need to fulfillment. On this journey, you'll create a sense of loyalty and trust that facilitates a buying decision when your prospect is ready to take that next step.

- How do you get to that point of commitment? First, you get to know your prospects. Think about who you're trying to reach, and ask yourself these questions:
- What types of content does my audience tend to engage with the most?
- Where does my audience hang out online, and how can I reach them most effectively?
- How does my audience interact with my website? With my content?
- How can I facilitate interactions with my audience through engaging, informative, and useful content?
- What tips a person over the edge from prospect to customer?

Not only is lead nurture an important follow up for the previous steps in this process; I would argue it's important for the success and longevity of your business as a whole. After all, businesses that know how to cultivate lead nurturing generate up to 50% more qualified leads than those who don't. Not to mention that this comes at a 33% lower cost, too, as Forrester Research has found.[51] You can't afford to spend the time, effort and manpower generating leads, only to let them sit untouched and unnurtured.

> **Businesses that have a solid lead nurturing process generate up to 50% more qualified leads at a 33% lower cost.**

The importance of lead nurture does not lie solely in the financial benefits. Lead nurture will contribute to your brand reputation and awareness. The stronger a brand you have, the more your organization's personality and the way you do business comes across to your prospects. The more they relate to your brand, the more you build their trust. A strong brand, founded on trust and loyalty, can lead your organization to more business.

How Lead Nurture Can Work for Your Business

If you type "lead nurture" into any search engine, you'll get back a wide range of results, ranging from automation to campaigns to software and strategy. Lead nurture can work on a variety of levels and just how it works will differ from company to company. The main objective remains the same in whatever form it takes: *lead nurture increases business by providing value, keeping your company top-of-mind, deepening relationships, moving people through the buying cycle, building your brand recognition, and creating loyalty and trust.*

Your whole team should be involved in lead nurture, both on the marketing and sales spectrums. When both sides of the house work together, it's more efficient. You can avoid duplicated effort, contacting leads multiple times, wrongly targeting messages, etc. The two departments must work together to create a system that is highly targeted, relevant, and guides

---

51 http://www.act-on.com/resources/whitepapers/introduction-to-lead-nurturing

prospects along the funnel in a way that doesn't feel forced, and is conscious of your prospects' typical behavior.

Many companies make the mistake of treating lead nurture inconsistently – an email here, a service update there, maybe a webinar over here. A good lead nurture program resembles a funnel, with every narrowing phase of the funnel connected to the previous, moving leads toward the sale.

Map out your ideal lead journey, from the first point of contact to other touch points along the way, until the point of conversion to happy customer. Put yourself in your prospects' shoes. What would they find interesting and relevant for the stage they're in? When you answer that, you can then set up a process to guide them where you want them to go.

The lead nurture funnel can look very different from industry to industry, and even within similar businesses. For example, B2B companies may have a far longer sales process due to the very nature of B2B purchasing, while B2C may not be as lengthy. Nonetheless, the general dynamic of lead nurture can be broken down into five basic phases:

1. Handshake: *"Nice to meet you"*

Goal: To attract and convert a casual visitor to an interested lead.

This is the first point of contact between you and your new prospect. The handshake can happen through a download on your website, a sign-up for your email newsletter, at registration for your webinar, or by simply completing a contact form. This is the first chance to introduce yourself and start the relationship off strong. Remember, first impressions matter – even on the Internet.

2. Conversation: *"Let's get to know each other"*

Goal: To build a relationship, inform, educate, and solve a problem.

Here is where the lead nurturing really begins. In this phase, you deliver content to your prospects, re-engage them on different platforms, and build a foundation of loyalty and trust. The Conversation phase often is the longest part of the process, during which you and your prospects figure each other out.

3. Contact: *"Tell me more"*

Goal: To convert a lead into a legitimate prospect.

This is when nurturing the Conversation Phase will start to pay off. You've proven yourself by providing content that was relevant to your prospect's interests, and you've compelled them to reach out for further information. The conversation doesn't stop here, though. You will continue to offer helpful, useful content throughout the Contact Phase to get to a point where a proposal is sent or a product purchase is more seriously considered.

4. Qualification: *"Are we a good fit?"*

Goal: To prove your expertise and usefulness specific to a lead's pain points and convert them to a customer.

Now that you've given your lead everything they need to understand what you do and what you offer, it's time to get personal. What do *they* want and need from you and how can you fulfill it? Your content plays a big role, shaping how your relationship will progress, as well as how your business development team handles the lead.

5. Close: *"Let's get started"*

Goal: To create a strong, happy customer relationship that naturally encourages further business.

You did it – you made the sale! Whether you closed a new client or sold a product, your relationship is now cemented. You built trust, provided useful content, and gained new business. But your work is still not over. Now you must *deliver on your promise* and *continue to build loyalty and confidence* so your customer never chooses to start a similar relationship elsewhere.

How a Prospect Moves through the Phases

The diagram below offers one example of a generic funnel of the 5 phases of lead nurturing. Let's imagine you've done all the pre-work to generate the actual lead, and this funnel starts when your prospect has made their first point of contact via your website.

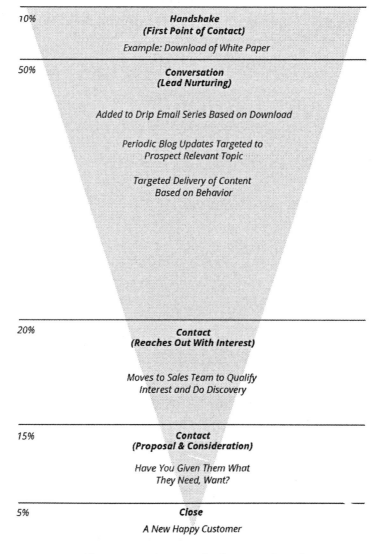

10%
Handshake
(First Point of Contact)
Example: Download of White Paper

50%
Conversation
(Lead Nurturing)

Added to Drip Email Series Based on Download

Periodic Blog Updates Targeted to Prospect Relevant Topic

Targeted Delivery of Content Based on Behavior

20%
Contact
(Reaches Out With Interest)

Moves to Sales Team to Qualify Interest and Do Discovery

15%
Contact
(Proposal & Consideration)

Have You Given Them What They Need, Want?

5%
Close
A New Happy Customer

Figure 54: A generic lead nurture funnel

The percentages in the figure above attempt to quantify the average time a prospect spends in each stage, but this isn't a linear process. The pace at which a prospect moves through the funnel will vary depending on your business. There's a big difference between selling hiking shoes and selling enterprise security software or consulting services, for example. At the end of the day, slow and steady wins the race when building a relationship.

According to SiriusDecisions research, 80% of prospects initially deemed to be "bad leads" by sales teams will go on to become a buying client within 24 months.[52] So the odds are that your efforts will prove their effectiveness over time, but a consistent, well designed lead nurture system can accelerate your prospects through each phase.

Become the Expert

Fundamentally, lead nurture is an educational process for your prospects. You are the teacher with the power to give them the information they are looking for. Education goes both ways too. You will learn about what your leads want, what they find interesting, and how you can best serve them. In turn, your prospects will learn more about your business, your brand, the services and products you offer, and the ways in which you offer them. The information you provide in the lead nurturing stage will pave the road for an easier sale. Therefore, the more quality content you provide, the better. Keep these guidelines in mind as you develop content:

Educate your prospects on your products and services. Give people the tools and information they need to make a purchasing decision.

Provide information that people can trust. When people trust your information, they trust you. When they trust you, they are more likely to buy from you.

Keep your prospects' needs at the top of your mind. In whatever content you create, your customer comes first. Meet them where they are and help them move forward.

---

52 https://smallbusiness.yahoo.com/advisor/beyond-batch-blast-launching-first-lead-nurturing-program-133028146.html

Remember, you're the expert. Prove it.

As my good friend and expert content marketer, Marcus Sheridan says, "If you can't answer the question 'What's in it for the buyer?' the messaging probably isn't valuable in your nurturing program."[53] Educate them. Be authentic. Give them what they're looking for.

Nurture Leads through Content Creation

Now that we've covered the high level overview of lead nurture, let's get into the specifics. Loyalty and trust are paramount, but how do you go about achieving them? There are many ways to reach your prospects, but this 8 Step process is about the creation of useful internet content so that's where we'll focus our conversation. Following are six types of content you can create for your lead nurturing systems. The types that you choose to implement depend on the many unique factors of *your* funnel and *your* goals.

E-Newsletters

In 2012, MarketingSherpa ran a survey for their Lead Generation Benchmark Report, asking people which content types were the most effective at nurturing their leads. The winners were not fancy infographics or tech-savvy podcasts (both of which were actually ranked at the bottom of the barrel). Instead, the overwhelming answer with 57% of the votes was email newsletters.[54]

57% of business vote that email newsletters are the best type of content for lead nurturing.

Email newsletters are a great way to generate leads, yet those leads can often be characterized as interested, but hesitant. Perhaps they saw your

---

53 http://www.thesaleslion.com/blogging-save-business-neither-content-marketing

54 http://www.marketingsherpa.com/article/chart/messaging-tactics-effective-lead-nurturing

sign-up form on your blog and decided to scope you out. They're curious enough to follow you, but not necessarily ready for commitment. Cater the newsletter to those who are looking for more information, but be sure to appeal to longstanding customers looking for updates, too.

Email newsletters can include many different elements:

- **Internal News**: hiring, changes/expansion of services, team photos, and more.

- **Content**: highlight of the top content you've created during the month to show what you've been up to and provide interesting material for your recipients.

- **Product or Service Updates**: announcements for expanded or new services and products is a great way to show your growth and offerings.

- **Events:** if you are participating in conferences, putting on workshops or seminars, this is the place to broadcast your involvement and show opportunities for further education.

- **Industry News**: larger news and shifts in your industry are useful snippets of content to provide timely information to people who may have not heard elsewhere.

Email newsletters are most often sent monthly, but can be more or less frequent, depending on your audience and how much content you choose to include. Some newsletters are very effective with a short blurb and one or two links, while others do well jam packed with content. Either way, email newsletters as part of a lead nurture program can drive website traffic, re-engage existing and prospective clients, and grow your brand awareness.

Email

Certain people have proclaimed email to be dead with the onset of social sharing, tweets, and other briefer forms of communication. But in content marketing, this is still far from the truth. Email plays a pivotal role in lead nurturing because it remains a strong form of business communication. As shown with the email newsletter format, it is still the most effective form of moving leads towards a sale.

Email marketing can take many forms, but one of the most powerful is the email drip series. A drip series is a series of periodic or automated emails targeted for precise time intervals and based on a lead's particular behaviors or lead segments. For example, a lead comes to you through the download of a free guide you created and housed on your website. After downloading it, the lead may experience the following touch points during the Conversation stage via an email drip series:

A drip series is tied to the original free guide download or other valuable content, and the resources within the drip must be packaged to follow up specifically on that content. Most importantly, the series must be planned out far before the first "thank you" email is sent. This takes foresight, content creation, and mapping out of what you think a prospect would need to move closer to taking action and move down the funnel from conversation to contact.

Keep your content educational. Keep it informative. Ask for the sale only after you've proved your helpfulness. Of course, not every business will maintain a long drip, and that's okay. Imagine, for example, that you sell hiking shoes. Your email series would need to be heavily tailored to your lead's interests. Find the right cadence and funnel for your company – you know your audience best and what they're looking for.

Blogs and Articles

Blogs and articles are beneficial when a lead is in the initial stages of their path to purchase. Blogs make for great awareness-building pieces and are perfect for educating your audience. If you're already creating content for your blog but not thinking about the lead nurture aspect – create a process to target your readers in a more strategic way.

Maybe you're building out a white paper on a very specific service offering you have. Why not create pre-launch articles to build up momentum, and post-launch articles that support different aspects of the whitepaper? As you engage and re-engage your audience on a topic in a variety of ways and mediums (think outside of the blog post to other formats like videos, graphics, etc.), you will create more and more awareness for your services and thought leadership within your field.

Product or Service Updates

The essence of lead nurture is simply keeping people up to date with what's going on. Just like you'd call up a friend when you have an exciting piece of news, the same goes for lead nurture and the relationships you're creating with your leads. Your business is continuously changing and evolving, and there is always something noteworthy you can share. Look for opportunities that arise naturally to show all that's going on in your business:

- New or expanded products/services
- Discounts, price changes, and special offerings (see Figure 55 on page 211)
- Hiring and internal changes
- Conferences and workshops
- Case studies

Keep in mind the mantra that your updates should always be done in a manner of helping, and not selling. This is your chance to provide informative content that encourages your prospects to keep up to date and commit to buy sooner rather than later. These kinds of updates can also be shared via social media, email, newsletters, or other targeted correspondence.

In all types of lead nurture content, use the perspective of "helping, not selling."

Figure 55: A discount email from Cafe Press

POV's, Whitepapers, and Free Guides

A Point of View document (or POV for short) is a document or content piece that clearly identifies the climate of your industry and demonstrates your point of view: your response, your opinion, your solution, and ultimately, your expertise. POV's tend to be very timely to gain the most traction, but can also be reflective of industry trends further down the road, opportunities, news, or other insights. Say you're a company in a shifting industry, like ours, and Google drops another algorithm bomb that affects many of your clients' search engine rankings. This is the perfect time to turn around a quick POV reaching out to your leads to give them your expert take on the situation:

- You're on the ball and up to date with the changing industry.
- You have your leads' best interests in mind by keeping them "in the know" on how the greater industry is addressing an issue.
- You prove authority by taking a strong stance on a hotbed issue.

- You provide useful recommendations and outline the best means to move forward.

The fact is, a POV doesn't only have to be in response to a problem or issue – it can be more proactive, showing how a certain technology has evolved to help businesses get ahead, or perhaps an educational perspective on best practices your prospects can implement.

Your leads will be grateful for the overview and analysis you provide. They may even use this as a first step to reach out for more information on your services; effectively moving themselves closer to a sale. POV's offer a chance to re-engage existing customers with new or evolved service offerings. Remember, lead nurture doesn't have to only be for new leads; it can apply to anyone in your database who could use your services, even if they are already loyal clients.

On top of POV documents, whitepapers and free guides make great lead nurture content, and as I detailed in Step 3, they can be some of the best lead generators around. Just like POV's, whitepapers and free guides build your authority and provide an in-depth exploration on a highly targeted topic that is helpful to your leads. Even though these act as hearty lead generators, you can also frame the creation of guides and papers within your lead nurturing process by targeting specific segments of your list with a topic that would be relevant to them at whatever phase of the funnel they're in.

Webinars

In Step 3, I covered how to create a webinar, but here I want to emphasize that hosting a webinar is one the best ways to nurture leads. Content Marketing Institute found that 62% of marketers used webinars/webcasts to prospect and/or nurture leads in 2013.[55] That's a 20% increase from 2010, when only 42% of companies did the same. By the numbers, webinars have proven to be viable conversion tools.

---

55 http://contentmarketinginstitute.com/2013/10/2014-b2b-content-marketing-research/

I suspect that the reason webinars are so successful as lead nurturing tools has to do with the very nature of webinars. They help put the "name with the face," so to speak. They bring your brand to life with an actual presence from your business – a voice on the other end of the line, an open conversation in real-time, a chance to prove your knowledge and professionalism, and an opportunity to show a little bit of your personality. Not to mention that your attendees also have to sign up in advance and set aside quality time to listen to you – a real commitment on their part. All of these factors are reasons why webinars can take you far, provide higher qualified prospects, and more quickly move your leads along the funnel.

> **What you do with these well-suited leads after the webinar ends is just as essential as the webinar itself.**

You've also got to consider the not-so-qualified leads that may be new to you or just looking for some solid information. Both groups are ripe for lead nurturing, but may each need a uniquely tailored approach. Throughout the webinar process, track who fits into what lead group and tailor your communication based on that data. The following guidelines can help ensure that you get the most out of each webinar from start to finish and beyond.

Discovery

From the outset, you have a chance to discover who your audience is via the registration form. Ask targeted questions to see what interests them, what brought them to you, and what they expect to learn. Keep it light – not too prodding – yet retrieve information that will guide you in the future. Many webinars have in-session polls and interactive question-and-answer sessions. This is yet another opportunity to gauge your audience and see where their interests lie, and where they may be within your funnel – anxious to fill their need or just looking for information. By being smart about the data you gather before and during the webinar, you can increase your ability to target your post-webinar lead nurture content.

Targeted ASAP Delivery

Timing is key. After a webinar ends, the session is still fresh in peoples' minds. Seize the opportunity to reach out before their busy lives sweep them away, and provide the type of targeted delivery that is personalized and helpful. You have two main groups to reach:

1. People who actually attended the webinar.

    ...and...

2. People who registered but never signed on to watch the webinar.

Send **attendees** high quality information – possibly recapping a few unanswered questions, providing a resource list or free download, and of course, mention how they can sign up for your next webinar. As for **registrants,** they need to be persuaded to take the next step and listen/ watch or review the presentation material. It won't hurt to provide additional resources here either, but remember the next step should be for them to understand and experience the value they missed.

Follow-Up Content

Don't stop at one targeted email – build a series of drip messages that provide even more content relevant to the webinar topic. Here is a good chance to include links to relevant blog posts you've written or an innovative infographic you designed on the topic. You could, for example, format your emails in the structure of "lessons" or "teachings" to really hone in on the idea that you are the expert and the educator. Keep track of the behavior that results from these follow-up emails – all of it helps you to discover what it is your leads are looking for.

Automated Lead Nurture

Automated lead nurture is one of the most potent ways to build out your funnel and move your leads closer to a sale. With their ability to streamline and automate content delivery based on specific actions taken by your leads, automation software can significantly reduce the headache. Do you *need* automation? No. But, it could make life a whole lot easier if you have the budget to invest in it.

Lead nurture automation will allow you to more accurately measure and track all of your efforts. To add to that, the ROI is there: businesses that implement marketing automation to nurture their prospects experience a 451% increase in qualified leads.[56] Yes that's right – 51%. Automation can be a critical piece of the lead nurturing puzzle.

Many customer relationship management systems (CRMs) have a built-in capability for automated lead nurture, but oftentimes they are limited to manual actions or small scale systems. If it is a right fit for your business, true automation software is really the way to go to get the most out of your lead nurture and take much of the pain out of the process. There are many software companies out there, and one may fit better for your business than another, so a little research and testing is needed. Here are a few we recommend looking into:

- Act-On
- HubSpot
- AWeber
- Eloqua
- InfusionSoft
- Marketo
- Pardot for Salesforce

Automation facilitates triggered delivery of relevant content based upon specific actions taken by your prospect, such as:

- They request information on your services and get an automatic email with related resources based on which checkboxes they select on your form.

- A coupon is sent for their next purchase when they complete

---

checkout on a similar product. The logic being that if they have found Product X to be of interest, a complementary Product Y will also have an immediate appeal.

- Automated lead nurture is not entirely hands off. You need to return frequently to your funnel to decide what it is the next step you want your prospects to take, and give them what they need to move forward.

An Automation Case Study

PumpOne stands out as a great example of triggered lead nurture automation. A leader in affordable, portable, personal training solutions, PumpOne uses Act-On to automate all four fitness programs that they offer through their mobile app, FitnessBuilder. Each automated process draws on user behavior from the app to deliver targeted and customized messages. For example, if the user has watched one video of a fitness class, he/she will receive a message asking how the workout went.

PumpOne focuses on two main elements essential to their programs' success: design and data. FitnessBuilder emails include a responsive design that escalates engagement across mobile and desktop devices. The careful use of subtle animated gifs in the emails also promotes a prolonged email view, which ultimately helps drive engagement. Each message includes an animated image showing how much time remains for the user on the Premium application. This helps keep users motivated and engaged, leading up to a strong call-to-action, promoting a purchase at the end of the trial period.

Data from the platform drives custom email messaging that encourages the next workout, or congratulates the completion of a recent one. Everyone receives unique email messages depending on the activity they log and the type of user they are: Individual Consumer, Physical Therapist, or Personal Trainer. All of the messages are dynamically produced, automated and deployed from within the Act-On platform. With the automated system, PumpOne has been able to run B2B, B2C, and even B2B2C lead nurturing campaigns concurrently, contributing even more to the campaign's effectiveness.

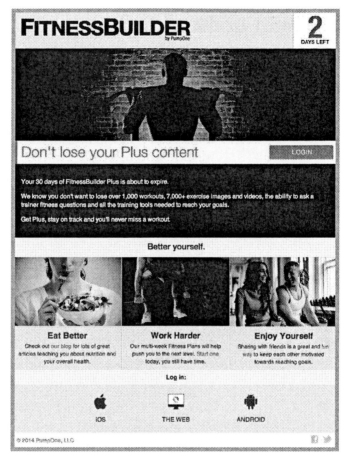

Figure 56: PumpOne automated lead nurture email

As for results, PumpOne's CEO, Craig Schlossberg, says they have been great: "We're getting much more engagement from the professional side of our user base. More and more personal trainers and physical therapists are giving us their logo to further customize the emails to appear as if they are coming directly from them. Also, our subscriber base continues to grow."

In the case of PumpOne, a triggered delivery of lead nurturing communication fits perfectly within their business model and resulted in a growing base of customers and brand loyalty.

A Real World Look at Lead Nurture

Not all companies can afford an automation system, but that doesn't mean lead nurture is inaccessible. Organizations like Minneapolis-based The National Theatre for Children, put together a lead nurture system that worked for their business, their constraints, and their end goals.

NTC is an organization that brings educational theatre into schools on behalf of corporate sponsors. NTC faced the challenge of putting together a content marketing piece to gain sponsors within the utility industry. To do this, they started with the creation of a free downloadable whitepaper with their marketing partner Maccabee, called "7 Strategies To Power Up Your CFOs Support: How To Get Money For Your DSM Program." The whitepaper covered strategies that would help utility marketers better partner with their corporate financial decision-makers. The eBook exceeded their lead generation goal, gathering over 190 eBook downloads, resulting in 55 highly qualified leads.

As Bob Beverage, Vice President of NTC, remarked:

"Not all leads are created equal."

At the start of the lead nurture process, Bob and his team segmented each lead one-by-one to understand if they were at all qualified and, if so, which of the 4 buckets they fit into within their CRM system:

- Current Account
- Former Account (either past sponsor or someone who had shown interest in the past)
- Unsolicited Leads (website lead, got a business card – no real conversation or interest)
- Everyone else

They focused on reaching out to the first three groups and segmented their list by industry, organization, and revenue. This segmentation guided the nuances in messaging so the content hit the right note with each recipient. Every two months, the NTC team put together content that they felt would be most effective for each segment. This included curated content, written articles, or something as simple as a press release.

Figure 57: NTC's "7 Strategies to Power Up" Free Guide

As Bob noted, he didn't have a fancy algorithm to score or prioritize leads or any other automated system. What he did have was a clear rationale guiding the analysis, a strong understanding of who he was reaching, and plenty of content to repurpose in interesting ways. NTC has expanded their lead nurturing system to a highly targeted outreach program sent six times a year.

Even if all leads are not created equal, all *qualified* leads are treated equally and put into a lead nurturing process. Every time they reach out to their leads, NTC receives at least 3-4 "raised hands" asking for more information or a call. Bob has found that NTC's lead nurturing process produces prepared leads who are interested, but not ready to buy, which means that their sales cycle is a long one – 12 to 18 months.

The "7 Strategies to Power Up" campaign was the first highly integrated campaign that NTC ran, and they've learned what worked, what didn't, and what they can do better next time. Bob reflected on the fact that even though his ROI results for this campaign may still be another six months out, its current value lies in the amount of information he's learned about his leads and the opportunity to create a relationship with prospects that will pay for itself when the time is right.

Measurement

NTC's story leads me to my next point – measurement is key to understanding ROI. Bob of NTC was tracking numbers at the end of the day, not individuals, so he could see what worked and what didn't. In order to know if your efforts are truly gaining more business, the answer is all in the data. Once you start measuring success, you may be surprised by what works and what doesn't. Sometimes expectations don't square with reality. We'll go into much more detail on this topic in Step 8, but the one thing to remember, from a lead nurture perspective, is that tracking is your lifeline to understanding your prospects. Analytics will tell you the story of how your relationship building is working, what people like, what doesn't resonate, and what captures conversions. From this data you will be able to more clearly paint a picture of your prospects' journey and tailor your funnel to help them towards a sale in the future.

You may be surprised what works and what doesn't. Sometimes expectations don't square with reality.

Returning to Marcus Sheridan's thoughts on the subject, lead nurture isn't really lead nurture at all; it's the *philosophy of building a relationship*. How you approach that is unique to your business.

Focus on your company's business philosophy and fulfill it for your leads. Don't think of yourself as a hiking shoe company – *you're the expert at creating great adventures!* Show your prospects your expertise and helpfulness in everything you do, and give them the information they need to go on that adventure with you. You're not just an enterprise security software provider – *you keep other corporations safe from harm*. Prove your authority, trustworthiness, solidarity, and help your audience understand how you can keep them secure. Discover your overall philosophy, and begin your lead nurture process from there.

I guarantee this approach is much more sustainable than just "creating great content" alone. When you're intentional with your strategy, concentrating on how your unique brand can serve your prospects, your strategy will guide you for years ahead, regardless of the platform. Build trust, create loyalty, and pave the way for your business to grow.

If you can't answer Marcus' original question of *what's in it for the buyer*, start over and get down to the basics. Lead nurture is its most effective when it's authentic, educational, and above all – useful.

STEP 8

MEASUREMENT
It's All About the Return on Investment

Everyone wants to know that their efforts bring back the best return possible. Most importantly, measurement and tracking using benchmarks and goals helps prove content marketing ROI – metrics that track content marketing shape, and lend efficiency to, future content development efforts.

Though there are a multitude of tools available to measure the effectiveness of your content, I'm going to limit this discussion to Google Analytics,[57] which is the "one stop shop" that most website owners use to measure their content's success. This user-friendly tool offers a wide variety of data, which has its ups and downs. Keep in mind that it can be difficult to determine exactly which metrics will be most valuable to track. However, there are many other analytics tools out there beyond Google Analytics, such as Omniture or Hubspot. They all can be very valuable from a data analysis perspective. The bottom line is, choose one that works for you and use it consistently.

Measuring Your Content's Overall Progress

If you want to find out whether your content has led to conversions such as product purchases through a shopping cart, lead generation from

---

57 http://www.google.com/analytics/

gated-content, or mailing list opt-ins, you will need to set up Google Analytics to track those metrics and measure how your content performs.

A good place to start is to look at the most popular content on your website. Navigate to Behavior > Site Content > All Pages.

Page		Pageviews	↓	Unique Pageviews
		83,146		73,145
		% of Total 100.00% (83,146)		% of Total 100.00% (73,145)
1. /		11,397 (13.71%)		9,456 (12.93%)
2. /content-editorial-calendar-template/		6,096 (7.33%)		5,547 (7.58%)
3. /resources/seo-tutorial-videos/using-h1-tag-improves-search-engine-ranking/		5,136 (6.18%)		4,803 (6.57%)
4. /contact-us/		2,534 (3.05%)		2,110 (2.88%)
5. /about-us/careers/freelance-content-writer/		2,183 (2.63%)		1,990 (2.72%)
6. /resources/seo-tutorial-videos/choosing-the-best-keywords/		1,892 (2.28%)		1,784 (2.44%)
7. /blog/		1,812 (2.18%)		1,535 (2.10%)
8. /about-us/our-team/		1,785 (2.15%)		1,224 (1.67%)
9. /about-us/		1,442 (1.73%)		1,102 (1.51%)
10. /services/		1,213 (1.46%)		835 (1.14%)

Figure 58: Google Analytics view of top page content

To see conversions based on landing page content, you will need switch to the Goal Set View.

The data you pull from just these two metrics can be eye opening, even surprising. You might learn throughout the content strategy that your most popular content is not your highest converting content. The trick is to find content that has a nice balance of traffic and conversions, which will guide your content development as you move forward with your strategy.

If one of your content goals is to increase the visibility of your brand in social media, then you'll want to know what content leads to the most social sharing. If you use WordPress for an external blog (self-hosted, not WordPress.com), or any other CMS, then you can use a plugin that is compatible with their format for social sharing. WordPress plugins can also track social shares of your content within the WordPress dashboard. When you sort your found metrics based on number of tweets, likes, +1's, or other social sharing stats, it can help determine which content resonates with specific social media audiences. It can give you an idea of what content works best within a specific network, so you can be smarter with your distribution efforts.

Onsite analytics measure user activity as they engage your website. They track each user's path through your content, revealing what's important to their experience and identifying areas where you could bring forward the content you want to emphasize. With Google Analytics, or similar tools, you can track all kinds of activity on your site. You can identify which pieces of content lead to the most visits per page and which ones lead to conversions. As you develop onsite analytics, you'll be more equipped to establish milestones for future content because you'll know exactly what you can measure. When you know what is measureable, suddenly you can determine with accuracy whether or not you are meeting your goals, what content works, and what needs improvement. By developing web forms on your site, you can gather precise metrics on user behavior. By tracking user interactions with forms, you can identify who's using your content, what kind of people are converting, what they want from your products and services, and a host of other possibilities.

Measurement always begins with establishing a baseline benchmark from your current analytics. Establishing a baseline is generally not difficult, especially if you've been monitoring at least some of the analytic data already. From the baseline, establish a goal and a timeline for achieving the goal. Generate your content and run the analytics according to your timetable. Here are some examples of objectives and some practical analytics you can run to measure success:

Let's imagine a company is ready to launch a new "free guide" and they want to get the word out and drive traffic to it. In this case, because it's new, the baseline is zero traffic and zero leads. After a set period of time, say six months, they can check back to see how their promotion efforts have been working. From web analytics, you have hard data on the number of visitors and the number of downloads (leads) of the free guide.

For web copy, you can use Google Analytics to check bounce rate of the traffic for that content page to see how visitors are behaving. Are they staying and engaging, continuing through your site, or are they bouncing away? Are they converting by purchasing, or filling out your web form? The answer will shape future web copy and help you tweak it to meet your goals. If the content does meet your goals, analytics will help confirm your decision to continue on the same path, or not.

If you're looking to increase branding, you can track an excellent metric, called "share of voice." Using tools like Trackur.com, Radiantsix.com and Moz.com's Fresh Web Explorer you'll get baseline metrics on how your product or brand name is mentioned around the internet. These services give you a rating, the sentiment, and the number of mentions on the social web. You can then take that data and compare against your competitors' mentions. Essentially, this will show you if the majority of people are talking about you or your competitor and how those mentions rate. After you've established a content plan to address your branding, set a goal period – say a year. At the end of the period, rerun the share-of-voice report and check how your brand is trending. If you see your share of voice increase, or your positive mentions go up, then you can attribute those results (at least in part) to your content efforts.

Another way to benchmark success for certain types of content is by measuring how many quality links the piece earned (backlinks). This is a popular metric to run, so there are a number of tools out there available for measuring backlinks. One such tool is OpenSiteExplorer.org. Just enter the URL for the content page and see how many backlinks it has received. If people are willing to link to your content, you can be certain that it's hitting that sweet spot where the content is meeting a need, not to mention all the added value the new links bring – increased traffic and better rankings in search.

Web analytics will help shape your vision for future content development. Therefore, all content you develop should work toward a measurable goal. By using analytics to establish your goal and measure your efforts, you can be smart about each new effort, freeing you up to follow bold, creative ideas with confidence.

Managing Traffic Patterns

Obviously, you want people to move through your site; you don't want to have them leave your content without engaging. The first dynamic to understand about site traffic is "bounce." *Bounce Rate* shows you the percentage of visitors who visit only one page on your site and then leave. For example, if you have a 15-page white paper that's received 8,000 unique views, a bounce rate of 20% and the *Average Time Spent* is six seconds on the landing page, you probably need to make some adjustments to that landing page. A bounce rate of 20% isn't terrible, but if the average visitor stays only 6 seconds, there may not be much on the page compelling them to stay. Both bounce rate percent and time spent metrics are great gauges of how relevant, engaging or useful your content is.

Google Analytics can offer in-page analytics to track click patterns. Such information is vital to understanding what your audience is looking for; what they find relevant. Knowing this will allow you to optimize your content marketing strategy. This is not just for onsite relevance, either – you can still measure the effectiveness of offsite content, whether in the form of guest posting or content placed on distribution sites. You can discover which content you published offsite drives the most traffic to your website by creating an *Advanced Segment* in Google Analytics. To create an Advanced Segment, click on Advanced Segments in your Google Analytics profile, name your segment appropriately and add each site where you publish content using the following setup (see Figure 59 on page 228):

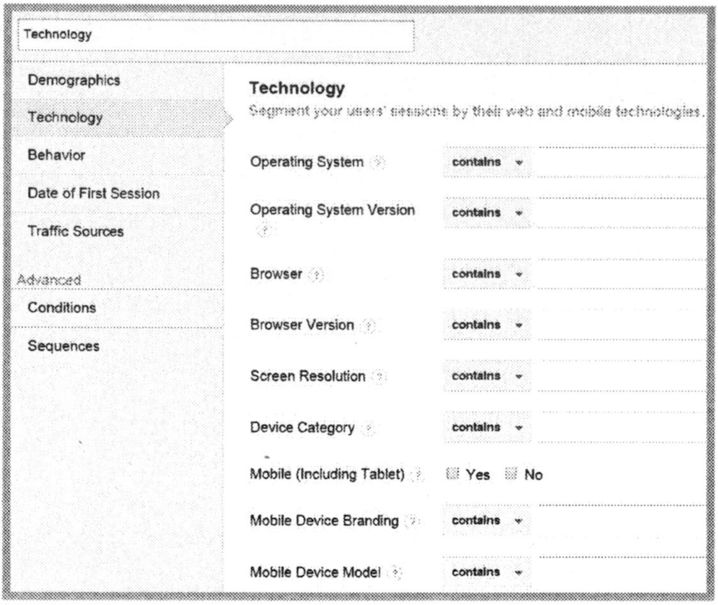

Figure 59: Setting up an Advanced Segment

Using this tool, you can track visitors from each of the sites where you have published content. If you regularly contribute to industry related sites, you can go to Acquisition > All Referrals, click on the site in question, and view the specific posts which have driven the most traffic and conversions to your website. This can help you identify topics to publish offsite that will drive qualified visitors back to your website. On the other hand, these metrics can lead you to stop wasting your time publishing on a particular site if you are not getting the results you expect.

Unique visits (users) are the standard measure of how many individuals have viewed your content within a given time frame. This key performance indicator provides a good baseline for which to compare different forms of content and trends. However, it is important to keep in mind that not all unique visits are the same. For example, a unique visit to a white paper might be much more valuable for lead generation purposes than a unique visit to a blog post – especially if a visit spends more time with the content.[58]

---

58 http://contentmarketinginstitute.com/2013/02/kpis-for-content-marketing-measurement/

Pageviews tends to be one key performance indicator that gets overlooked. If you have a lot of page views and unique visits, there's a good chance that your audience is engaged. Quite often this means that they are moving through your website to find more information. This metric can also give you a good picture of just how far a user reads through a publication. Did they only read four pages of an 8-page article before leaving? It's up to you to figure out why.

Google Analytics also provides page-level details of geographic information to help understand where around the world your content is being read. This certainly helps content marketers optimize for specific geographical locations, i.e. geo-specific content.

In addition to "unique visits" to your content, you should keep in mind *how* your content is accessed. What percentage of these visits comes from mobile devices? This is a huge consideration when moving forward with your strategy because it will directly impact the type of content you develop and how you promote it. Content is consumed very differently on a mobile device compared to a desktop computer.

Measuring Traffic and Time on Page

Sure, every company wants more traffic to their site, but traffic alone is not a great indicator of content marketing success. If it's coupled with other metrics, it can, however, be particularly insightful. For example, your home page is probably one of the most visited pages on your site — but this isn't always due to the content found there. This could be because you're a strong brand and visitors begin at your home page before moving on to other pages on your site.

In order to use traffic volume to measure content marketing success, compare pages of similar content to each other, because all pages are not created equal.

The graph below shows a huge spike in overall traffic to my company's site, occurring during the week of March 1. Data such as this should prompt the website owner to take a deeper look at Google Analytics data to determine what caused such an anomalous spike.

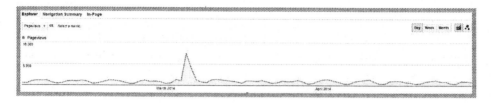

Figure 60: A traffic spike in Google Analytics

In this instance, we determined that the traffic spike could be attributed mainly to one of our blog posts that was shared on a popular Facebook page. As you can see in the screenshot below, a certain company shared our post. They had a very active community, which prompted many "likes," comments, and shares. All of this activity contributed to of the spike in traffic. Because of this post, other Facebook users and pages shared the link with their audiences and so on. As a result, this post continues to garner a few visits a day, despite it being published months ago.

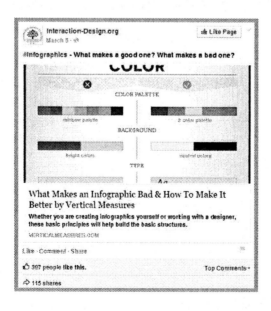

Figure 61: The Facebook post that drove a huge traffic spike

A piece of content or web page that attracts a high volume of pageviews can likely be considered a strong content page, since it obviously draws interest from your audience. But another metric to consider on high-traffic pages is the *Average Time on Page*. When the average time on a particular page is much higher than your site-wide average, it suggests that this page is grabbing and keeping visitors' attention more than other pages, indicating that the content there is worth analyzing more deeply to see what additional insights it might provide.

Let's look at another example. As you can see from the image below, the average time on page for our infographic post was nearly twice that of our site-wide average at the time. This told us that audiences were interested in the content we published on that page, which gave us a benchmark for comparisons to other content we plan to publish on our blog as part of our content marketing strategy.

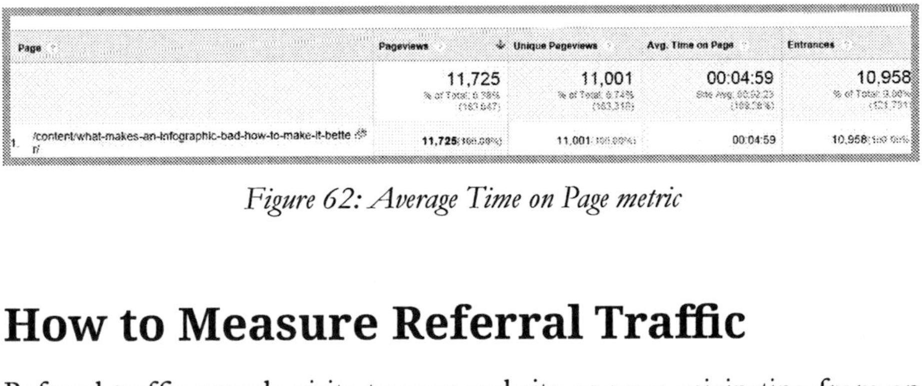

Figure 62: Average Time on Page metric

How to Measure Referral Traffic

Referral traffic reveals visits to your website or page originating from an outside source. For example, if a visitor clicks a link that leads to your website via a social media site like Facebook or Twitter, that visit is considered a "referral" since the social media site referred the visitor to your site. Measuring referral traffic in Google Analytics can be done in many different ways, such as the referral traffic report (under "acquisition"), by choosing "referral path," or "full referrer" from the list of secondary dimensions.

By now, you should have a content promotion and/or distribution strategy in place to get awesome content in front of your audience – as we've covered, if it's valuable, your audience will share, email, and bookmark your content on their own. As sharing increases, your promotional efforts will likely result in more referral traffic. Referral traffic can testify to the effectiveness of your efforts at promotion and distribution by providing insights into which sites refer the most traffic to your site as well as the timing of the traffic being referred.

As an example, the following screenshot shows referral traffic to an infographic from a "full referrer" secondary dimension report gathered from Google Analytics. The infographic has received 8,451 pageviews (7,609 unique users), with referral traffic from a variety of sources. As you can see in the Full Referrer column, the infographic received many visits as a result of being shared on Facebook and StumbleUpon, as well as from the blogs that linked to it. Because of this, the website owner may consider submitting similar content to StumbleUpon and comparable sharing sites to get its future content efforts in front of those same engaged audiences.

	Page	Full Referrer	Pageviews	Unique Pageviews
			8,253	7,397
			% of Total: 9.74% (1,114,815)	% of Total: 9.76% (97 1,802)
1.	/search-optimization/infographic-the-aut hority-building-machine/	(direct)	2,138 (25.81%)	1,949 (26.31%)
2.	/search-optimization/infographic-the-aut hority-building-machine/	stumbleupon.com/refer.php	1,629 (19.74%)	1,431 (19.35%)
3.	/search-optimization/infographic-the-aut hority-building-machine/	google	736 (8.92%)	659 (8.91%)
4.	/search-optimization/infographic-the-aut hority-building-machine/	stumbleupon.com/su/8z36y8/www.verticalmeasures.com/search-optimization/infographic-the-authority-building-machine/	651 (7.89%)	636 (8.60%)
5.	/search-optimization/infographic-the-aut hority-building-machine/	pointblankseo.com/link-building-strategies	240 (2.91%)	234 (3.16%)
6.	/search-optimization/infographic-the-aut hority-building-machine/	seo.com/blog/5-content-pieces-build-site-authority/	195 (2.36%)	172 (2.33%)
7.	/search-optimization/infographic-the-aut hority-building-machine/	stumbleupon.com/toolbar/litebar.php	148 (1.79%)	145 (1.96%)
8.	/search-optimization/infographic-the-aut hority-building-machine/	facebook.com/l.php	121 (1.47%)	115 (1.55%)
9.	/search-optimization/infographic-the-aut hority-building-machine/	Google Images/imgres	121 (1.47%)	92 (1.24%)
10.	/search-optimization/infographic-the-aut hority-building-machine/	searchenginewatch.com/article/2125584/Using-Social-Media-to-Build-Site-Authority	112 (1.36%)	104 (1.41%)

Figure 63: Full referrer Analytics information

Measuring Your Content Downloads

It's common practice in content marketing to create downloadable content for audiences to digest offline, including things like free guides, mobile apps, or PDFs. More often than not, these downloadable content pieces are kept behind a gated page, which means that visitors must fill out a contact form in order to gain access to the content. On the other hand, visitors are sometimes allowed to download content without providing any additional information. If you want to keep tabs in those instances, it would be necessary to set up *Event Tracking* in Google Analytics, which allows you to capture the incidence rate of your content being downloaded.

Per Google Analytics Support, "Event tracking is available for both web and app properties but requires additional technical set up that should be completed by a qualified developer." Google also says, "Although Event tracking requires a little extra work to set up, we strongly recommend you use it. Events are a flexible way to collect data about interactions specific to your site or app that might not otherwise be tracked."[59]

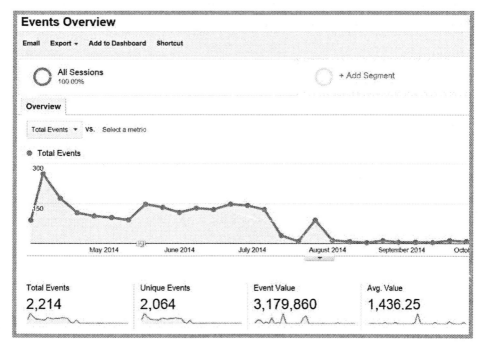

Figure 64: Event Tracking dashboard in Analytics

Once you have event tracking set up, you can establish an event *Goal* to track downloaded content conversion rate. To set up a goal in Google Analytics, go to Admin > Goals > Create a Goal and follow the step by step

---

59 https://support.google.com/analytics/answer/1033068

instructions. You can use a template or create a custom goal. Then, setting a value for the goal is optional, but highly recommended. The value is a monetary amount that you assign to a goal in order to see how much the conversion is worth to your business. In the case of measuring downloads, the event will be the act of downloading the piece of content.

After your event goal is set up, you will be able to find the number of people who are actually downloading your content, without requiring any additional contact information from your visitors if your prefer. This data can be used in conjunction with other metrics (like page views and time on page) to measure the success of your content offering. Let's take a look at another example: A piece of content we produced was downloaded 5,438 times, as measured by event tracking in Analytics. A goal was set up to register when that event (someone downloading the content) took place. A total of 16,719 sessions, 15,243 unique visitors and 5,434 downloads were captured.

To calculate the conversion rate for this example:

Conversions (downloads) 5,438 / Unique visitors 15,243 = 35%

Using this information, be sure to evaluate the conversion rate by measuring it against conversion rates of similar content pieces to get a full sense of its impact. In cases where the content is not gated, conversion rate is especially telling because there is no risk to the user associated with downloading the content piece.

Maintain Your Content to Get the Most Value From It

Remember, once you've created a piece of useful content and published it to the web, you aren't done with it. Content needs continuous maintenance to be successful. When your team starts paying attention and tracking the results of all your content efforts, you'll discover what works, and you can strive to create even better content for your audience.

It's your job to ensure that your content remains up to date, accurate, and relevant to your visitors. In the dynamic world of the Internet, content can quickly become irrelevant, possibly to the detriment of your brand. Often we focus on delivering new content, but to go back and ensure that what we've created remains useful to visitors? Well, that can seem like a chore.

In our industry, we call this level of content quality assurance *governance* because it's about actively setting and enforcing standards and policy that will ensure your content is peak quality at all times. While "web governance" can be defined in a number of ways, we're looking at it strictly from a content perspective. I suggest that you appoint someone to keep your content updated and maintained properly. This person will serve as a content governor or web managing editor and will be in charge of ensuring that all published content conforms to the standards you've set for your content strategy. If you don't have the resources to appoint someone to the role, you will have to add one more hat to the many your content strategist already wears. It's not a task you can ignore.

You must ensure that your brand is always associated with expert industry knowledge and your content is the primary place to support that association. Any time a searcher finds old, inaccurate or irrelevant content, it undermines the expertise you've been working to demonstrate. Your web managing editor will constantly patrol your content looking for content pieces that need to be updated or removed. While there are many content issues out there that need monitoring, some common issues are:

- Broken links within the content
- Outdated or inaccurate information
- Policy changes that may affect the content
- Inconsistency with branding style
- SEO/metadata updates to adapt to changes in search

To ensure that content is up to date, monitor your existing content assets through frequent audits. This is tied to the content inventory discussed earlier in Step 1. You can use the inventory more efficiently to review every piece of content to identify where content needs updating.

The audit schedule is cyclical. Rather than randomly cleaning up of your assets, you should conduct routine audits to keep your content in healthy condition. Your audit schedule should be incorporated into your editorial calendar; in fact, I recommend that it's the first thing you populate when you set up for a new year. You might want to perform semi-annual audits, say in the spring and the fall. On the other hand, conducting an audit every six months may not be enough. Certain major events within your organization, such as a major shift in policy or branding update, might make it necessary to audit off cycle. When you audit, update your content inventory. Having a current inventory will make the audit smoother and be more organized.

Naturally, the more content you generate, the more you will need to maintain and keep up to date. It follows, then, that the more you have to keep updated, the more frequently you will want to conduct audits. There's an old adage that says to keep a house painted, you should paint one side every year. Every four years, then, you've painted the whole house. Thus by breaking down a large job and tackling portions on a cycle, you make the job more manageable. One way to manage a large volume is to section off your content and cycle through areas of your site. If you are going to approach your audit schedule this way, you will reduce the load for each audit, but you'll want to increase the frequency within the schedule so that you're keeping everything up to date and not letting any one section sit for too long. You just can't ignore this regular content maintenance. Your content represents your brand and your expertise; your ability to meet the needs of your customer.

Defining Your Content Marketing Success

Early on in your content strategy, you defined what success looks like for your goals and your business. Success in content marketing will always relate to goals, reinforcing the need to track all your efforts and measure your return on the objective. As I stated earlier, you need to establish clear, measurable objectives and then use analytics to compare performance to objective.

- **Define what success means for your content and how you will measure it.**

- **Establish a timetable for measuring and using web analytics to gather data on the activity on your site.**

- **Use analytic data to adapt future content for optimal performance.**

How do you know if you're meeting the goals you've established in the first step? If your goal is to increase traffic to your site, for example, at what point have you achieved that goal? Every goal should be contextualized to include measurable milestones so that you can clearly see your success rate.

If you want simply to increase traffic to your site, set one or more milestones that establish a timetable and measurable benchmarks. Articulate these goals so that they are clearly established, and try to make them as specific as possible. For example, if your goal is to "increase traffic to our site," you should articulate the benchmark: "Show a 30% increase in traffic to our 'Contact Us' page in 12 months." This restated goal specifies what area of your site you'll focus on, it gives a firm, measurable definition of what level of increase you're looking to achieve, and it establishes a date at which you will be able to determine the success.

Take What You Have Learned and Adapt

As I've said before, in content marketing the mantra is "be willing to try new ideas, and keep moving."

> **But it's not about trial and error. It's about trial and testing.**

It's not exactly *science*, but you shouldn't have to take a shotgun approach, either. It's far more efficient to take rifle shots. In other words, you can generate targeted content that has been informed by experience and research. Through measurement, you can hone in on the kinds of content that have historically worked for you and for your competitors. You have the ability to use analytics to adapt your content toward what is likely to work and not waste as much time producing content that doesn't have a chance at success.

Test Everything!

A/B testing is a great way to test content by analyzing two versions of a web page – an A version (the control) and a B version (the variation). It's a method to validate that any new design or change to an element on your webpage is improving your conversion rate before you make that change to your site code. A/B testing allows you to show visitors two versions of the same page and measure which version is determined the winner.

Multivariate testing is, as the name implies, testing different combinations of many variables on a page. Instead of showing you which version of a page performs best, multivariate testing shows you the page elements that are responsible for having the most impact.

Consistently testing and optimizing your page can increase engagement and leads, while providing you with valuable insight about your site's visitors. There are a number of tools available for A/B testing, with different focuses, price points and feature sets:

- **Google Website Optimizer:** This is a free A/B testing tool and an excellent option to get started, but it lacks advanced features.
- **Optimizely:** An easy-to-use A/B testing tool; includes click maps. Multivariate testing also available.
- **Unbounce:** Landing-page creator with integrated A/B testing.

These resources help test for the following:

- Content placement
- Design elements
- Content copy

- Privacy policy
- Load speed and submission speed

> **"Without testing you're leaving money on the table, no business wants that. Take the time to set up proper tests, whether A/B or multivariate. Test often. Let data tell you what works and what doesn't, don't assume you know what will work."**
>
> **– Kaila Strong, Senior Director of SEO Services, Vertical Measures (@cliquekaila)**

Depending on the goal, there are numerous ways to measure the effectiveness of content marketing strategies, and there are a variety of tools available to collect the data. Even so, there's one tool that is used by more than 10 million websites to get most or all the metrics they need: Google Analytics. From measuring overall traffic and time-on-page to conversions, referral traffic and so much more, Google Analytics provides a wealth of resources to gauge content marketing success.

Through measurement, you can hone in on the kinds of content that have historically worked for you and for your competitors. Analytics enable you to adapt your content to what is likely to work so that you don't waste time producing content that has no chance of success. From traffic and time on page, to referral traffic and number of downloads, much of the data needed to measure against a range of possible content marketing goals is available in Google Analytics.

Return on Investment

Ultimately, the steps in this process lead up to achieving a return on your content marketing investment. There are numerous metrics that might be important to your organization, such as organic traffic, brand awareness, social shares, revenue, and of course leads – all of which can be used to determine ROI.

Since we get asked about leads the most, let me give you an example of how you might show an ROI for lead generation via your content marketing efforts:

One way marketers attribute leads to content is through lead-capture forms, trading your content for contact data to sign up for a newsletter, etc. It's up to you and your team to close the lead, but the content acts as the carrot. The second way marketers attribute a lead to a particular piece of content is by tracking the originating source of the lead. A visitor may happen across a great video you developed and in turn, goes to your "contact us" or similar page for more information. The video content was consumed and directly helped produce a lead. Cookies can also track visitors on your site and indicate which pages they viewed prior to filling out the form – even if they don't do so on their first visit. Ensure your site is set up to track these events and understand the value each lead provides to your company. Regardless of the method, it's important to set up your site with the correct goals to track and measure leads and attribution. Bottom line: once you are set up to track activity, it's easy to calculate ROI.

If a piece of content costs $3,000 to produce and you spend $4,000 to promote it, your total investment is $7,000. Say each lead you get has a value of $70; to break even on your investment your content piece must generate 100 leads. The key is to understand your lead-value price. If you haven't yet determined your lead-value price, I recommend you do so; otherwise, you won't be able to fully understand your ROI.

To effectively measure ROI, you need to dissect the path customers take from the first site visit to the closing sale. Eventually, you will be able to see what types of content your customers consumed throughout the sales cycle, and assess which content influences sales the most. An additional benefit to tracking the entire sales cycle is seeing where leads drop off by tracking the last piece of content viewed and the steps taken to get there. With this data, you will better understand your customers and can use that knowledge when strategizing future content marketing projects.

Though it seems like great deal of work, the point I want make clear is that measuring content marketing ROI is possible with the right mindset, strategy and tools in place. While it may take some time up front to define metrics and set up the necessary tools, these steps are necessary to ensure your content marketing plan meets business goals and provides an accurate representation of ROI.

What Can You Measure?

Goals:

- Brand awareness
- Engagement
- Lead Generation
- Lead Nurturing
- Revenue
- Upsell
- Customer Retention
- Customer Mentions

Measurement:

- Benchmark lift of company awareness
- Benchmark lift of product/service awareness
- Website traffic
- Time spent on website
- Inbound links
- SEO ranking
- Sales lead quality (e.g., sales accepted leads)
- Sales lead quantity
- Higher conversion rates
- Customer renewal rates
- Revenue
- Subscriber growth
- Qualitative feedback from customers
- Cost savings of client services

Together, consumption, lead-generation, sharing and sales metrics can help you measure your success and provide insight for future content marketing endeavors, which is surely worth the investment.

HOW TO CONVINCE YOUR BOSS TO INVEST IN CONTENT MARKETING

"No matter how great an idea you may have, if you can't present a convincing case, you can't sell it."[60]

If you've made it this far in the book without skipping any chapters, then you should have found numerous resources, ideas, and tools to help convince your boss to invest in content marketing. The one thing left to do now is to pull it all together and actually meet with the decision maker! In this last chapter, I'll outline nine points for getting your boss to go all in with content marketing:

1. Personalize your pitch for the decision maker(s)

2. Educate them on what content marketing really is

3. Prove the value of content marketing

4. Face objections on budget, ROI, implementation, and more

5. Identify gaps and opportunities to rank ahead of your competition

6. Lay out your plan, specific to your business and end goals

7. Design and build out your presentation

60 https://www.americanexpress.com/us/small-business/openforum/articles/7-tips-for-proposals-pitches-and-presentations/

8. Ask for buy-in

9. *Convince Your Boss!*

With all that you've learned so far, I trust you will knock the socks of your boss and launch a content marketing pilot program, or get buy-in for something even more extensive. If you're not there yet, make sure to check our companion website *HowToConvinceYourBoss.com* to read up on commonly faced objections, research the resources available to you, and discover stats that will support your case. Ready to convince your boss?

1. Know your Audience: Make a Personal Pitch

As with any sales pitch, convincing your boss means you have to think about your audience:

- What do they want?
- How can you most effectively reach them?
- What do you need to do to educate, inspire, and engage?
- How do you tip them over the edge from hesitant to interested?
- What most likely are going to be their objections?

Once you've answered those questions, it's time to get personal. Think about your boss as a person (sometimes that's tough, I know) and see what stands out to you in terms of their personal interests. Maybe you've noticed that they have a hobby, like golf, given their vacations, client outings, and that Golf Magazine sitting on their desk. Ask them about a recent article they read on golf, where they read it, why they chose that specific outlet, and if it has influenced any of their decisions when it comes to what clubs they buy, shirts they wear, trips they take, etc. Lead them on a journey that starts with content and ends with a sale, all within the realm of their personal experience.

To relate it specifically to your business, perhaps they were involved in your last major IT purchase. Did they do any research? How did they learn about the available options? Use real world examples of how content helped them make critical business decisions. Who provided that content?

> **Pitch Tip:** Personalization is power. Bring it home for your boss by relating it to their life and interests, and show them the power of content marketing that is already happening in their life. Integrate this interest throughout your pitch.

2. Educate: What Is Content Marketing?

If your boss doesn't understand content marketing, *educate them*. If your boss is already familiar with content marketing, *encourage them to dive deeper* to see how it can work for your business. Nowadays, more and more C-level executives know that content marketing is "out there," but haven't yet experienced it within their own business. Or they may have wrong perceptions of what content marketing means. You can illuminate their path to content marketing enlightenment by ensuring that you're both talking about the same thing. Here are a few points to hit:

Content Marketing

- Content marketing is the art of providing relevant, **useful content** to your customers without selling or interrupting them.

- Instead of pitching your products or services, you deliver information that makes your customers **more informed** before they buy.

- If you deliver valuable information on a consistant basis to your customers, they ultimately reward you with their **business and loyalty**.

> **Pitch Tip:** Give your boss a "broad strokes" vision of the philosophy of content marketing. If you can paint a picture of the vision and intention behind content marketing, they are more likely to see the value that it has to your business as a whole. Don't tell them that the company needs a blog, instead tell them they need to create a learning center for prospects and clients. Be the knowledge center for your industry. Remember to bring in your personal interest example to prove how content has had value for them in their purchasing life. Show them some case studies found earlier in this book, or at HowToConvinceYourBoss.com.

3. Prove Value

To prove value to someone on the fence, you have to know what they want. Here are common goals we've come across:

- More leads (quantity and/or higher qualified)
- More conversions (faster, better, stronger)
- Brand awareness
- Expertise and thought leadership
- Better customer service
- Customer loyalty, retention, and upsell

You can show your boss the value of content marketing through hard, statistical data which supports your business goal. If your marketing goal is to gain higher qualified leads, then tell your boss that *people go through 57% of the buying process before even talking to a sales person.*[61] "So, boss, you want more qualified leads? Let's give our future customers content that tells them what they need to know during that 57% and pave the way to reach out to us when the time is right."

That being said, don't limit yourself to what you think your boss wants. Go above and beyond and show them what they *should* want. If they're

---

61 http://www.executiveboard.com/exbd-resources/content/digital-evolution/index.html

focused on ROI, show them that becoming the expert in your field is the way towards more business. Distributing content across the web not only increases traffic and leads, it shapes your brand recognition. All paths converge in content marketing, so the more you can show how one goal connects to others, the more your boss will see the value of content marketing in a holistic way.

> **Pitch Tip:** Don't forget that even though all goal paths lead to one another, the main destination is more business for your company. Continue to integrate the overarching vision into the details and supporting facts.

4. Confront Objections

Here comes what is often the toughest part of your content marketing trek – *confronting doubts*. Companies both large and small are challenged with obstacles when forging ahead with content marketing. The more objections your boss presents, the harder it will be for you to move forward.

Because you so expertly convinced them on your stellar golf personalization, the decision maker in your company knows the value and buy-in to the concept; nonetheless, you may not have hit a hole-in-one when it comes to budget, ROI and implementation. They may come back with, "We don't have money for this." One of the most common objections that bosses have comes down to budget. But, you have the tools in your pitching arsenal. Most often, fear of the unknown can be assuaged by facts. Find the stats that ease their budgetary qualms (like the fact that using inbound tactics saves an average of 13% in overall cost per lead according to Hubspot.)[62] Show how their objection is valid, but can be countered.

The same tactic goes for other objections, whether they are implementation, ownership, ROI, etc. Follow this process to prepare and you'll clear this hurdle without tripping up:

---

62 http://www.stateofinboundmarketing.com/

1. **Identify probable objections** based on your business and boss

2. **Find supporting stats** that prop up your point against the objection

3. **Create an explanation** that not only confronts the objection, but educates your boss on the why's and how's

4. **Integrate your specific business' data points** (if available) that are relevant to your existing marketing or content efforts to show what has already worked

Pitch Tip: You will face numerous objections, but if you come equipped with the power of intelligent information, supporting data, and a persuasive presentation, your pitch will stand out. Again, be sure to check our companion website **HowToConvinceYourBoss.com** for more help in this area.

5. Show Them What They're Missing

Some bosses can be convinced by knowing the value and data of content marketing. But when it comes to others, a little competition might spark their fire. Is your boss in that bucket? Always eager to outperform close competitors and find different marketing opportunities? Use that competitive edge for fuel in your pitch:

- Find what your direct competitors are doing well with their content and what falls flat
- Identify gaps you can fill
- Build on their successful ideas and show how it can evolve and become your own

Pitch Tip: Bring in screenshots or live examples of your competitors nailing their content marketing strategy. By using visuals and specific samples with names that your boss is already familiar with, you will show exactly what your company has been missing out on.

6. Lay Out your Plan

Now that you've proved value of, and addressed any objections to the basic philosophy behind content marketing, you're going to need a well thought out plan to grab the attention of your boss. The following three items will need fleshing out for your particular enterprise:

Strategy

- How you will implement content marketing within your company
- What type of content will be created, promoted, distributed
- Set timelines and goals

Implementation

- Who owns what on your team
- What internal resources need to be mined for content
- Day to day management needs

Measurement

- How you will prove the return on investment
- What benchmarks will you hold your plan up to
- Timeline for testing and tracking reports

> **Pitch Tip:** Refresh yourself on Steps 1 and 2 of the strategy earlier in this book to understand how to craft your strategy and gather ideas for content.

7. Craft Your Presentation

Impress your boss with a stellar presentation (both visually and intellectually), and you will make great strides towards achieving buy-in. Craft a presentation that highlights the main points you're trying to hit, with specific examples, stats and visuals.

> **Pitch Tip:** A visual supplement like slides or handouts will go far to give your boss a better idea of what they're looking at (literally and figuratively). Don't overload your visuals with lots of text — let your voice do most of the work, and let your visuals complement you.

8. Ask for Buy-In

Regardless of your company's size, and regardless of your marketing budget's resources, you need at least some of the funds to make your plan come to life. It's up to you to figure out a ballpark estimate of the costs involved, both in time and hard money spent. Pin down who will own what aspects of the work so your boss knows what internal resources will be used up. And most of all, ask for what you want! Be confident in what you're requesting — you've already done the work to prove your case.

> **Pitch Tip:** All good sales people know to ask for the sale, and this is no different. Ask for buy-in, be specific, and lay out a timeline for the first measurements to be reported.

9. Convince Your Boss

You've done all the hard work, thought through every step, and now it's time to walk into the meeting with confidence and passion for your plan. Many years ago, I jotted down this observation, and I suspect it will be good for *your* boss to hear it: "**The fundamental difference between two individuals is the order of their priorities.**" Let's look at our priorities and go all in with content marketing! Go for it!

Visit HowToConvinceYourBoss.com

THE ALL IMPORTANT CONCLUSION

We did it! We've walked through each important step in the path to content marketing success, and considered point-by-point how you can convince your boss to get on board. If I could leave you with one parting thought, it would be this: *You are now in the publishing business.*

My goal in writing this book is to get you thinking like a publisher and to encourage you to take on a content marketing mindset. By embracing this approach, you'll find inspiration in the possibilities all around you. Above all, I want to get you excited about creating.

Successful publishing is about consistent quality. When you do it right — when you strive for quality — you'll produce content that compels people to share it on social media, attracts links, and that meets the real needs of your customers, positioning you as the critical solution provider. The bottom line is that you publish in order to stimulate conversations in which you can engage as the expert.

Once you start thinking like a publisher, get organized like a publisher! Just ask a sharp content strategist and they will tell you that you'll never get a content marketing strategy off the ground without being organized. You need to have a plan. At the center of any publication, and the key to keeping it organized, is the editorial calendar. I can't emphasize that enough. **The editorial calendar is the hub of activity for your online publishing effort.** The beauty of the editorial calendar is that it highlights the publication process, revealing where you're succeeding and where you can find ways to improve your efforts.

When you step back and look at all that's going on in the steps I've described in this book, developing a content marketing strategy can seem daunting. And to be honest, it *is* – if you aren't organized. There are simply too many moving parts. An editorial calendar will help you visualize the process and will help you manage the content cycle. From research to content development to promotion and distribution, it all falls on the calendar. Plot out your calendar, and you'll see the convergence of search, social, and content marketing right before your eyes. As you see the steps in the process working together (strategy, ideation, content creation, optimization, promotion, distribution, nurture, and measurement), it will become clear why I say, "It's a continuous process."

BUT YOU CANNOT DO IT ALL. Even though I have tried to cover everything related to search, social and content, you just cannot do it all. Our company does not do it all and I doubt very few large organizations do it all. Just pick a few types of content that you think you can move all the way through the process with a high degree of quality and consistency and focus on those.

If there is one single thing I would recommend you start with, it's your blog. Get one on your website and commit to posting something new two or three times per week. If you can do that, you are off and running. Publishing is about finding opportunities to be creative. Every piece of content is an opportunity for *more* content. It's inspiration for your next piece. Repurposing is an awesome way to multiply your creative efforts by spreading the excitement to new forms on different channels. Before long your creative ideas will spread out in ways that might surprise you right now.

Hey, at the end of the day, creating engaging content is fun! It's your business to demonstrate that you have expert industry knowledge, and that's not only something to be proud of, it's something to have a good time with.

We at Vertical Measures considered the occasion of publishing this book an opportunity to create new content that would excite our audience. It opened an avenue to put some of our online content *in the book!* From this standpoint, you could say that this book accomplishes what it promotes. On the other hand, you could just say that we have a content marketing mindset!